I0153108

Arts 1

Pillars of Society: Ibsen, Shaw, Brecht; Essays in Dramatic Criticism

Pillars of Society: Ibsen, Shaw, Brecht; Essays in Dramatic Criticism

James R. Russo

© Individual author and College Publications 2022
All rights reserved.

ISBN 978-1-84890-404-0

College Publications
Scientific Director: Dov Gabbay
Managing Director: Jane Spurr

http://www.collegepublications.co.uk

Cover produced by Laraine Welch

-

All rights reserved. No part of this publication may be reproduced, stored in a retrieval system or transmitted in any form, or by any means, electronic, mechanical, photocopying, recording or otherwise without prior permission, in writing, from the publisher.

TABLE OF CONTENTS

List of Illustrations

ACKNOWLEDGEMENTS

My deep gratitude goes out to my first, now late teachers on the subjects of Ibsen, Shaw, and Brecht: Leon Katz, Stanley Kauffmann, and Eric Bentley. My thanks, also, to Methuen Publishing for permission to reprint translations by John Willett and Robert Conard.

INTRODUCTION

"Ibsen, Shaw, Brecht: Form, Idea, Influence"

Ibsen and Shaw

George Bernard Shaw decried the nineteenth-century practices of both melodrama and the well-made play as churned out by Victorien Sardou and Eugène Scribe, even coining the term Sardoodledom to describe their well-oiled but trivial machinations. He called such works "cats' cradles, clockwork mice, mechanical rabbits" with plots like "jig-saw puzzle[s]" (West, 268). In 1894 he wrote that "stage realism is a contradiction in terms," and thirty years later, in a letter to Alexander Bakshy, he asked, "Have I ever been what you call a representationist or a realist?" (Russo, 212). Martin Meisel points out that Shaw objected to the well-made formula, in that "any serious play whose ultimate dramatic values lay in an intriguing situation and its circumstantial plausibility was likely to depend upon conventional moral and social values in its characters and its audience" (Meisel, 80). In other words, realistic plots support status-quo attitudes. Philosophically, the comfort of realism—the way in which realism echoes the lives and experiences of the audience—anesthetizes rather than provokes.

Shaw, however, considered himself more old-fashioned or classical than avant-garde. He listed as his influences "Shakespeare . . . the Bible, Bunyan, Walter Scott, Dickens and Dumas *père*, Mozart, and Verdi" (West, 268). He wished to return to a pre-realistic style, when actors were trained in the art of rhetoric and unafraid of "heroic acting"; Shaw sought "drunken, stagey, brass-bowelled barnstormers" who could break through the fourth wall (Meisel, 94). His works are not particularly radical in terms of structure; instead, they subvert familiar contemporary forms—melodrama, the drama of adultery, romantic drama—even in some cases taking plots directly from the popular plays of Dion Boucicault and Lord Byron in order to lure the audience into the theater (Meisel, 94). Within the play, he would reverse plot or characters and thus upset expectations. In *Misalliance* (1910), for example, inverting the expectations of romantic comedy, the women are in pursuit of the men: the young woman tries to seduce the older man; the same woman later in the play proposes to her intended; and the aviatrix, Tarzan-style, slings Bentley over her shoulder and carries him off.

It was Henrik Ibsen's skillful manipulation of the gears and cogs of the (so-called) well-made play that first evoked Shaw's admiration:

> Formerly you had in what was called a well-made play an exposition in the first act, a situation in the second, and an unraveling in the third. Now you have exposition, situation, and discussion; and the discussion is the test of the playwright. . . . The discussion conquered Europe in Ibsen's *Doll House* [1879]; and now the serious playwright recognizes in the discussion not only the main test of his higher powers, but also the real center of his play's interest. (Shaw, *Quintessence of Ibsenism*: 135)

Shaw embraced Ibsen in the lecture (quoted directly above) that became *The Quintessence of Ibsenism* (1891), the first book in English on the subject, a study that through its insights and its partialities opened paths for the critics who followed. Shaw's subsequent writings on Ibsen, both when he was a theater critic and after he himself had become a world-rank dramatist, confirmed what he had learned from the senior man.

Above all, the views of the two dramatists were comparable on a curious but revelatory point: their attitudes toward conventional nineteenth-century dramaturgy. The hoariest critical commonplace about *A Doll House*, for instance, is that, until the great final scene, the play is a creakily contrived, nineteenth-century *pièce de théâtre*. The first critic to point out this creakiness, and to scoff at those who were put off by it, was Shaw in *The Quintessence of Ibsenism*. Up to a point, wrote Shaw, this is "a play that might be turned into a very ordinary French drama by the excision of a few lines and the substitution of a sentimental happy ending for the famous last scene." But, says Shaw, it was that last scene through which the play "conquered Europe and founded a new school of dramatic art" (*Quintessence*, 219).

To understand why the iconoclastic Ibsen wrote two thirds of this play like a "very ordinary French drama," look at his earlier theater life. In 1849, at the age of twenty-one, Ibsen began his playwriting career with *Catiline*, which was published in Christiania (today's Oslo) but not produced. His second play, *The Warrior's Barrow*, was produced the following year and helped to get him a job at the theater in the small city of Bergen. There, in 1851, he became a jack of almost all theatrical trades. One way or another, except as actor, he was involved for the next six years in the production of many dozens of plays in Bergen, a few of them his own. In 1857, he returned to Christiania to do similar work in theaters there. Through all his years in those two cities, patching and cutting and expanding plays in the popular repertory whenever commercial viability required it, Ibsen kept on writing plays of his own, often in verse and in large forms. Several of them were produced, a few of them with some success. In 1864, when he was thirty-six, his historical drama *The Pretenders* helped towin him a government pension. Living in Germany and Italy, Ibsen continued writing in large-scale mode through 1873 when he completed *Emperor and Galilean*, an extensive "world-historical drama," as he called it in a subtitle. It was published but not produced.

Then Ibsen changed modes. He had already given signs of it in *Emperor and Galilean*. Edmund Gosse, a prophet for Ibsen in Britain, wondered in a review of the (published) play why it had not been written in verse. Ibsen wrote to Gosse:

> Here I must differ with you. As you must have observed, the play is conceived in the most realistic style. The illusion I wished toproduce was that of reality. . . . If I had employed verse, I would have counteracted my own intention and defeated my purpose. (*Letters and Speeches*, 144)

We can justly make an assumption here, I think. Ibsen's grander work had achieved substantial recognition, through grants and appointments; he had even been given an honorary doctor's degree. (He had also published a book of poetry.) But apparently he decided that the general large-scale conception and execution of those earlier plays was keeping him from immediacy with the changing world around him. In any case Ibsen was completely revising his methods, not to quell the fire that burned inside him but to use it in more practical theater form. He put aside the figurative and the formally poetic, and he turned to the workaday theatrical craft that he had learned in the Bergen and Christiania theater: Ibsen used the popular well-made play, but he used it for new, radical ends. In 1877 he completed *Pillars of Society*, the first of his twelve contemporary plays in prose. When he sent this manuscript to his publisher, he said: "It is modern in all respects and completely in tune with the times" (*Letters and Speeches*, 165).

As Ibsen wrote those twelve plays, he was inferably thinking that, if producers and audiences preferred stage contrivance in the manner of Sardou and Scribe, the two chief contemporary play manufacturers (whose work he had once called "dramatic candy-floss"), he could provide it—but only as a means of lulling the audience into coziness until the dramatic bomb exploded. The second of these old-new plays was *A Doll House*. In *A Doll House* the Sardou-Scribe mechanics are thick. The vindictive Krogstad threatens Nora Helmer with a paper that she once signed illegally. As he presses her, hoping to revenge himself for injuries he has suffered, Mrs. Linde arrives, a woman whom Krogstad once loved and who is conveniently in time to mollify his vengeance. There is a good deal of further contrived suspense about a fatal letter that is waiting in the Helmer letter-box. And so on.

The audiences of the nineteenth century recognized all this Sardoodledom (again, Shaw's term) clearly enough: more, they welcomed it. This, for them, was what the theater *was*. Then, while they were snuggled in their seats enjoying the usual, came the last scene. After the threat against Nora has evaporated, she refuses reconciliation with the husband who had declined to stand by her in her trouble. She leaves their home. The slam of that front door has echoed ever since.

It is wonderfully fitting that the first critic to point out the juxtaposition of old and new dramaturgy in *A Doll House* was Shaw because, in his own way, he soon did the same thing. From his boyhood in Dublin through his youth and early manhood in London, Shaw had loved the popular theater, but this very love hobbled his interest in playwriting. Until his mid-thirties he wrote novels (unsuccessfully) and, though he dabbled a bit with plays, he never actually finished one. He was seriously ambitious as a writer, and he thought that the theater of his day had become exclusively the province of the popular. He enjoyed it, certainly, but he couldn't feel that playwriting was an apt field for him, just as a talented young writer today might enjoy television without wanting to write for it. (Later, in 1907, he said: "The genius of Dickens, who at first wanted to write for the theater, was lost to it because there was no theater available in which his art could have breathed" [Shaw, *Drama Observed*: 1149].) When Shaw became a theater critic, which he did before he completed his first play, he often spoke of his long-term enjoyment of the theater, of acting, despite the mediocrity of current plays.

Then, around 1885, William Archer, who knew Norwegian, introduced him to the work of Ibsen, much of which had not yet been translated. Through Ibsen's work, Shaw became convinced that seriousness was possible, was urgently needed, in the contemporary theater. Ibsen showed him that this gravity was especially possible if a dramatist used the theater's very own commercial devices to present it. In the 1890s, the first decade of Shaw's playwriting life, he wrote *Mrs. Warren's Profession* (1893), which focused on the then-voguish "fallen woman" idea, except here it was used to prove that the woman was right; *Arms and the Man* (1894), about a military hero with more canniness than dash; *You Never Can Tell* (1897), a summery seaside romance that turned out to include a drama of deep change in man-woman relationships; and *The Devil's Disciple* (1897), a melodrama that echoed Dickens' *A Tale of Two Cities* (1859) except that this hero was more ironic than noble.

Shaw continued with this symbiotic procedure, with old bottles for new wine, through much of his career. (Meisel explores the subject thoroughly in *Shaw and the Nineteenth-Century Theater.*) Shaw thus echoed Ibsen's style in certain of his own plays, categorized by scholars as "discussion plays" in which "discussion is primary, plot is sometimes of little importance, sometimes of none; the two are loosely connected, sometimes not at all" (Dukore, 190). The London critics' blindness about his method tickled Shaw so much that he exposed their myopia. In 1911, he wrote an epilogue to *Fanny's First Play* (1911), his first real hit, in which critics appear to discuss the play they have just seen. These critics (caricatures of well-known figures) concentrate on the play's advanced views; but then one of them discloses the antique theatrical devices through which the author has deployed those views.

This particular critic says the following:

> Here you have a rotten old-fashioned melodrama acted by the usual stage puppets. The hero's a naval lieutenant. All melodramatic heroes are naval lieutenants. The heroine gets into trouble by defying the law (if she didn't get into trouble there'd be no drama) and plays for sympathy all the time as hard as she can. Her good old pious mother turns on her cruel father when he says he's going to put her out of the house, and she says she'll go,too. Then there's the comic relief: the comic shopkeeper, the comic shopkeeper's wife, the comic footman who turns out to be a duke in disguise, and the young scapegrace who gives the author his excuse for dragging in a fast young woman. All as old and stale as a fried fish shop on a winter morning. (*Fanny's First Play*, 241)

All true. All the devices are stock items. And the basic fun is that the audience hasn't been aware of it: Shaw has tossed the old ingredients so deftly that the dish seems fresh—until he himself points out his recipe.

Hence there is a shared paradox in Ibsen and Shaw—trenchant and amusing. These two masters, who irrevocably altered the theater, did it, in considerable part, with devices lifted from the theater warehouse, dusted off and used to new purposes. Quite obviously Ibsen and Shaw were also dramatic innovators. Ibsen pioneered both before and after he transmuted the old. Such plays as *Peer Gynt* (1876) and the ultimate *When We Dead Awaken* (1900) were explosions in theatrical imagining. Shaw innovated soon after he began playwriting, with *Man and Superman* (1903), and again much later, with *Back to Methuselah* (1920). But both dramatists, one of them patently and the other slyly, often used the old theater against itself. Both of them found a way to the theater's future through its past.

Interval

Shaw, like Ibsen, embraced several different styles of playwriting. Over the long course of his career, his dramas encompassed social realism, symbolism, even absurdism—sometimes within the same play. *Man and Superman* (1903), *John Bull's Other Island* (1904), *The Apple Cart* (1928), *Too True to be Good* (1932), and *Heartbreak House* (1919) have long been considered plays that presaged Samuel Beckett, Bertolt Brecht, and Eugène Ionesco's avant-garde techniques of absurdism and "alienation." In "The Avant-Garde Shaw," Stanley Weintraub notes the playwright's declaration in 1926 "that the sort of theatre his new plays needed was one that had to 'combine' the optics and acoustics of a first-rate lecture theater and a first-rate circus" (Weintraub, 230). He describes how Shaw anticipated several later and more commonly acknowledged "experimental" playwrights such as Jean Genet in addition to Beckett, Ionesco, and Brecht, asserting that "after his first decade as a dramatist Shaw had already outgrown even Ibsenite realism." Weintraub further remarks on Shaw's insistence that "the more scenery you have, the less illusion you produce," concluding, "He wanted his characters to be able to step out of their roles now and then to become bigger than life" (Weintraub, 224-225). Shaw, John Gassner notes, was always

> ready to stop the overt action for a good discussion or good lecture, or even step out of the proscenium frame to harangue the audience in behalf of a relevant philosophy or sociology, which is beyond, if not indeed antithetical to, the illusion achieved by plodding realists and the designers who provide scenic realism (Weintraub, 229).

Shaw, writing in 1908, saw the following as key features of classical plays: "Not... a plot or a story but an argument... lasting three hours, and carried on with unflagging cerebration by twelve people and a beadle" (Weintraub, 230). This idea of plays as arguments would come full circle in the twentieth century in the theories of Brecht. Of all of the avant-garde dramatic approaches, Shaw's anti-illusionist ideas connect most specifically with twentieth-century epic theater—the theater of Bertolt Brecht. In a 1926 article titled "Three Cheers for Shaw," Brecht observes that Shaw realized that "the mere reproduction of reality does not give an impression of truth" (*Brecht on Theatre*, 11). Both men saw theater as an instrument of debate leading to social change rather than a trivial display of either "Sardoodledom" or the emotional excesses of melodrama. Brecht, in fact, refers (in *Brecht on Theatre*, 11) to Shaw as a "terrorist" who "creates a play by inventing a series of complications that give his characters a chance to develop their opinions as fully as possible and to oppose them to our own." (The dilemma in staging is that directors can become entranced with the complications that are Shaw's "bait" without allowing opportunities to bring forth the opinions.)

Brecht himself took specific steps in his dramaturgy of epic theater to ensure an aesthetic distance from the plays of the era—specifically their heavy reliance on linear plot. His plays are organized around episodes, avoiding the artificiality of causal and/or climactic plotting. He decried the use of realistic settings, asking that the theater be purged of "magical" and thus "hypnotic tensions": "It is of course necessary to drop the assumption that there is a fourth wall cutting the audience off from the stage and the consequent illusion that the stage action is taking place in reality and without an audience" (*Brecht on Theatre*, 136). Brecht hoped to separate the audience from emotionally identifying with the characters or conflicts through a series of "alienation" techniques, including projected titles, gestic music, and actors' stepping out of character to address the audience.

The characters of *Misalliance*, for one Shaw play, while compelling, are not particularly empathetic, supporting Brecht's ideas of "alienation." In Brecht's theater the actors use "a definite gest of showing" exactly what they are doing, *as actors* (*Brecht on Theatre*, 136). Each character can be seen as emblematic of an idea, a class, a gender—similar to characters in expressionistic drama. Bentley may represent the Brain; Johnny, the Natural Man; Lina, the Exotic Woman; Lord Summerhays, the Aristocrat; Hypatia, the Ingenue; and Tarleton, the Nouveau Riche. Shaw described Lina, the aviatrix, as a type: "the St. Joan of Misalliance . . . a religious force" (Laurence, 180-181). Relationships are instantaneous; motivations and conflicts are superficial and quickly resolved. Hypatia, for example, ricochets from Bentley, to Summerhays, to Percival. Both Gunner's socialist revenge plot and the potential lost-child revelation (a staple of melodrama) dissolve. What remains, then? An opportunity to raise questions and discuss opposing views through thesis and antithesis.

What are the questions raised in the play *Misalliance*? In other words, what is it that Shaw would want us to be thinking about through these "alienation" techniques? Metatheatrical critiques of melodrama are unquestionably present in the play; witness the lost child, the stage machinery, the gun that in fact does not go off at the end of the play, the received ideas about the call of the blood, and the intense "natural," emotional connections between parent and child. Shaw even has his characters draw attention to the dramaturgy of the play they are in. Johnny says to Tarleton: "I like a book with a plot in it, you like a book with nothing in it but some idea that the chap that writes it keeps worrying. You look on an author as a type of god. I look on him as a man . . . I pay . . . to amuse me and take me out of myself and make me forget" (*Misalliance*, 28).

Shaw thus pokes fun at his own plot as the one readers are most interested in, a plot that labors over "which particular young man some young woman will mate with," to which Percival replies, "As if it mattered" (*Misalliance*, 93). But Shaw's greatest questions in *Misalliance* come in his satirical treatment of any unexamined ideals, seen in the attempt at a duel over Hypatia's "honor," Gunner's fervent espousals of socialism (resulting in a headache), and, finally, what Tarleton sadly refers to as the lack of "paternal sentimentality" (*Misalliance*, 98) when he calls for a future in which "no man should know his own child! No child should know its own father. Let the family be rooted out of civilization!" (*Misalliance*, 100). In a realistic production, these statements would carry inappropriate emotional heft. In epic theater, we see them as ideas or notions to be questioned and considered.

The greatest danger in using Brecht's "alienation" techniques in any production is that the audience may be alienated beyond intellectual engagement. Surely, though, Shaw's ideas, characters, and language are resilient enough to survive and disclose new insights through new types of production. Shaw and Ibsen embraced the *democracy* of realism, the opportunity to place middle- and working-class characters onstage, to talk about unspoken social realities, particularly how money controls our relationships. But fourth-wall realism—as though we were peeking into someone's house—is not the essential vehicle for portraying social problems drawn from everyday situations. If one could produce, say, a Brechtian *Misalliance*, why not frankly symbolist depictions of *Candida* (1894), expressionist mask work to highlight the layered characters in *Mrs. Warren's Profession* and *Major Barbara* (1905), and surrealist dreamscapes for *Arms and the Man* or *You Never Can Tell*? Shaw warned that what he was planning was nothing less than "a siege laid to the theater of the nineteenth century by an author who had to cut his way into it at the point of a pen" (Meisel, 66). His works merit such a siege to nineteenth-century realism, which must needs be superseded by twentieth- and twenty-first-century directorial approaches.

Shaw and Brecht

At first glance, neither the men, Bertolt Brecht and Bernard Shaw, nor their works seem to have much in common. Shaw was an apostle of the "Life Force," a puritan vegetarian, and somewhat of a loner who had something to say about practically every topic from vivisection to the creation of a new alphabet (for which purpose he left part of his estate). Brecht, on the other hand, was a gregarious and epicurean Marxist who basically had only one subject—the creation of a society based on Marxist-Leninist principles—and who cared little for alphabets and grammar. When one compares works like Shaw's *Candida* with Brecht's *Mother Courage and Her Children* (1941), the only similarity would seem to be that both protagonists are women. Yet in the realm of dramatic form and technique, as well as the history of drama, Brecht assigns Shaw an important position. The previously cited "Three Cheers for Shaw" bears testimony to this, and it is significant that it was written when Brecht was beginning to talk and write about his epic theater (Hecht, 4). It is in their dramatic concepts, then, that the two playwrights, in spite of all their other differences, have many things in common.

Through comic elements, first of all, a deeper relationship between the works of these two playwrights can be established. Indeed, there is a close affinity among the comic spirit, satire, and the "alienation effect"; the elements of contrast, distance, and surprise are characteristic of all three. Like Shaw, Brecht often uses humor or satire to achieve the *Verfremdungseffekt*. As Shaw himself argued, "The function of comedy is nothing less than the destruction of old-established morals" (Enck, 41). At the same time, he deplores the attitude of British theatregoers, who tolerate an attack on established conventions only "when it is done seriously, or even grimly and terribly as they understand Ibsen to be doing it" (Enck, 41). Like Brecht, Shaw stresses the importance of levity, which, however, the general public scorns as being too cynical: "But that it should be done with levity . . . is too scandalously wicked, too cynical, too heartlessly shocking to be borne" by the general public (Enck, 41). Brecht recognized the same problem in the German theater. Both playwrights regarded the theater as a forum, a platform for propaganda, and the comic spirit as well as the *defamilarization* (a better word) effect as means to an end: namely, to instruct and entertain at the same time.

In his struggle with the "ewige Meiningerei" (a type of staging that stressed pomp and seriousness), Brecht found an ally in Shaw: "If one adds to this his exploding of the thoughtless, habitual assumption that anything that might possibly be considered venerable should be treated in a subdued manner instead of energetically and joyously; if one adds to this his successful proof that in the face of truly significant ideas a relaxed (even snotty) attitude is the only proper one, since it alone facilitates true concentration, it becomes evident what measure of personal freedom he has achieved" (*GW* 15, 97-98; my trans., here and throughout, unless otherwise noted). Brecht's statement about Shaw's work, which could be supplemented by many remarks of a similar nature on his own work (e.g., "But it is especially necessary to treat serious matters in a light vein" [*GW* 7, 2992]), reveals Shaw's as well as Brecht's own dialectic method: both playwrights invert generally accepted modes of thinking; they "take delight in upsetting our habitual prejudices" (*GW* 15, 99), and hope that the audience replaces its worn-out convictions with theirs. To achieve this, the theatergoer "must not hand in his brains along with his coat at the cloakroom," as Brecht pointed out (*GW* 15, 189). Shaw expected the same of his audience: "And so effective do I find the dramatic method that I have no doubt I shall at last persuade even London to take its conscience and brains with it when it goes to the theater, instead of leaving them at home with its prayer book as it does at present" (Preface to *Mrs. Warren's Profession*, 221).

One method of upsetting old-fashioned concepts, as noted earlier, is to give a new interpretation of well-known subjects and to use topics that are commonly known but regarded as non-literary or even un-literary. Indeed, creative originality in the Aristotelian sense of *inventio* meant nothing to either Brecht or Shaw. Accusations of plagiarism were brushed aside with remarks such as "Shakespeare was a thief, too" (Brecht, in Willett: 124), and "I do not deny [the charge] as I possess in a marked degree that characteristic of Shakespeare . . . which is described as picking up a good thing when you find it" (Shaw, in Henderson: 704-705). One familiar literary topic both playwrights employed was the Saint Joan theme. Here again, what Brecht writes about Shaw with reference to Saint Joan is also true for his own works: "These complications can never be old and familiar enough to suit Shaw" (*GW* 15, 99). Examples of non-literary and un-literary topics that Brecht and Shaw exploited for their own purposes are the Salvation Army, boxing, and prostitution.

Brecht was so fascinated by the Saint Joan theme that he used it three times: in *Saint Joan of the Stockyards* (1929-31), in *The Visions of Simone Machard* (1941-43), and in an adaptation of Anna Seghers' radio play *The Trial of Joan of Arc at Rouen, 1431* (1934/1952). Shaw's *Saint Joan* was written in 1923 and soon became one of his best known plays. In 1905, moreover, Shaw gave his interpretation of the role of the Salvation Army in a capitalist society in *Major Barbara*. Brecht's *Saint Joan of the Stockyards* combines the Saint Joan theme with that of the Salvation Army; his Saint Joan is an officer of the Black Straw Hats, as he called this Christian organization.

In these works, both playwrights avoid painting in black and white: they recognize weaknesses in their "heroines" and human traits in their "villains." They also pursue a similar objective in their plays: they take the familiar subject of Joan of Arc in order to demonstrate the need for social change. Brecht's and Shaw's interest in the topic of Joan of Arc reveals yet another similarity, namely their historical and dialectic approach in the tradition of G.W.F. Hegel and Karl Marx. Hegel had pointed out that history advances through clashes of contradictory forces. Brecht and Shaw, who knew their Hegel well, illustrate these dialectics of progress in the conflict between Joan and the ruling classes.

Neither Brecht nor Shaw sees the Salvation Army, for its part, as a charitable organization that strives to improve the lot of the poor; rather, they consider it the complete opposite. Its activities only help to sustain a corrupt system by pacifying the impoverished masses with promises that the meek shall inherit the earth. For both writers, the Salvation Army and all other religious organizations are instruments of capitalism. And the real gods of capitalist society are money and profit. Thus money occupies a central role in many of Brecht's and Shaw's works, particularly in the former's *Saint Joan* and latter's *Major Barbara.* Yet neither playwright condemns material possessions for the sake of a blissful state of innocence in poverty. Poverty is "the vilest sin of man and society" (Preface to *Major Barbara*, 122), and in order to abolish it, a redistribution of income is essential. According to Brecht and Shaw, this change will not be brought about by peaceful means. Major Barbara's father, Undershaft, recommends gunpowder, Brecht's Black Straw Hats call for tanks, cannons, planes, and warships (cf. *GW* 2, 702).

Two additional topics that Brecht and Shaw used to counter the traditional concepts of *belles lettres* were boxing and prostitution. The boxing motif achieved two purposes: it brought some freshness into an otherwise sterile atmosphere, and it served as a metaphor for the fight for survival in a capitalist society. For one of his early novels, *Cashel Byron's Profession* (1882), Shaw chose a boxer with the suggestive name of Byron as a hero. In this novel, Shaw applies the Darwinian principle of the survival of the fittest to Victorian society. Cashel points out to wealthy Lydia: "What is life but a fight? . . . You were born with a silver spoon in your mouth. But if you hadn't to fight for that silver spoon, someone else had" (Zeiger, 504). In 1926, Brecht wrote a short story called "The Uppercut" (*GW* 11, 116-120) and a poem about boxing ("Memorial," 307-310), and he started to write the biography of the German middleweight champion Paul Samson-Körner.

As for prostitution, Brecht's *The Good Person of Setzuan* (1940, a.k.a. *The Good Woman of Setzuan*) flies in the face of bourgeois morality when Brecht maintains that Shen Te, the prostitute, is the only decent person in the capital of Setzuan. Almost fifty years earlier, in 1893, Shaw, too, had made a prostitute the "heroine" of a play. His main intention in *Mrs. Warren's Profession* was to create a "counter-portrait to the general image of the romantic, sentimentally attractive courtesan of the stage" (Meisel, 146). Like Brecht, he based his play on economic realities. Through Shen Te and Mrs. Warren, both playwrights demonstrate that it is impossible to be decent in a society that is solely directed towards profit. Both of these women have to sell themselves in order to survive. But for Brecht and Shaw, the term "prostitution" is not restricted to these "immoral" activities. For them, marriage in its traditional form as the sacred institution of bourgeois life is also a sort of prostitution.

In *The Philanderer* (1893), for example, Shaw talks about "the grotesque sexual compacts made between men and women under marriage laws" (Preface to *Plays Unpleasant*, 726). In a poem, Brecht follows Kant and defines marriage as: "The pact made for mutual use of fortunes and sex organs" (*GW* 9, 609; cf. also *The Tutor* [1950], *GW* 6: 2384). Yet prostitution takes on an even more general meaning; it becomes a key word for capitalistic society in general. Shaw maintains that "we have great prostitute classes of men . . . who are daily using their highest faculty to belie their real sentiments: a sin compared to which that of a woman who sells the use of her person for a few hours is too venial to be worth mentioning, for rich men without conviction are more dangerous in modern society than poor women without chastity" (Preface to *Plays Unpleasant*, 726-727).

The concept of prostitution illustrates particularly well how both playwrights use a traditional mode of thinking and turn it into a club to castigate conventional bourgeois society. This device of inversion or counter-convention in Brecht's works can be detected even in the details of language and word formation. The same principle is also characteristic for Shaw's language: "One of Shaw's favorite habits was the use of common words in an uncommon manner; he particularly enjoyed inverting the ordinary usage of terms" (Abbott, 73). Thus Brecht talks about "hired heads" (*Kopflanger*) and Shaw about "the son of a downstart gentleman" (Preface to *Buoyant Billions*, 891). The inversion of ordinary usage of language points out the wrongs in society in the following quote from Brecht's *The Caucasian Chalk Circle* (1945): "Terrible is the seductive power of goodness" (*GW* 5, 2025), and from *Mrs. Warren's Profession*: "But Lord help the world if everybody took to doing the right thing!" (92).

Sudden, unexpected turns themselves run counter to expectation and thus create distance. Mother Courage claims: "I won't touch Army stuff. Not at that price" (*GW* 4, 1369). Undershaft does not exactly flatter politicians when he says about his son, Stephen, "He knows nothing and he thinks he knows everything. That points clearly to a political career" (*Major Barbara*, 490). Well-known quotations, especially from Shakespeare, the Bible, and the German classics, provided both playwrights with an abundance of material. In Brecht's *Saint Joan*, for instance, Graham's description of the stock market echoes the familiar lines from Friedrich Hölderlin's "Hyperion's Song of Fate" (1800):

> Unto prices it was given
> to fall from quotation to quotation
> like water hurtling from cliff to cliff
> deep down into infinity. They didn't stop . . .
> (*GW* 2, 767; *Saint Joan of the Stockyards*, 109)

After Sir Ralph Bloomfield Bonington has "experimented" Dubedat to death in Shaw's *The Doctor's Dilemma*, Sir Ralph proclaims the following from Shakespeare's *Macbeth* (1606):

> Tomorrow and tomorrow and tomorrow
> After life's fitful fever they sleep well
> And like this insubstantial bourne from which
> No traveller returns
> Leave not a wrack behind. (*Doctor's Dilemma*, 541)

The principle of inversion is also at work in larger structural units in the work of Brecht and Shaw. It even determines the structure of whole plays in those cases where the dramatist bases his play on a well-known theme or another play. Examples of Brecht's "counter-plays" are the 1923 *Baal* (to Hanns Johst's *Der Einsame* [*The Lonely One*, 1917]) and the 1956 work *The Days of the Commune* (to Nordahl Grieg's *Die Niederlage* [*The Defeat*, 1937]). Shaw is less radical in his inversions—he often remains within the structural confines of the theatrical convention he attacks, which, to repeat, is mainly the nineteenth-century well-made play. But, as Martin Meisel pointed out in his excellent *Shaw and the Nineteenth-Century Theater*, Shaw nevertheless uses inversions quite effectively: "Even in his primary phase of 'bluebook' drama, Shaw turned to the popular genres of the nineteenth-century theater to provide the vehicle for his social and intellectual concerns. The simplest way of exploiting a popular genre for revolutionary purposes was by the method of systematic counter-convention, by the creation of a genre anti-type" (Meisel, 141). According to Meisel, *Mrs. Warren's Profession* is an anti-type of the courtesan play in general, and of Pinero's *The Second Mrs. Tanqueray* (1892) in particular; *Captain Brassbound's Conversion* (1900) is an anti-type of the adventure melodrama, and *Arms and the Man* an anti-type of romantic comedy and the military melodrama.

Brecht's *Saint Joan* itself re-forms German classical elements—particularly Friedrich Schiller's romantic tragedy *The Maid of Orleans* (1801). And, as Shaw informs us in his preface to *Saint Joan*, his version of the Maid is directed against her treatment in other literary works, especially Schiller's: "When we jump over two centuries to Schiller, we find Die Jungfrau von Orleans drowned in a witch's cauldron of raging romance. Schiller's Joan has not a single point of contact with the real Joan, nor indeed with any mortal women that ever walked this earth" (Preface to *Saint Joan*, 616).

Other structural forms that both playwrights used to create their type of drama are parables, prologues, epilogues, interludes, and the play-within-a-play; intrusion of the author, contrast of form and content, comments on the action by one of the characters, and trial scenes. These all help to create distance and to prevent or diminish empathy. Parables are especially suited to Brecht's and Shaw's didactic theater in that they demonstrate a moral truth by transposing it to a different milieu, in time or place. Thus, Brecht's Setzuan and his Chicago (from *In the Jungle of Cities* [1923]) stand for the world of capitalism and exploitation, and in the Polynesian island of Shaw's *Simpleton of the Unexpected Isles* (1934) and the nameless tropical country in *Too True to be Good* (1932), we recognize his native Britain. Prologues as in Brecht's *Mr. Puntila and His Man Matti* (1948) and Shaw's *Caesar and Cleopatra* (1898), epilogues as in the former's *The Good Person of Setzuan* and the latter's *Saint Joan*, and interludes as in Brecht's *A Man's a Man* (1936) and Shaw's *Man and Superman*—all are instrumental in destroying theatrical illusions of reality.

The play-within-a-play is a particularly effective means of making the audience realize that it is witnessing a play and not reality. It sees its position as an audience watching a play repeated onstage. In Brecht's *The Caucasian Chalk Circle*, members of the collective farm Rosa Luxemburg perform the play of the chalk circle for the entertainment and instruction of the collective farm Galinsk on the stage, as well as for the audience in the theater. In Shaw's *Fanny's First Play*, Count O'Dowda's daughter, Fanny, puts on a play for the benefit of four eminent critics who, as previously indicated, discuss its merits in the epilogue. This structural device provides Shaw with an excellent opportunity to exploit the idea of a "discussion play" and to show the reactions of contemporary critics. Needless to say, the critics who condemn the play are thoroughly satirized. To increase the satirical effect, Shaw even introduces his own name into the discussion.

The critics in *Fanny's First Play* are supposed to try to guess who the author of the play was. Gunn notices "the hackneyed old Shaw touch," but Vaughan opposes: "Rot! . . . Poor as this play is, there's the note of passion in it. . . . Now I've repeatedly proved that Shaw is psychologically incapable of the note of passion" (*Fanny's First Play*, 682-683). Brecht uses the same technique of introducing his name in *Roundheads and Peakheads* (1936), in which one of the landlords has a pointed head "because Mr. Brecht wishes it that way" (*GW* 3, 912), and in *A Man's a Man*, wherein Leokadja Begbick informs the audience:

> Mr. Bertolt Brecht claims: a man is a man.
> And that is something anybody can claim.
> But Mr. Bertolt Brecht then proceeds to prove
> That you can do almost anything with a man. (*GW* 1, 336)

A form closely related in structure to the play-within-a-play is the trial scene, which can be regarded as a central dramatic form of Brecht's theater. In fact, his whole work can be understood as an indictment of the society in which he lived: "Just as with Kafka, the world of Brecht's characters is the legal world. Every one of Brecht's works could be called *The Trial*" (Anders, 24). Trial scenes also provide an excellent forum for argumentation and demonstration of conflicting ideas. They involve the audience intellectually, not emotionally. Even if a play contains no formal trial scene, judgment is passed on society, as in *Saint Joan of the Stockyards*. But in the majority of Brecht's plays, the trial either constitutes one part of the play, as in *Rise and Fall of the City of Mahagonny* (1930) or *The Exception and the Rule* (1929), or it shapes the structure of the whole play, as in *The Measures Taken* (1930) or *The Trial of Lucullus* (1940). Shaw uses the trial scene for similar reasons. *On the Rocks* (1932), *Major Barbara*, and *Widowers' Houses* (1892) are indictments of the society in which he lives, without containing formal trials. In *Saint Joan* and *The Devil's Disciple*, the trial is actually a part of the play; in *Geneva* (1939), the trial determines the whole structure.

Another important feature of both playwrights' anti-illusionary theater is their development of character—or rather the lack of it. Neither Brecht nor Shaw endeavors to present his characters in such a way that the spectators can wholly identify with them. On the contrary, their characters are a "very real conglomeration of contradictory traits" (*GW* 15, 99). These "contradictory traits" are particularly noticeable in Mrs. Warren of *Mrs. Warren's Profession* and Shen Te of *The Good Person of Setzuan*, Undershaft in *Major Barbara* and Mauler in *Saint Joan of the Stockyards*. There is no gradual, organic development but, instead, an abrupt clash of opposites. Mrs. Warren and Shen Te, as well as Undershaft and Mauler, are victims and, at the same time, beneficiaries of a capitalistically organized society. The system forced Shen Te and Mrs. Warren into prostitution, but it also allowed them to become ruthless capitalists—Mrs. Warren the operator of an international call-girl trust, and Shen Te/Shui Ta the boss of a big tobacco factory. Both Undershaft and Mauler, for their part, are driven by the almost pathological fear of poverty, "the worst of all crimes" (*Major Barbara*, 498).

These characterological contradictions are not explained in psychological terms, but by sociological and political circumstances. The system, not the individual characters in the play, is the common target of both Brecht's and Shaw's attack. In the preface to his *Plays Unpleasant* (1898), Shaw warns his readers that "my attacks are directed against themselves, not against my stage figures. . . . The guilt of defective social organization does not lie alone on the people who actually work the commercial makeshifts . . . but with the whole body of citizens" (Preface to *Plays Unpleasant*, 727). Similarly, Brecht's Saint Joan appeals to the audience to bring about change: ". . . and nothing henceforth be considered honorable except what changes this world once for all: it needs it (*GW* 2, 780; *Saint Joan of the Stockyards*, 120).

Because of their dramatic techniques and their antagonism to the dominating art forms of their time, both Brecht and Shaw were accused of not being "realists." Both refuted these accusations with very similar arguments, thereby providing us with valuable insights into their own views of what a drama should be. According to Shaw, it is the function of a playwright not simply to mirror the world, but to interpret it: "Holding up a mirror to nature is not a correct definition of a playwright's art. A mirror reflects what is before it. Hold it up to any street at noonday and it shows a crowd of people and vehicles and tells us nothing about them. A photograph of them has no meaning. . . . The playwright must interpret the passing show by parables" (Meisel, 92-93). Time and again, Shaw emphasizes that it is the duty of responsible playwrights to point out social injustices and remedies for them: "If people are rotting and starving in all directions, and nobody else has the heart or brains to make a disturbance about it, the great writer must" (West, 64).

Only when the social problems are solved can the dramatists turn their attention to other subjects again: "When we succeed in adjusting our social structure in such a way as to enable us to solve social questions as fast as they become really pressing, they will no longer force their way into the theater" (West, 64). As a dramatic realist and social critic, Shaw sees himself in the tradition of Miguel de Cervantes, Percy Bysshe Shelley, Jonathan Swift, John Gay, Pierre Beaumarchais, and Samuel Butler. In his essay on "The Problem Play" (1895), for example, he reveals his indebtedness to Shelley: "In short what is forcing our great poets to follow Shelley in becoming political and social agitators, and to turn the theater into a platform for propaganda and an arena for discussion, is that . . . the political machinery . . . is so old-fashioned . . . that social questions never get solved" (West, 64). Because Shaw wants to analyze rather than reflect reality, his dramatic technique comes close to what Brecht called *Experimentaldramatik*: "The dramas of Ibsen, Tolstoy, Strindberg, Gorky, Chekhov, Hauptmann, Shaw, Kaiser, and O'Neill are experimental dramas. They are great attempts to capture the problems of the time in dramatic form" (*GW* 15, 288). Shaw himself was quite aware of the experimental nature of his own plays, as he implied in the essay "How to Lecture on Ibsen" (1895): "The drama progresses by a series of experiments made on the public by actors and actresses with new plays" (West, 54).

By calling his plays "experiments" (*Versuche*), Brecht places himself in the very same tradition. Like Shaw, he emphasizes the didactic and dialectic nature of his definition of the art of the realistic playwright: "The term realistic means that the playwright is consciously influenced by reality and, at the same time, deliberately attempts to influence reality" (*GW* 19, 356). In explaining his concept of the realistic playwright, Brecht also uses the argument that a mere reflection of reality is meaningless: "The situation is so complicated that a simple rendition of reality has less meaning than ever. A photograph of the Krupp works or A.E.G. [Allgemeine Elektricitäts-Gesellschaft] reveals hardly anything about those institutions. . . . Thus it is indeed necessary to create something 'artificial'—to create art" (Žmegač, 16). To support his concept of realism, Brecht also points to some of the same writers Shaw mentioned as his literary ancestors, particularly Shelley and Cervantes. Shelley's ballad "The Mask of Anarchy" (1819) was the model for Brecht's poem "Freedom and Democracy" (1947; *GW* 9, 943-49); in this connection, Brecht introduced "the reader to a writer of past ages who wrote differently from other bourgeois authors but he must still be called a great realist. The name of this great revolutionary English poet: P. B. Shelley" (*GW* 19, 340). Cervantes' novel *Don Quixote* (1605/1615) is called upon as witness to Brecht's view that "realism does by no means exclude imagination and invention" (*GW* 19, 371).

In addition to using the dramatic devices described above, which allow the audience to rationalize and analyze actions on the stage, many of Brecht's and some of Shaw's works have open endings that are designed to induce the audience to find solutions to the problems presented in the play, along the lines suggested by the playwrights. Both Brecht's *The Good Person of Setzuan* and Shaw's *Saint Joan*, for example, end with passionate pleas to the audience. Not only the plays, but the stage, too, had to be changed to suit these playwrights' purposes. The audience should be made comfortable and the "peephole" of the "fourth wall" should be replaced by a modern version of the Shakespearean stage. "I am in favor of making the playgoer comfortable," Shaw writes in his essay "Playhouses and Plays" (1926), and he continues: "The auditorium must combine the optics and acoustics of a first-rate lecture theatre and a first-rate circus. There must be a forestage extending on occasion to the occupation of all the floor level" (West, 181). The *dramaturg* in Brecht's *The Purchase of Brass* (a.k.a. *The Messingkauf Dialogues*, 1939-42) also points to Shakespeare's theater: "People smoked in these theaters . . . the action took place in the closest proximity to the audience" (*GW* 16, 586-587).

Since neither Brecht nor Shaw wanted a spellbound spectator caught up in an illusion, but rather one who left the theater with a better understanding of the world around him, the Aristotelian tradition had little to offer either man. They dealt with this subject in numerous articles, although Brecht was much more thorough and systematic in his discussion of the Aristotelian theater. Both dramatists even brought the discussion of Aristotelian principles onstage in *Fanny's First Play* and in the dialogue fragments of *The Purchase of Brass* (staged 1963), respectively. Brecht's and Shaw's characters, for instance, do not suffer from a tragic flaw (*hamartia*) within themselves, as Aristotle postulated. In the case of Brecht's Saint Joan, Shen Te, or Grusche (of *The Caucasian Chalk Circle*), and Shaw's Saint Joan, there is, indeed, an inversion of Aristotelian *hamartia*, since trouble arises not from the vices, but from the virtues of the protagonist; the "flaw" lies in the prevailing social and political power structure. Brecht's and Shaw's opposition is especially directed, however, against the central purpose of Aristotelian drama: catharsis. Brecht's criticism of Aristotle's *Poetics* (330 B.C.) begins with an attack on the concept of catharsis: "The spectator's completely independent and critical attitude, which is bent solely on the solution of problems here on earth, is no basis for a catharsis" (*GW* 15, 241).

Shaw, too, is critical of the Aristotelian concept of catharsis, as revealed in this sentence from the essay "About Actors and Acting" (1929): "In the old days Aristotle said that tragedy purged the soul with pity and terror; . . . I have never regarded that as a permanent definition" (West, 197). Like Brecht, he argues that pity and fear only serve to obstruct the all-important social mission of the theater:

> I do not want there to be any more pity in the world, because I do not want there to be anything to pity; and I want there to be no more terror because I do not want people to have anything to fear. . . . You may throw

> pity and terror to one side, and you can reveal life, and you can stimulate thought about it, and you can educate peoples' senses. (West, 197-198)

Like Brecht, Shaw topples the pyramidal structure of Aristotelian drama: "The writer who practices the art of Ibsen therefore discards all the old tricks of preparation, catastrophe, *dénouement*, and so forth without thinking about it.... Hence a cry has arisen that the post-Ibsen play is not a play; and that its technique, not being the technique described by Aristotle, is no technique at all" (*Quintessence of Ibsenism*, 183).

Both writers discarded the Aristotelian unities of time, place, and action, as illustrated by Brecht's *The Caucasian Chalk Circle* and Shaw's *Saint Joan*. It should be noted, however, that Shaw had to be much more cautious since, in order to win a foothold in the theater of his time, he had to devise "certain expedients calculated to make his radically unconventional plays more tolerable to conventional people" (Carpenter, 18). For Aristotle, epic elements had no place in a "unified" drama. Yet Brecht talked about his theater as epic theater and many of Shaw's plays obviously contain epic elements, such as his long prefaces and stage directions. Shaw's play *Back to Methuselah* itself is conceived as a dramatized epic modelled after the Pentateuch. Shaw thus observes in "My Way with a Play" (1946): "The art of all fiction, whether made for the stage, the screen, or the bookshelf, is the art of story-telling. My stock-in-trade is that of Scheherazade and Chaucer no less than of Aristophanes and Shakespeare" (West, 269).

However far both playwrights are removed from Aristotle's *Poetics*, their art and their techniques are new only to the stage of their day—their roots lie in the tradition of Aristotelian rhetoric. In one of his major theoretical works, *The Quintessence of Ibsenism*, Shaw makes it quite clear which line of tradition he follows:

> The new technique is only new on the modern stage. It has been used by preachers and orators ever since speech was invented. It is ... a forensic technique of recrimination, disillusion, and penetration through ideals to the truth, with a free use of all the rhetorical and lyrical arts of the orator, the preacher, the pleader, and the rhapsodist." (*Quintessence*, 184)

Brecht, too, uses many rhetorical devices to convince his audience. His technique of "alienation"—of defamilarization or estrangement (making the familiar strange)—probably the most characteristic feature of his dramatic technique, can be regarded as an excellent rhetorical device to gain the attention of the audience and to persuade it to adopt the author's views. In fact, Aristotle himself suggested a very similar method in his *Rhetoric* (4th century B.C.): "It is therefore well to give to everyday speech an unfamiliar air: people like what strikes them, and are struck by what is out of the way" (*Rhetoric*, 167). The so-called *Verfremdungseffekt* therefore can be classified under the rhetorical category of *persuasio*, the art of convincing an audience. Of the subdivisions of the rhetorical device of *persuasio, docere* and *delectare* rather than *pathos* are the main purposes of Brecht's and Shaw's theater.

Finale

It should be stressed here that there are nevertheless considerable discrepancies between the dramas of Brecht and Shaw. Indeed, the times in which the two playwrights lived and the audiences for which they wrote were quite different. At the end of the nineteenth century Shaw's Britannia still ruled the waves, while in young Brecht's war-ravaged Germany, bourgeois society had begun to disintegrate—a process that was hastened by the defeat of 1918. Shaw directed his works mainly towards British middle-class society, whereas Brecht envisioned a more proletarian, anti-bourgeois audience. In 1898, when Brecht was born, Shaw was already forty-two years old; moreover, the latter was a successful literary critic who had just achieved his first recognition as a playwright. In short: Shaw's dramatic or theatrical concepts were largely formed in the nineteenth century, whereas Brecht profited from new literary and performance developments in the twentieth century.

Some of the discrepancies between Brecht and Shaw can certainly be attributed to differences in temperament. To a large extent, however, they are due to historical, political, and sociological circumstances. Both playwrights had similar intentions and used similar dramatic techniques. One could almost say that exactly those things they have in common separate them from each other: that is, each addresses a certain, singular type of audience in a certain, particular historic situation in order to change the political and social structure of his country. Yet the numerous parallels and similarities in Brecht's and Shaw's dramatic techniques and intentions point to a close affinity, for these two writers belong to the same tradition. Brecht writes, "The line of attempts to create better theatrical productions on the subject of social relations runs from the English Restoration comedy via Beaumarchais to Lenz. Naturalism (of the Goncourts, of Zola, Chekhov, Tolstoy, Ibsen, Strindberg, Hauptmann, and Shaw) shows the influence the European labor movement has had upon the stage" (*GW* 16, 1). Brecht saw himself as a successor to the writers mentioned—particularly Ibsen and Shaw—but he assumed a radically different point of view regarding social class.

We can be sure that Brecht was influenced by some aspects of Shaw's work, not in a narrow, positivistic sense, but in the form of catalytic impulses as they originated from new and pioneering dramatic concepts. Although to a somewhat lesser extent than in the works of Frank Wedekind, Georg Kaiser, or William Shakespeare, Bertolt Brecht found in the works of Bernard Shaw (and to a lesser extent Henrik Ibsen, in such epic dramas of his as *Brand* [1866], *Emperor and Galilean*, and *Peer Gynt*) a confirmation and a reinforcement of his own ideas about drama, particularly during the incubation period of his epic theater.

What follows, in *Pillars of Society: Ibsen, Brecht, Shaw*, is a collection of essays on the plays *Pillars of Society, Ghosts* (1881), *A Doll House* (1879), and *Hedda Gabler* (1890); *The Philanderer, Candida, The Doctor's Dilemma, Androcles and the Lion* (1912), *Major Barbara, Misalliance, Saint Joan*, and *Pygmalion*

(1913); *A Man's a Man, Mother Courage and Her Children, The Caucasian Chalk Circle, Life of Galileo* (1939), *Saint Joan of the Stockyards* (1929), *The Trial of Joan of Arc at Rouen, 1431* (1934/1952), and *The Visions of Simone Machard* (1943); and on the subjects of tragedy, comedy, realism, theatricalism, feminism, and adaptation.

Pillars of Society features close analysis of individual plays by Ibsen, Shaw, and Brecht, plus readable, comparative surveys of these writers' *oeuvres* and careers. Shaw wrote about Ibsen's incipient influence on him in *The Quintessence of Ibsenism*; early in his career, Brecht wrote the aforementioned essay about Shaw titled "Three Cheers for Shaw." These three modern dramatists are thus linked in their common moral, social, and political concerns, as well as in their bridging such dramatic movements as naturalism, symbolism, epic theater, even absurdism. As Brecht and Shaw (and probably Ibsen) would surely want, I'll leave it to the reader to make further connections among the three playwrights, their plays, and their ideas.

Works Cited

Abbott, Anthony S. *Shaw and Christianity*. New York: Seabury Press, 1965.

Anders, Günther. *Bert Brecht: Gespräche und Erinnerungen*. Zürich: Arche Verlag, 1962.

Aristotle. *Poetics*. Trans. Ingram Bywater. New York: Modern Library, 1954.

----------. *Rhetoric*. Trans. W. Rhys Roberts. New York: Modern Library, 1954.

Brecht, Bertolt. *Brecht on Theatre: The Development of an Aesthetic*. Trans. & ed. John Willett. New York: Hill & Wang, 1964.

----------. *Gesammelte Werke* [*Collected Works*]. 20 vols. Ed. Elisabeth Hauptmann. Frankfurt am Main: Suhrkamp Verlag, 1967.

----------. "Memorial for 12 World Champions." *Gesammelte Werke* [*Collected Works*]. Vol. 8. Ed. Elisabeth Hauptmann. Frankfurt am Main: Suhrkamp Verlag, 1967. 307-310.

----------. *Saint Joan of the Stockyards*. Trans. Frank Jones. Bloomington: Indiana University Press, 1969.

Carpenter, Charles A. *Bernard Shaw and the Art of Destroying Ideals*. Madison: University of Wisconsin Press, 1969.

Dukore, Bernard. *Shaw's Theater*. Gainesville: University Press of Florida, 2000.

Enck, John J., *et al.*, eds. *The Comic in Theory and Practice*. New York: Appleton-Century-Crofts, 1960.

Gassner, John. *Dramatic Soundings.* New York: Crown, 1968.

Hecht, Werner. *Brechts Weg zum epischen Theater.* Berlin: Henschelverlag, 1962.

Henderson, Archibald. *George Bernard Shaw: Man of the Century.* New York: Appleton-Century-Crofts, 1956.

Ibsen, Henrik. *Letters and Speeches.* Ed. Evert Sprinchorn. New York: Hill & Wang, 1964.

Laurence, Dan H., ed. *Shaw: Collected Letters.* Vol. 4. New York: Viking, 1988.

Meisel, Martin. *Shaw and the Nineteenth-Century Theater.* 1963. New York: Limelight, 1989.

Russo, James R., ed. *Drama According to Alexander Bakshy, 1916-1946.* Washington, D.C.: Academica Press, 2021.

Shaw, Bernard. *Misalliance, Fanny's First Play,* and *The Dark Lady of the Sonnets.* New York: Brentano's, 1910.

----------. *The Quintessence of Ibsenism.* 1891. New York: Hill & Wang, 1957.

----------. *The Complete Plays of Bernard Shaw.* London: Paul Hamlyn, 1965. Source for all quotations in the text, except in the cases of *Misalliance* and *Fanny's First Play.*

----------. *The Complete Prefaces of Bernard Shaw.* London: Paul Hamlyn, 1965.

----------. *The Drama Observed.* Volume 3: 1897-1911. Ed. Bernard Dukore. University Park: Pennsylvania State University Press, 1993.

Weintraub, Stanley. *The Unexpected Shaw: Biographical Approaches to G.B.S. and His Work.* New York: Frederick Ungar, 1982.

West, E. J., ed. *Shaw on Theater.* 1958. New York: Hill & Wang, 1965.

Willett, John. *The Theatre of Bertolt Brecht: A Study from Eight Aspects.* 1968. London: Methuen, 1977.

Zeiger, Arthur, ed. *Selected Novels of G. Bernard Shaw.* London: Caxton House, 1946.

Žmegač, Viktor. *Kunst und Wirklichkeit. Zur Literaturtheorie bei Brecht, Lukács, und Broch.* Bad Homburg vor-der-Höhe: Gehlen, 1969.

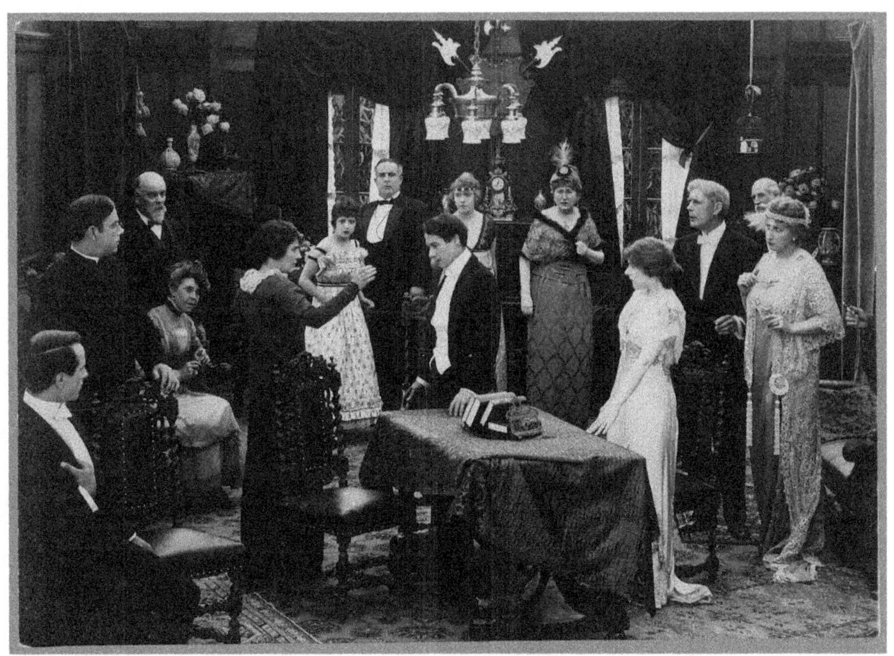

1. *Pillars of Society*, dir. Raoul Walsh, 1916

2. *The Philanderer*, Yale Repertory Theatre, 1982

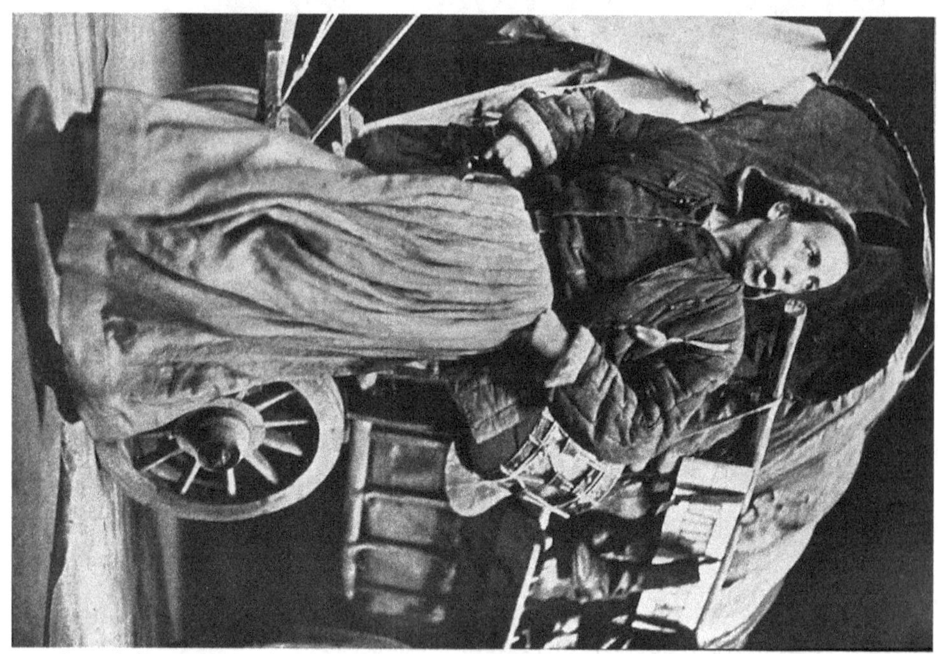

3. Helene Weigel, *Mother Courage and Her Children*, 1949

4. Charles Laughton, *Life of Galileo*, 1947

5. Mary Shaw & Frederick Lewis, *Ghosts*, 1903

6. Dooley Wilson & Add Bates, *Androcles and the Lion*, 1938

PRELUDE

"To the Survivors" (1860), by Henrik Ibsen

Now they sing the hero loud;
But they sing him in his shroud.

Torch he kindled for his land;
On his brow you set its brand.

Taught by him to wield a sword;
Through his heart the steel you drove.

Trolls he smote in hard-fought fields;
You bore him down 'tween traitor shields.

But the shining spoils he won,
These you treasure as your own.

Dim them not, so that the dead
May rest, appeased, his thorn-crowned head.

(Translated by Fydell Edmund Garrett in *Lyrics & Poems from Ibsen*. New York: E. P. Dutton, 1912.)

"The Pillar of Ibsenian Drama: Henrik Ibsen and *Pillars of Society*, Reconsidered"

Pillar or Weak Link?

Pillars of Society is the most ignored of the dozen major Ibsen prose plays. Written between 1875 and 1877, it was an immediate success and made Ibsen the champion of radical artists and social reformers throughout Europe, especially in Germany. Within four months of its publication in October 1877, it was being performed simultaneously at five different theaters in Berlin alone; within a year it had been produced by twenty-seven German-speaking theaters, besides productions in Norway, Denmark, and Sweden. *Pillars of Society* remained part of the standard Ibsen repertory through the first several decades of the twentieth century and was produced a number of times in England and America. But it is rarely presented in English today. Indeed, to take a prominent example, the American Conservatory Theater's revival of the play in 1974 was the first major American production of it in over half a century.

Critically the play has fared no better. *Pillars of Society* was the work that got William Archer excited about Ibsen, and it was the first Ibsen play to be translated into English—by Archer—but a few years after his translation he declared that British theater audiences had grown so advanced and enlightened that "the play already seemed commonplace and old-fashioned" (Archer, xviii). Most modern critics seem to agree, by default if nothing else. To wit: no major critical essay or article on the play has been published in several decades, and even full-length books on Ibsen usually either pass over it entirely or grudgingly accept it as another one in the long bumbling series of Ibsen's "apprenticeship plays." Again and again we hear the same litany of complaints that includes its "creaky plot," its improbabilities, its psychologically unjustified final reversal, its superficial idealism—all colored, of course, by our glib, liberal self-assurance that modern, enlightened contemporary Western society is leagues beyond the short-sighted, conservative, repressed, hypocritical world presented in the play. Moreover, *Pillars of Society* is still approached as a "problem play" in the narrowest definition of that term. (Writing about Shaw—and, as it were, speaking for him—J. L. Styan was correct in pointing out that, actually, all good plays are "problem" plays [Styan, 125].) From this point of view, the meaning of the play indeed becomes simplistic, i.e., that bourgeois society is hypocritical and its leaders are often corrupt. But, as Horatio advised Hamlet long ago, "There needs no ghost, my lord, come from the grave /To tell us this" (*Hamlet*, I.v.129-130; p. 1686).

Ibsen worked longer (over two years) on *Pillars of Society* than on any of his twenty-six plays; five rough drafts of it survive, more than of any other drama of his. Upon its completion, Ibsen said that *Pillars of Society* was "of all my works the one composed with the greatest artistry" (*Oxford Ibsen*, V: 430). Far from being an apprenticeship play, then, it is the mature work of a dramatic genius on which he brought all his imaginative powers to bear—the first time, in fact, that Ibsen's manifold creative talents become totally fused in the same work.

The Road to *Pillars of Society*

Pillars of Society is the first of the twelve-play series of realistic plays referred to by Ibsen himself as his "prose cycle," which he regarded as a single dramatic entity unto itself. It was immediately preceded by the play Ibsen considered his masterpiece, the massive *Emperor and Galilean* (1873). *Emperor and Galilean*, subtitled "a world-historical drama" (*Oxford Ibsen*, IV: 195), deals with the fourth-century A.D. Roman emperor Julian the Apostate, who disavowed the official state religion, Christianity, and tried to reestablish the worship of Dionysus and other pagan deities. The conflict of the play, as outlined below by Julian, is the struggle between Dionysus (the First Empire) and Christ (the Second Empire):

> All human emotions have been forbidden since that day the seer of Galilee began to rule the world. With him, to live is to die. To love and hate are to sin. But has he changed man's flesh and blood? Is man still not earthbound as before? With every healthy fiber of our being we revolt against it; . . . and yet we are told to *will* against our own will! Thou shalt, thou shalt, thou shalt! (*Oxford Ibsen*, IV: 309)

Julian tries to grab hold of the reins of history but is crushed between two monolithic imperatives, each of which makes absolute and contradictory demands. The dialectic is not resolved, and no synthesis emerges; the resolution of this great world-historical dialectic will be the Third Empire, for which the world is still waiting. *Emperor and Galilean* is the dead center of Ibsen's dramaturgy. In fact, one could say that the entire prose cycle is a rewriting of this single play, on a seemingly lesser scale but still featuring conflicting categorical imperatives that are in the end irreconcilable. Put another way, *Emperor and Galilean* is Ibsen's Dantesque *Divina Commedia* (1472) and the prose cycle his Balzacian *Comédie Humaine* (1799-1850). (Interestingly, the play was published one year after Nietzsche's *The Birth of Tragedy* [1872].)

At first glance, *Emperor and Galilean* and *Pillars of Society* seem worlds apart. *Emperor and Galilean* is written in ten acts (it is over 250 pages long in some published texts), employs ten different settings, a cast of over seventy parts plus dozens of supernumeraries, and is set in ancient times. Moreover, although mainly prose, its language is consciously poetic and far removed from that spoken in real life. No wonder that most critics address the two plays, when they address them at all, as if they were the works of two different playwrights. The point, however, is that they were written by the same man.

Some features of *Emperor and Galilean* that are integral to an understanding of Ibsen's dramaturgy should be noted. It is a work of immense scope: its dramatic axis is the collision of world orders and systems of values. The play presents the moral and social consciousness of man, not as something foreordained or established in a system of immutable value, but as something that changes and evolves through the resolution of contradiction—that is, through dialectics or, in dramatic terms, conflict. Finally, in a dramatic text that is already highly referential or allusive, the setting and design are time and again overtly symbolic, metaphorical, or even allegorical.

After completing *Emperor and Galilean*, Ibsen returned to Norway in July 1874 for the first time in a decade and stayed for almost nine months. He had become a celebrity in his homeland. After a performance of *The League of Youth* (1869), he was honored by the students of Oslo with a torchlight procession through the streets that included songs, a poem composed for the occasion, and speeches. This event may well have inspired the final scene of *Pillars of Society*. It was at this rally where he made his famous declaration that the task of the poet was "to see, not to reflect," which he repeated in 1871 in a letter to Georg Brandes (*Correspondence of Henrik Ibsen*, 215). In the spring of 1875 Ibsen left Norway for Germany, where he saw a production of Björnson's *The Bankrupt* (1875). In this play, as in *The Editor* (1874), Björnson had abondoned verse and historical drama to write a contemporary social-problem play that questioned the hypocrisy of bourgeois society. Ibsen would follow the artistic lead of his fellow countryman, but in the process he would "up the ante" considerably,

In 1875, as Ibsen grappled with the problem of form, he was in the middle of his career. He had written fourteen plays, all but one either totally or partially in verse, and over seventy poems. Although he was no longer active in the practical theater, he had directed over 100 plays and done the set and costume designs for dozens of others. But Ibsen was concerned that he was losing touch with the modern theater. *Brand* (1866) and *Peer Gynt* (1867) themselves had not been written for the stage, and no one would even consider a production of *Emperor and Galilean* for over twenty years. As he sought to find the future direction of his work, in 1875 Ibsen wrote his last two poems of any length, "Song of Greeting to Sweden" and a rhymed letter written for the wedding of the son of Frederik Hegel, Ibsen's publisher. Here is a short excerpt from each, both, significantly, touching on the theme of the new or the future:

> Spring-songs, newly turned and cheering
> through our times now wend; —
> singers must be keen of hearing,
> heed what they portend.
> Our blithe song-birds are the youngsters;
> in the people's view
> it's the singer's task amongst us
> to sing in the new. ("Song of Greeting to Sweden," *Collected Poems*: 278)

> Look, my dear friend, "Europa" puts to sea
> full steam ahead for some new destination,
> and we've bought tickets, booked for you and me
> a space up on the poop-deck's privacy. ("A Verse Letter," *Collected Poems*: 275)

Next Ibsen set to work on his new play, *Pillars of Society*, a serious drama in prose set in contemporary times, which he said would be "new and appropriate to the present day in every respect" (*Oxford Ibsen*, V: 430). The most difficult and important decision of his literary career, Ibsen's resolve to abandon verse was based largely on his belief that verse and a literary vocabulary were no longer functional in the modern theater. In an 1883 letter to the actress Lucie Wolf he would write that for verse he could "scarcely find any application worth mentioning in the drama" (*Oxford Ibsen*, VI: 439), and that "the poetic objectives of the future will surely not be reconcilable with it" (*Oxford Ibsen*, VI: 439). In this same letter he advised this same actress that "a true artist of the stage, whose repertoire is the contemporary drama, should not be willing to let a single line of verse cross her lips" (McFarlane, *Ibsen and Meaning*: 369)—quite a declaration from the author of *Love's Comedy* (1862), *Brand*, and *Peer Gynt*.

The choice of dramatic realism and a language close to the vernacular denied Ibsen the lexicon of the great dramatic poets who had preceded him. Instead of traditional poetic diction, Ibsen sought to formulate a new poetic vocabulary rooted in the modern theater and suited to dramatic realism—a poetry of things or objects, let us say, more than words. He would have to bring every element of the theater to bear in order to create this new theatrical poetry: the set, stage directions, props, costumes, and lighting as well as the actual spoken lines of the text and the subtextual or unspoken dialogue that would often lie beneath it.

Ibsen had first started thinking about the play that would eventually become *Pillars of Society* after he had completed *The League of Youth*, a Scribean satirical comedy about contemporary politics. In 1870 he wrote the preliminary notes for a new contemporary comedy: "the theme of the thing generally must be that of women's modest position in society amongst all the bustle of the men and their petty aims" (*Oxford Ibsen*, V: 424). These notes turned into a three-page outline, which he put aside when he started working on *Emperor and Galilean*. Ibsen returned to this outline in 1875, and for a year and a half he worked meticulously on the new play. In 1876, while laboring over the fourth draft of *Pillars of Society*, Ibsen went to Berlin to see the Meiningen Company's acclaimed production of his play *The Pretenders* (written in 1863, immediately before *Brand*). Even though this drama is set in Norway's Viking past, he was struck by the company's use of three-dimensional realistic scenery, their advanced staging techniques, and their prototypical deployment of ensemble playing. Ibsen was not often pleased when he saw his own plays performed, but he called this production "brilliant and spectacular" (Meyer, *Plays of Ibsen*, II: 128). George II, Duke of Saxe-Meiningen, invited the playwright to visit him and study the Company's work in closer detail, which Ibsen did that summer. When he returned to Munich, he scrapped his last working draft of *Pillars of Society*, which called for four different settings, and rewrote the play for a single set.

Ibsen drew on many real-life parallels for the play. The small coastal town in Norway where the action takes place is modeled on Grimstad, where Ibsen had worked for six years as a young man. Edmund Gosse described the town (with a population of less than a thousand) as "a small, isolated, melancholy place, connected with nothing at all, visitable only by steamer" (Gosse, 10). The *Palm Tree* in the play was an actual Grimstad ship, and Karsten Bernick was based on the Grimstad shipping and business tycoon Morten Smith-Petersen. Aune, Bernick's foreman, was very likely drawn from the radical labor organizer Marcus Thrane, whom Ibsen had met. The character of Lona Hessel (Mrs. Bernick's elder half-sister) was suggested by Aasta Hansteen, who herself was involved in the struggle for Women's Emancipation. The practice of superficially patching up unseaworthy ships, insuring them to the hilt, and then sending them out to sea in the hope of their sinking was a common way for shipowners to "cut their losses." This dubious practice received a lot of attention in the press during Ibsen's nine-month stay in Norway in 1874, and the issue reached the level of an international scandal in July 1875, when Samuel Plimsoll unleashed a savage attack in England's Parliament on the "murderers" and "scoundrels" (Lavery, 230-231) who employed such tactics.

Before going further, let me summarize the action of *Pillars of Society* for those who do not know or remember the play. Karsten Bernick is the most prominent businessman in a small coastal town in Norway, with interests in shipping and shipbuilding in a long-established family firm. Now he is planning his most ambitious project yet, backing a railway that will connect the town to the main rail line and open up a fertile valley that he has been secretly buying up. But suddenly Bernick's past comes back to haunt him. Johan Tønnesen, his wife's younger brother, returns from America to the town he fled fifteen years earlier. At the time it was thought he had tried to escape with money stolen from the Bernick family business, as well as to avoid a scandal connected with his affair with an actress. But none of this was true. He left town to take the blame for Bernick, who was the one who had actually been having the affair and was nearly caught with the actress. Besides, there was no money for Johan to take, since at the time the Bernick firm was almost bankrupt.

With Tønnesen from America comes his half-sister Lona, who once loved and was loved by Bernick. But he rejected her and married his current wife for money so that he could rebuild the family business. In the years since Tønnesen left, the town has cultivated ever-greater rumors of his wickedness, helped by Bernick's studious refusal to reveal the truth of the matter. This particular dramatic potion only needs a spark to explode, and it gets one when Tønnesen falls in love with young Dina Dorf, who is the daughter of the actress involved in the scandal of fifteen years ago, and who now lives as a charity case in the Bernick household. Tønnesen demands that Bernick tell the girl the truth; Bernick refuses. When Tønnesen then says he will go back to the United States to clear up his affairs and then come back to town to marry Dina, Bernick sees his chance to get out of this mess of his own making.

His yard is repairing an American ship, the *Indian Girl*, which is deeply unseaworthy. Bernick orders his yard foreman to finish the work by the next day, even if it means sending the ship and its crew to certain death, because he wants Tønnesen to die on board. That way Bernick will be free of any danger of exposure in the future. But matters do not work out quite in the way he wants. Tønnesen runs off with Dina on board another ship that is safe, leaving word that he will be back. And Bernick's young son stows away on the *Indian Girl*, thereby seemingly heading for certain death. Bernick discovers that his plot has gone disastrously wrong on the very night the people of the town have gathered to honor him for his contribution to the city.

The whole of the action in *Pillars of Society* is thus set up for a tragic conclusion, but suddenly Ibsen pulls back from the brink. The yard foreman gets an attack of conscience and rows out to stop the *Indian Girl* from heading to almost certain disaster at sea; Bernick's son is brought back safely by his mother; and Bernick addresses the community, telling them most of the truth and getting away with his sins of the past. His wife even greets the news that he married her only for money as a sign there is now some hope for their marriage.

Pillars of Society, Per Se

In a single stroke *Pillars of Society* transformed the Western stage and moved bourgeois drama onto a new level and into an entirely new frame of reference. Although the specifics of its action are extremely particularized and the characters fully-drawn psychologically, the scope of the drama is huge in its implications and resonances. Remember, Ibsen had said that the mission of the poet was "to see, not to reflect" (*Correspondence of Henrik Ibsen*, 215). His purpose was not to create yet another version of bourgeois mimesis, but to use the stage itself as metaphor; dramatic realism in this case was not the aesthetic end, but the means. I wish to clarify this statement through a close examination of the first few scenes of the play.

The setting is the garden-room in the home of Bernick the shipbuilder. There are large glass doors and windows upstage through which a spacious garden is visible. Beyond the garden is a fence and "a street, on the far side of which is a row of small, gaily painted timber houses" (*Oxford Ibsen*, V: 23), where we can get a glimpse of "people going about in the heat of the day, sweating and straining over their petty affairs" (*Oxford Ibsen*, V: 26), as the schoolmaster Rørlund describes the scene. The room is only partially lit by the bright, early afternoon sunshine coming from outside. Onstage a group of the town's civic-minded women is sewing clothes for distribution to the poor. Even though it is warm and sunny outside—a rare thing in Norway—everyone is seated inside. During the scene the curtains are even drawn such that the room is lit solely by artificial light. Rørlund stands reciting aloud from a book; and upstage in the garden, young Olaf (the Bernicks' thirteen-year-old son) runs around playing with a toy crossbow, a weapon suggestive of Norway's Viking past.

Within the first few lines of the play, Aune, who is almost an out-and-out socialist, tries to get in to see Bernick and argues with Krap (Bernick's confidential clerk) about his right to do as he pleases in his "free time," which leads to a hackneyed discussion about the very notion of freedom. Rørlund himself praises the small community for its moral fiber, it faith in the old, traditional values, and its resistance to the new and immoral ideas running rampant in the world outside, which has "no moral foundation under its feet" (*Oxford Ibsen*, V: 25). Throughout the scene we hear muffled voices coming from Bernick's inner office. Finally, the "pillars" of this particular society, Bernick and the merchants Rummel, Sandstad, and Vigeland, come slinking out of the smoke-filled room. From this moment on, the contradictions in this society become more and more visible, and they are exposed by Ibsen with ferocious irony as well as uncanny accuracy.

The world of the play creates a microcosm of Norwegian society, and, appropriately for the first play in a prose cycle that will explore the nature of human consciousness, the inhabitants of this society operate on the most primitive level of social and ethical consciousness. It is not that people here do not have good intentions, or that they never take moral action. This is not so much an immoral world as an amoral one; and before there can be morality, there must be the consciousness of morality. Henry James himself praised *Pillars of Society* for "its large, dense complexity of moral cross-references . . ." (James, 252), but the society the play depicts happens to be a sub-ethical "community of animals" (as Hegel described the most primitive level of human social consciousness; see Johnston, *The Ibsen Cycle*: 41-43).

Yet bear in mind that the play depicts *bourgeois* society, which, perhaps more than any other segment, seeks to re-create the world in its own image or likeness. It considers itself, not just one of many potential ways of structuring society, but the absolute pinnacle of all human thought and development. In an act of self-preservation, bourgeois society creates a mythos, an idealized image of itself that progressively has less and less to do with reality. In the process language is turned on its head, and vocabulary becomes little more than just another bourgeois manifestation or extension of itself. Thus, blatant, unrestrained economic exploitation is called "free trade," acts of naked military aggression become "protective reactions" or "self-defense," etc. Although this idealized mythos grows more and more elaborate, and may even seem at times to be anti-bourgeois, the reality is that, in all its interactions, bourgeois humanity's relationship to its environment and to the rest of mankind is defined exclusively in terms of self-interest and utilitarianism. It is this gap between the bourgeoisie's idealized image of itself and the actual reality of human existence that *Pillars of Society* seeks to explore.

It's worth noting at this point that the existence of bourgeois, capitalist society depends at least as much on the exploited as it does on the exploiters. None of the "exploiters" in *Pillars of Society*, for example, makes it a conscious goal to commit evil. In fact, everyone here feels that he or she is doing the proper thing. Some of them do commit crimes out of necessity—Aune does not want to be an accessory to mass murder, but he does want to protect his family. Others are blind or consistently able to see the world as the world is not—an ability, according to Rørlund, that is partly an inborn gift and partly an acquired trait. But the most dangerous are those who alter the definition of right and wrong to accommodate their own needs or desires, like Bernick.

One of the most disturbing aspects of the play is that when morality does triumph, it does so only accidentally. Some hope initially seems to lie in individual acts of moral courage: for example, Aune's boarding the *Indian Girl* after it has set out, which prevents what would be the ultimate calamity of the play—the death of a number of people, including Olaf. Ironically, Aune's action also saves Bernick and alters what had appeared to be the inevitable tragic design of *Pillars of Society*. But what Aune does is not truly moral or heroic, for it was really Betty Bernick's pleas that got him to disobey her husband's orders. What would he have done if left solely to his own devices?

These and other characters make up a cast of remarkably drawn individuals woven into a complex web of interaction and motivation. Hilmar Tønnesen (Mrs. Bernick's cousin), for his part, is a harmless, domesticated Viking who calls for daring and adventure but who has completely assimilated bourgeois values and prejudices. Johan Tønnesen operates as a sort of psychic double for Bernick: in simplistic terms, something like the good part of him; Lona, spurned by Bernick, has spent the last fifteen years educating his alter ego. But Bernick, when he gets desperate, decides that he must kill off this alter ego—Johan—in order to save himself. Rørlund is perhaps even more complex than these figures. He spouts the most moral platitudes in the play, and he actually believes himself. Indeed, he could be termed the Bard of the Bourgeoisie—the most valuable tool of the "pillars of society" because he doesn't have to be bribed, blackmailed, or bullied into helping them with his words. Yet Rørlund is at the same time a watered-down Brand who lashes out at the modern world as weak and unclean. He sees industrialization and technology, for example, as another form of idolatry and is against the railroad, which will cut through the virgin countryside and better link his community with the outside world.

Some of the women in this society offer the major hope for change, partly due to their superior instincts and partly due to their centuries of exploitation. Only the women in the play are self-sacrificing, and a few are courageous in their attempts to break the shackles of social and sexual bondage. I am referring not just to Martha Bernick (Karsten Bernick's sister) and Dina Dorf, the only persons in the community who really question what is happening around them, but also to Lona Hessel, the sole character in the play to have reached a new and higher level of consciousness. Mrs. Rummel, Mrs. Holt, and Mrs. Lynge, the chorus of gossipmongers whose prototypes may be found in *Love's Comedy*, themselves have been brainwashed to worship their otherwise meaningless roles as appendages to the men who run the bourgeois world. Ironically, these women imitate their male counterparts and build their own caste system: just as the men send the women out of the room when they talk business, for example, the women send Dina and their daughters (Hilda Rummel and Netta Holt) out of the room when they talk gossip.

Dina Dorf, a lass of spunk and courage, is clearly tied to Højrdis of *The Vikings at Helgeland* (1857) and Svanbild of *Love's Comedy*. In two years she will be the Nora who slams the door on the doll house. Martha Bernick is akin to the Thea of *Hedda Gabler* (1890)—both of them strong women who may not initially appear to be so. Martha's sister-in-law, Betty Bernick, herself might have been an independent person of substance, but instead she has lived the dutiful, self-abnegatory myth of the bourgeois wife. Lona, for her part, is a woman from the New World, a location whose name speaks for itself. Like Apollo or Athena, Lona is the "bringer of light"; her entrance is prepared for by the closing of all the windows and the pulling shut of the curtains. She enters, then parts the curtains to let the light in and opens the windows to air out the room. Ironically, Lona was first mentioned in the play by Mrs. Rummel as the "dark spot" ("sun spot" in Norwegian; *Oxford Ibsen*, V: 34) on Bernick's happiness.

The plot of the *Pillars of Society*, rather than being "creaky," is one of the clearest indications of Ibsen's mastery of his medium. There is a late point of attack, with the action of the play gaining momentum at the same time as (figuratively speaking) it moves backward in time, growing more and more complex, and expanding its radius of implications. What is actually a long series of subplots is unified into a single, ever-widening, and whole action, with each complication a cog in the wheel that drives the catastrophe forward even as it simultaneously refers back to, or threatens to reveal, some previous lie, deception, or crime. For example, Aune's moral crisis over the fate of the *Indian Girl* and its crew triggers a further moral crisis in Bernick, pushing him to make the decision that human life must be sacrificed for the greater good of society. Krap's own attempt to be conscientious (or is he just trying to get Aune fired?) reveals Bernick's automatic, almost unconscious ability to manipulate indiviuals and events.

Bernick sinks lower and lower in the audience's estimation as the plot forces him into corner after corner and he responds with greater and greater moral audacity, if not arrogance. Step by step he is pushed beyond the boundaries of any locus of moral values. By the end of Act III, Bernick has become a trapped, raging animal who takes for granted that his actions are beyond good and evil because he is working for the good of society—providing jobs, bringing prosperity to the community, and aiding progress in general. If this type of reasoning sounds familiar, that is because the same arguments are used every day to justify the creation of neutron bombs and the rape of the natural environment. Far from being outdated or simplistic, the strategic maneuverings of the characters and the conspiratorial nature of their business affairs in *Pillars of Society* are precisely in line with the contemporary reality of politics, technology, and commerce.

Structurally, the public nature of Acts I and IV of the play are balanced against the private nature of Acts II and III, which are composed almost entirely of scenes between two or three individuals. (Imagistically, this public-private opposition is complemented by the opposition or struggle between light and darkness.) This balance aside, the great structural problem in *Pillars of Society* has always been the ending, where the play seems to shift gears. To paraphrase one nineteenth-century critic, Ibsen planned a tragedy and bouleversed it into a farce (*Oxford Ibsen*, V: 434). A momentous inevitability, a tragic force that has been building up for two-and-a-half hours, is suddenly reversed in the last ten minutes. How, then, are we to take the ending of the play and Bernick's apparent epiphany? Is Ibsen trying to drive home some naïve, idealistic point about man's ability to change and ultimately to change the world? Can years of deception and crime be atoned for so easily and bloodlessly? In his great confessional scene, Bernick claims to be coming clean, but can he or should he be taken totally at his word? He is remarkably vague about the past and Johan's role, or non-role, in it, he does not even mention Lona, and he conveniently skips over the affair of the *Indian Girl* and his thwarted attempt at mass murder. This last scene demands closer examination, since it is the single most important critical—and directorial—problem in the drama.

The action of *Pillars of Society* has been propelled relentlessly forward to what is clearly intended to be a *scène à faire*. Lona stands clutching the letters that can expose and destroy Bernick. Johan and Dina, not to mention Olaf, seem to be on their way to certain death. Up the street come parade banners and a torchlight procession. Although this final movement thus seems like something out of the well-made play, Ibsen undercuts every one of the potentially melodramatic or sentimental elements in it. Lona tears up the letters; Olaf, Johan, and Dina are saved, as is the *Indian Girl*; the parade and festivities lose all direction. As Bernick prepares to address the crowd, he stands behind a large curtain like an actor about to enter the stage and play a grand scene. Rørlund even lays the icons of civilization at the feet of this "pillar of society": the silver goblet and coffee service (crafts), an album of photographs (technology), and a "volume of sermons, printed on vellum and luxuriously bound" (art and religion; *Oxford Ibsen*, V: 120). The encomium by Rørlund is the longest speech in the play and is followed by Bernick's own lengthy and platitudinous confession, which wins over the townspeople. Then there is the final tableau of Bernick surrounded by his family, in addition to the sententious exchanges with Lona that remind us of the optimistic, concluding couplets of much eighteenth-century drama.

If this last scene is not ironic, and even comic (recall that in 1870 when Ibsen began work on *Pillars of Society*, he called it a "comedy" [McFarlane, *Cambridge Companion to Ibsen*: 75]), then there is no such thing as irony. Bernick may well believe every word he says, but the fact is, he has just pulled off another grand political coup, the greatest of his career, and he has turned to advantage even his own guilt. Far from being naïvely idealistic, the play's ending poses a paradox, further underscores the inherent contradictions on which this society is based, and stresses the helplessness of humanity in the hands of a "pillar of society" like Bernick. As Rolf Fjelde points out in his introduction to the play, "Bernick is that most dangerous type of public man, the born opportunist who, with the agility of a dropped cat, can turn even contrition to his own advantage. Undoubtedly, he must continue to be closely watched" (*Complete Major Prose Plays*, 12).

Pillars of Society and the Prose Cycle

I cannot think of another playwright whose work is as self-referential as Ibsen's. It is as if, for his entire career, he were rewriting a single *Ur*-play. Ibsen himself said that "only by grasping and comprehending my entire production as a continuous and coherent whole will the reader be able to receive the precise impression I sought to convey in the individual parts of it" (*Letters and Speeches*, 330). He also said that in order to be understood, his plays had to be read "in the order in which I wrote them" (*Letters and Speeches*, 330). It is therefore important to look at *Pillars of Society* in relation to the plays that follow it, especially the next three, *A Doll House* (1879), *Ghosts* (1881), and *An Enemy of the People* (1882). Together they form a tetralogy linked structurally as well as thematically. Furthermore, the conflict in each play leads to a dialectical synthesis that serves as the "given" (or thesis) for the next play. The opening work, *Pillars of Society*, begins on the most primitive level of social and ethical consciousness, as I have discussed. Then each play in the tetralogy takes this consciousness one step farther, as personified in the protagonists: after Bernick, Nora, Mrs. Alving, and Dr. Stockmann; in this scheme, Bernick's crude, naïve fascism develops into Stockmann's scientific, impassioned vision of a moral Platonic dictatorship. The public-private structure of the four acts of *Pillars of Society* itself is a paradigm of the structure of the first four plays in the cycle taken together; i.e., the large-cast, externally driven plays, *Pillars of Society* and *An Enemy of the People*, are balanced by the two small-cast, inner-directed plays, *A Doll House* and *Ghosts*.

As early as 1882 Ibsen was already referring to his prose plays as "a series" (*Oxford Ibsen*, V: 1). After the completion of *Ghosts*, in correspondence with an American publisher, he insisted that the three plays (*Pillars of Society*, *A Doll House*, and *Ghosts*) be published in the order in which they were written: "This one [*Ghosts*] goes the furthest, and ought therefore to be the last of the series. This should, I suggest, open with *Pillars of Society*, after which should come *A Doll House*, since this forms as it were an introduction to, or preparation for, *Ghosts*" (*Oxford Ibsen*, V: 1). Each of these three plays has a single set, and all are set indoors (as is *An Enemy of the People*). Each of the dramas centers on the family as the paradigmatic unit of society; *Ghosts* is even subtitled "a family drama" (*Oxford Ibsen*, V: 345). Karsten Bernick himself declares that "the family is the core of society" (*Oxford Ibsen*, V: 41)—so much so in *Pillars of Society* that at least half of the large cast is related by birth or marriage. And *Pillars of Society*, like *An Enemy of the People* at the close of the tetralogy, ends with a final tableau of the family huddled together. In the course of the first three plays in this tetralogy, the scope of the action is wound tighter and tighter, as the casts shrink from nineteen to seven to five. The length of the action is itself reduced, as *Pillars of Society* takes place over five days, *A Doll House* three days, and *Ghosts* a single night. (This last play, incidentally, observes all three classical unities.)

In each of the first four cycle plays, an alien, a visitor returning or coming from afar—Lona Hessel, Mrs. Linde, Oswald Alving, Thomas Stockmann—brings with him or her a new, enlightened code of ethics or system of values and thereby sets in motion the dialectical conflict of the drama. Each of these characters arrives armed with a new outlook on life that challenges or calls into question the existing social and moral order. In *Pillars of Society*, Lona brings the ideals of truth and freedom and comes from a mythical American West—the New World or the Land beyond the Horizon, where people are genuinely liberated. These ideals of truth and freedom then return with a vengeance in the next three plays, as they also do later in *The Wild Duck* (1884).

Each of the four plays in the tetralogy also revolves around a central dramatic or poetic metaphor. In *An Enemy of the People* it is the metaphor of the Baths. The Baths are the lifeblood of the community, but they are poisoned: instead of cleansing and healing as they should, they cause harm. Stockmann, as a scientist, proposes his new plan for the ideal Baths, a plan suggestive of the ideal Hellenic society he envisions. In *Ghosts*, the central metaphor is worship of the dead, sociologically a ritual that has developed in every culture and civilization on earth—except that here that worship is extended to include dead ideas and dead values. This metaphor is coupled with the most savage and uncompromising one in Ibsen's dramatic *oeuvre*: congenital syphilis, or one generation's tainted legacy to the next. In *A Doll House*, of course, the title refers to a house built for dolls in which people are trying, and ultimately failing, to live.

Aside from its own central metaphor, which I shall discuss below, *Pillars of Society* contains a number of motifs and parallels found in Ibsen's other plays. Most obvious is the situation of the two women (Lona Hessel and Betty Bernick) in love with the same man, which we see in *Hedda Gabler*. The most significant parallels to *Pillars of Sociey*, however, are to be found in *John Gabriel Borkman* (1896)—the last play before the epilogue of the cycle in 1899, *When We Dead Awaken* (subtitled "a dramatic epilogue" [*Oxford Ibsen*, VIII: 235]). The protagonist of each drama, a captain of industry, has married for money, not love. *John Gabriel Borkman*, written almost twenty years after *Pillars of Society*, is a reexamination of a Bernick who has fallen from power. Betty, excluded from this Bernick's life and work, has here grown into the bitter, vengeful Gunhild. Olaf has grown up into Erhart in *John Gabriel Borkman*: each has been groomed to carry on the life's work of his father, but both wind up running away from home. Bernick's prosaic enthusiasm about the railroad plan should be compared to Borkman's own aria as he surveys his kingdom for the last time:

> BERNICK. . . . Just think of the huge tracts of forest it will open up! Think of all those rich mineral deposits that can be worked! Think of the river, with one waterfall after another! What about the industrial development that could be made there! (*Oxford Ibsen*, V: 41)

> BORKMAN. I feel the veins of metal, reaching their curving, branching, beckoning arms out to me. . . . (*His hands outstretched.*) But I'll whisper to you here in the silence of the night. I love you, lying there unconscious in the depths and the darkness! I love you, you riches straining to be born . . . I love you, love you, love you! (*Complete Major Prose Plays*, 1021)

The central metaphor of *Pillars of Society* is the *Indian Girl*, a ship whose hull and substructure have rotted away entirely but which is made to look seaworthy by superficial patching or "bandaging." It is not surprising, of course, that a Norwegian writer should use a ship as a symbol; Ibsen did it often in his poetry. The image of the ship, which Shaw himself used in *Heartbreak House* (1919), stands for the "ship of state" or the state of society. The talk about the *Indian Girl* in *Pillars of Society* may seem literal, but in the context of the play, it is designed to extend beyond the realm of realism:

> AUNE. That boat's hull is absolutely rotten, Mr. Bernick. The more we patch it, the worse it gets. (*Oxford Ibsen*, V: 52)

> KRAP. I'm very sorry . . . but that's the honest truth. Something funny's going on, I tell you. Been no new timber put in at all, as far as I could judge. Just been plugged and caulked and patched with bits of plating and tarpaulin and that sort of thing. All faked up! The *Indian Girl* will never make New York. She'll go to the bottom like a sprung bucket. (*Oxford Ibsen*, V: 80)

Ibsen is implying that if we want to change society, we must bring new "timber" and rebuild from the inside out, not just continue to repair the faulty exterior. I am reminded here of the letter (to Georg Brandes) where he expressed a similar lack of faith in political movements: "Everyone wants their own special revolutions, always in external things. What is really needed is a revolution of the human spirit" (*Letters and Speeches*, 106-107). Pillars of society, indeed.

Works Cited

Archer, William. Intro. *The Collected Works of Henrik Ibsen:* The League of Youth *and* Pillars of Society. Vol. 6. New York: Scribner's, 1906. vii-xxiii.

Gosse, Edmund. *Henrik Ibsen*. New York: Charles Scribner's Sons, 1907.

Greenblatt, Stephen, *et al.*, eds. *The Norton Shakespeare*. New York: W. W. Norton, 1997. 1668-1756 (*Hamlet*).

Ibsen, Henrik. *The Oxford Ibsen:* An Enemy of the People, The Wild Duck, Rosmersholm. Ed. & trans. James Walter McFarlane. Vol. 6. London: Oxford University Press, 1960.

----------. *The Oxford Ibsen:* Pillars of Society, A Doll's House, Ghosts. Ed. & trans. James Walter McFarlane. Vol. 5. London: Oxford University Press, 1961.

----------. *The Oxford Ibsen:* The League of Youth, Emperor and Galilean. Ed. & trans. James Walter McFarlane. Vol. 4. London: Oxford University Press, 1963.

----------. Letter to Georg Brandes dated Dec. 20, 1870. In *Ibsen: Letters and Speeches.* Ed. Evert Sprinchorn. New York: Hill & Wang, 1964. 105-107.

----------. *The Oxford Ibsen:* Little Eyolf, John Gabriel Borkman, When We Dead Awaken. Ed. & trans. James Walter McFarlane. Vol. 8. London: Oxford University Press, 1977.

----------. Letter to Georg Brandes dated May 18, 1871. In *The Correspondence of Henrik Ibsen.* Ed. Mary Morison. 1905. New York: Haskell House, 1978. 213-215.

----------. *Ibsen: The Complete Major Prose Plays.* Trans. Rolf Fjelde. New York: Farrar, Straus, & Giroux, 1978.

----------. *The Collected Poems of Henrik Ibsen*. Trans. John Northam. 273-278. https://www.hf.uio.no/is/tjenester/virtuelle-ibsensenteret/ibsen-arkivet/tekstarkiv/oversettelser/34498.pdf
accessed online Aug. 29, 2022.

James, Henry. "On the Occasion of *Hedda Gabler*" (1891). In James, Henry. *The Scenic Art: Notes on Acting and the Drama, 1872-1901*. New York: Hill & Wang, 1948. 243-260.

Johnston, Brian. *The Ibsen Cycle: The Design of the Plays from* Pillars of Society *to* When We Dead Awaken. 1975. University Park: Pennsylvania State University Press, 1992.

Lavery, Brian. *The Conquest of the Ocean: The Illustrated History of Seafaring*. London: DK Limited/Penguin Random House, 2013.

McFarlane, James Walter. *Ibsen and Meaning: Studies, Essays, and Prefaces, 1953-87*. Norwich, U.K.: Norvik, 1989.

----------, ed. *The Cambridge Companion to Ibsen*. New York: Cambridge University Press, 1994.

Meyer, Michael, trans. & intro. *The Plays of Ibsen*. Vol. 2. New York: Washington Square Press/Pocket Books, 1986.

Styan, J. L. *The Dark Comedy: The Development of Modern Comic Tragedy*. 1962. Cambridge, U.K.: Cambridge University Press, 1968.

"Bernard Shaw, *The Philanderer*, and the (Un)Making of Shavian Drama"

Dramatic Beginnings

> "For the right moment you must wait, as Quintus Fabius Maximus did most patiently when warring against Hannibal . . .; but when the time comes you must strike hard, as Fabius did, or your waiting will be in vain, and fruitless."
> —Motto of the Fabian Society and epigraph of the first Fabian tract, January 1884.

Shaw was thirty-seven years old in 1893 when he started work on *The Philanderer*, his second play after *Widowers' Houses* (1892). In 1893 Shaw was known in London intellectual circles as a respected music critic, an accomplished orator, and a Socialist propagandist. He had written five novels, two of them published, both unsuccessfully. In 1889 he had edited and contributed two essays to the enormously influential *Fabian Essays in Socialism*, which went through three editions within a year. On July 18, 1890, Shaw delivered his famous lecture on Ibsen to an enthusiastic audience at St. James Restaurant; this lecture was then expanded and published in 1891 as *The Quintessence of Ibsenism*—the first full-length study of Ibsen in the English language.

Shaw's writing of *The Philanderer* in 1893 began, as he himself put it, "with a slice of life; most of the first act really occurred" (Henderson, *Fortnightly Review*: 439). Here is how it did so: at the age of twenty-nine, Shaw had lost his virginity to an insistent, passionate, strong-willed widow named Mrs. Jenny Patterson, who was twelve years his senior. Mrs. Patterson, one of his mother's singing students, invited the shy young man over to her London apartment one afternoon for tea. Shaw accepted the invitation, and before the afternoon was over the aggressive woman had almost literally raped him. Shaw did not resist her advances. "I permitted her," he told Ellen Terry in a letter of October 12, 1896, "being intensely curious on the subject" (St. John, 90).

When Frank Harris asked him forty years later what his affair with Jenny Patterson was like, Shaw responded in a letter dated June 20, 1930: "If you want to know what it was like, read *The Philanderer*, and cast her for the part of Julia, and me for that of Charteris" (Harris, 30). He also wrote to Hesketh Pearson that "Mrs. Patterson was my model for Julia; and the first act of *The Philanderer* is founded on a very horrible scene between her and Florence Farr" (Pearson, 123). Besides supplying Shaw with the opportunity to break off with Jenny, this incident supplied him with the opening situation for his new play. On June 27, 1893, *The Philanderer* was completed, four and a half months after Shaw had started work on it. But the four acts of the final version of the play (published in 1898) were originally conceived as three acts; and in 1930 Shaw made minor changes to the play for his *Collected Works* and recompressed Acts II and III into a single act, thereby turning *The Philanderer* back into the three-act work it was intended to be. His seriousness about the play is evidenced by the fact that the revisions and alterations to its various drafts are more extensive than those for any of his fifty-two plays, with the possible exception of *Heartbreak House*.

Dealing with the serious literary and academic criticism of *The Philanderer* is a swift and easy task, because very little exists. Pick up any number of the full-length critical books on Shaw, and you will find that either they do not even mention the play or it is written off in a few sentences or even phrases. Here are a few of them: "a self-congratulatory piece of autobiography" and "a retrogressive step in Shaw's career as a dramatist" (Wilson, 115); "an apology for his own comprehensive philanderings" (Valency, 89); Shaw's "worst play" (St. John Ervine, 108). Even in the massive field of Shaw scholarship, then, there is no large body of critcism to plough through; *The Philanderer* is only grudgingly accepted into the Shavian canon. This judgment began to be altered in the late 1970s, it's true, when there was a resurgence of interest in the play and it was performed at the Roundabout in New York, Britian's National Theatre, and at the Yale Repertory Theatre. Later, serious studies of *The Philanderer* started to appear in such books as J. Ellen Gainor's *Shaw's Daughters* (1991) and Peter Gahan's *Shaw Shadows* (2004). Nevertheless, the play is still seen as inferior to Shaw's major works, as a mere preparatory sketch for the larger canvases of his subsequent dramatic masterpieces.

Now a deadly critical distortion occurs when critics take an author's greatest works and set such "masterpieces" up as literary peaks, in relation to which all his other work is viewed as either an ascent toward these heights or a descent from them. Thus, *The Philanderer* is usually approached simply as an amateurish, rough, flawed version of *Man and Superman* (1903), *The Doctor's Dilemma* (1906), or *Getting Married* (1908), depending on the individual critic's bent. Putting a playwright's work into the perspective of his career as a whole can indeed be valuable and illuminating, but it is not useful or valid to say that *Ajax* (450-430 B.C.) is not a good play because it is not *Oedipus* (430 B.C.), that *Little Eyolf* (1894) is a bad play because it is not *Hedda Gabler* (1890), or that *Andromache* (1667) is somehow flawed because it is not *Phaedra* (1677).

We all bring expectations and preferences to the theater, critics no less than audiences; this is especially true for a playwright with whose work we are familiar. In fact, to facilitate the clarification and definition of our expectations, we invent adjectival forms of the playwright's name—Brechtian, Shavian, Shakespearean, Aristophanic, Racinian, Pinteresque, Beckettian. Without realizing it, we start approaching a playwright's work, not on its own terms, but solely in terms of how much or how little it fits the ideal Shavian, Sophoclean, or Chekhovian model. In Shaw criticism, the holy trinity consists of *Major Barbara* (1905), *Heartbreak House* (1919), and *Saint Joan* (1923), so the critics evaluate and discuss his entire dramatic *oeuvre* on the basis of how similar or dissimilar any given play is to these works. And since *The Philanderer* is quite dissimilar to each of the three plays named, it is considered an inferior drama.

To be sure, critical perceptions of *The Philanderer* have been severely altered by what seemed to be Shaw's own disowning of the play in a letter to Ellen Terry in August of 1896:

> To tell you the truth, I have had a shock down here. In the evenings they make me read plays to them; and the other night I had to fall back on my Opus 2, a comedy called *The Philanderer*, now some years old. It turned

> out to be a combination of mechanical farce with realistic filth which quite disgusted me; and I felt that if my plays get stale at this rate, I cannot afford to postpone their production longer than I can help. (St. John, 38)

This letter has been quoted dozens of times by disparagers of the play. However, we must bear in mind the context of the letter. Shaw was writing it to persuade Terry to undertake the role of Candida, so what was wrong, in this instance, with talking down one of his other plays that had a tempting part for an actress?

On April 19, 1898, *The Philanderer* was published in *Plays Unpleasant*. This volume also included *Widowers' Houses* and *Mrs. Warren's Profession* (1893); on the same day *Plays Pleasant* was also published, including *Arms and the Man* (1894), *Candida* (1894), *The Man of Destiny* (1895), and *You Never Can Tell* (1897). Shaw became a literary sensation as a result. The most favorably received play in these two collections was *Candida*, and the most savagely attacked was *Mrs. Warren's Profession*—in relation to which *The Philanderer* fared only slightly better. *The Academy*'s critic, for one, charged Shaw with ignoring the emotions of his audience in this work:

> *The Philanderer* is professedly the study of a male flirt. . . . The defect of the play seems most clearly to exhibit Mr. Shaw's own main defect—the utter want of any real experience in life. . . . he has not understood, has not sympathised . . .; it does not move him at all on the side for which theatre mainly exists, that of the human emotion. (Murray, 614)

Shaw would hear this charge again and again—that he was heartless, cold-blooded, inhuman, unrealistic, merely delighting in paradox. But, in his "Author's Apology" (1902) for *Mrs. Warren's Profession*, he pointed out that his plays seemed paradoxical and inhuman not in relation to real life, but only in relation to the sentimental, romantic, idealized theatrical notions of human behavior that "did not exist off the stage." Shaw went on declare "that the real secret of the cynicism and inhumanity of which shallower critics accuse me is the unexpectedness with which my characters behave like human beings, instead of conforming to the romantic logic of the stage" ("Author's Apology" for *Mrs. Warren's Profession*, xxiii).

The Philanderer as/at Play

> "If you marry, you will regret it: if you do not marry, you will also regret it. Believe a woman, you will regret it, believe her not, you will also regret it. Hang yourself, you will regret it, do not hang yourself, and you will regret it: this is the sum and substance of all philosophy." —Søren Kierkegaard, *Either/Or*, 1843 (54).

To the play itself: the world of *The Philanderer* is that of the middle and upper-middle class, and the opening presents a light scene of lovemaking between Grace and Charteris, two intelligent people. This first scene appears to be one of high comedy, very sophisticated and with an emphasis on verbal wit. As the scene gathers momentum, it is interrupted by Julia, and a scene of sharp contrast follows, one that seems almost farcical on account of its total reversal of the expected male-female roles of pursuer and pursued. As this scene approaches its climax, it too is interrupted: by the entrance of Craven and Cuthbertson, two long-lost friends. The Ibsenite Realist, Charteris, is now surrounded by Idealists: a Romantic Idealist, Julia, who believes in the ideal of "depth of feeling" as the guarantee that she is a special human being with a "soul"; a Military Idealist, Craven, who sees society as one large barracks and the observing of social conventions and proprieties as the equivalent of "following orders"; and a Theatrical Idealist, Cuthbertson, who believes that life should aspire to the ideals of a sentimental play. Charteris makes a partial revelation about the preceding action to Craven and Cuthbertson, followed by a full revelation to Cuthbertson, which is a good outline of Act I:

> CHARTERIS. Julia wants to marry me: I want to marry Grace. I came here tonight to sweetheart Grace. Enter Julia. Alarums and excursions. Exit Grace. Enter you and Craven. Subterfuge and excuses. Exeunt Craven and Julia. And here we are. (*Philanderer*, 38)

In Act II the action moves into a polyphonic series of duologues, and the love triangle expands to a quartet. The opening scene introduces Sylvia, Julia's younger sister (a female Realist), and Dr. Paramore (a male Idealist). It is possible that Sylvia is actually a "closet Idealist"; her ardent feminism may well be just another ideal, for she still defines herself as an "unwomanly woman" rather than as an individual human being. To her mind, to be treated as a "man" means that she is accepted as a human being. Paramore is a Scientific Idealist who, generally, perceives other human beings in the same way that he views microbes in his laboratory. Interestingly, although he is in many ways unsentimental and probably an atheist, he still believes in the sentimental ideal of romantic love.

Enter Cuthbertson, and we see that the two Idealists are at perfect ease with each other. We then discover that Paramore is in love with Julia but doesn't think he has a chance. With the entrance of Craven and the exit of Paramore, the two men—fathers both (Craven to Julia, Cuthbertson to Grace)—talk "man to man," and, by adopting the familiar attitude of male cynicism, briefly enter into the world of the Realist without realizing they are doing so. Although both of them believe absolutely in the romantic ideal of the institution of marriage, Craven confides to Cuthbertson, "Well, Jo, I may as well make a clean breast of it—everybody knew it. I married for money." Cuthbertson responds encouragingly, "And why not, Dan? Why not? We can't get on without it, you know" (*Philanderer*, 41).

This moment is complicated by the fact that Cuthbertson married the woman with whom Craven was in love, but it is still the only moment in the play where these two characters let the masks fall away; it is also the only scene in which they are together onstage alone. With all social pretense gone, they speak to each other as two men in a bar would. Enter Charteris, who explains his dilemma frankly to Craven and Cuthbertson, hoping for some advice from two "men of the world." But suddenly, they are fathers again, and each is shocked that Charteris wants to talk "man to man" about the communications he has received from both Grace and Julia since he saw them in Act I. Cuthbertson and Craven can respond only with fatherly sentiment, as the latter does here:

> CRAVEN. Charteris: no woman writes such a letter to a man unless he has made advances to her.
> CHARTERIS (*mournfully*). How little you know the world, Colonel! The New Woman is not like that.
> CRAVEN. I can only give you oldfashioned advice, my boy; and that is that it's well to be off with the Old Woman before youre on with the New. (*Philanderer*, 43)

Julia arrives, and Cuthbertson and Craven go to lunch while Julia finds a pretense to lag behind. Once again the play approaches farcical dimensions as Charteris tries frantically to get out of the clutches of Julia, upsetting all our theatrical expectations of male-female role models. The scene culminates in a line spoken by almost every heroine of nineteenth-century melodrama, but now it is the man who protests: "Unhand me, Julia. If you don't let me go, I'll scream for help" (*Philanderer*, 43). Here, again, a scene building to a climax is interrupted, and the final confrontation between Charteris and Julia is postponed by the reappearance of Cuthbertson, who reminds Julia that her "lunch will be cold" (*Philanderer*, 44).

Sylvia and Charteris are subsequently left alone. They are at ease with each other, and for once Charteris can have a "man to man" talk with someone:

> SYLVIA (*thoughtfully*). . . . I don't think you care a bit more for one woman than for another.
> CHARTERIS. You mean I don't care a bit less for one woman than another.
> SYLVIA. That makes it worse. But what I mean is that you never bother about their being only women; you talk to them just as you do to me or any other fellow. Thats the secret of your success. You cant think how sick they get of being treated with the respect due to their sex. (*Philanderer*, 44)

This characteristic of his is the key to Charteris's successful philandering, but it also makes him prey to a woman like Julia, who sees him as the ultimate challenge.

Julia is convinced that Charteris's advanced theories about male-female relationships and his objections to romantic love are due to the fact that he simply hasn't yet found the right woman—a woman, like her, of sincerity and depth of feeling. But, no matter who the woman may be, Charteris appears to be uncompromising in his refusal to act upon romantic, sentimental, and idealized assumptions as if they were real. The point is not that he is heartless, cruel, unfeeling—Charteris *does* have emotions, and he does love Grace—but that he refuses to make his intellect subservient to his emotions, i.e., he refuses to become a character in a popular sentimental drama.

Grace soon arrives and Sylvia leaves. The scene that follows is a very sophisticated intellectual chess game during which Grace counters Charteris move for move. Although neither one is posing, Charteris does at times slip into the clichéd speech of the romantic lover—partly as a game but also partly to test Grace, to see if she really is the New Woman. Ironically, the more Grace refuses to marry Charteris, the more he is attracted to her, to the "newness" in her womanliness:

> GRACE. Oh, Leonard, does your happiness really depend on me?
> CHARTERIS (*tenderly*). Absolutely. (*She beams with delight. A sudden revulsion comes to him at the sight: he recoils, dropping her hands and crying.*) Ah no: why should I lie to you? My happiness depends on nobody but myself. I can do without you.
> GRACE (*nerving herself*). So you shall. Thank you for the truth. Now *I* will tell you the truth.... I love you.... but I'm an advanced woman. I'm what my father calls the New Woman. I quite agree with all your ideas.
> CHARTERIS (*scandalised*). That's a nice thing for a respectable woman to say! You ought to be ashamed of yourself.
> GRACE. I am quite in earnest about them too, though you are not. That is why I will never marry a man I love too much. It would give him a terrible advantage over me: I should be utterly in his power. That's what the New Woman is like.... And so we must part. (*Philanderer*, 45-46)

The second act of *The Philanderer* thus ends with the posing of the paradox that a true marriage is possible only between people who do not love each other.

Act III begins on a note of gloom with a discussion of Craven's supposed terminal illness—"Paramore's Disease" (*Philanderer*, 44, 47)—and the change in eating and drinking habits he has been forced to accept. Then comes the revelation that Paramore's Disease has been disproved and that Craven is a perfectly healthy man. (Paramore's Disease, incidentally, is supposed to be a disease of the liver—traditionally the seat of the passions.) Craven's continued insistence on vegetarianism and abstinence, not because he now has to live in such a way but on moral principle, gives us a key to the Idealist mentality:

> CUTHBERTSON (*chuckling*). Aha! you made a virtue of it, did you, Dan?
> CRAVEN (*warmly*). I made a virtue of necessity, Jo. No one can blame me. (*Philanderer*, 47)

No one will blame him, indeed, because society operates on this principle of convincing people that what they have to do is what they ought to do.

Paramore and Charteris are now by themselves for the first time, and Charteris tries to get Paramore to propose to Julia. This little moment contains another insight into the Idealist, who looks at everything in abstract terms. Paramore is angry that Craven's life is no longer in danger, because it has struck a blow to the progress of medical science:

> CHARTERIS. . . . Didn't you congratulate him?
> PARAMORE (*scandalised*). Congratulate him! Congratulate a man on the worst blow pathological science has received for the last three hundred years!
> CHARTERIS. No, no, no. Congratulate him on having his life saved. (*Philanderer*, 50)

Grace enters and takes Paramore aside to chat, followed by the entrance of Julia, who, jealous to see Grace speaking with Paramore, throws a fit. The men leave and the stage is now set for the great confrontation scene in the play, an agon between the Realist Woman and the Idealist Woman:

> GRACE. . . . How I hate to be a woman when I see, by you, what wretched childish creatures we are! Those two men would cut you dead and have you turned out of the Club if you were a man, and had behaved in such a way before them. But because you are only a woman, they are forbearing! sympathetic! gallant! Oh, if you had a scrap of self-respect, their indulgence would make you creep all over. I understand now why Charteris has no respect for women.
> JULIA. How dare you say that?
> GRACE. Dare! I love him. And I have refused his offer to marry me.
> JULIA (*incredulous but hopeful*). You have refused!
> GRACE. Yes; because I will not give myself to any man who has learnt how to treat women from you and your like. I can do without his love, but not without his respect; and it is your fault that I cannot have both. Take his love then; . . . Run to him, and beg him to take you back. (*Philanderer*, 52)

Julia concludes with "Thank Heaven, I have a heart: that is why you can hurt me as I cannot hurt you" (*Philanderer*, 52), after which Grace turns away from her contemptuously.

The masks have been ripped away during the above exchange, and we are completely immersed in the world of sexual power politics. Julia shows that she is far from the naïve romantic she has seemed to be. She is not a Nora, for she is fully conscious of her ability to use her sexuality to manipulate men in order to get what she wants. Grace, for her part, loses her temper without realizing it, in her own way thereby sinking just as low as she thinks Julia has sunk. Perhaps she too, like Craven, has made a virtue of necessity since she doesn't have Julia's innate sex appeal. They are both stripped naked, in any event: two women fighting over a man just as shamelessly as a pair of animals fighting over a piece of meat. In its dissection of character and laying bare of human emotion, this scene is far from being merely cleverly comic.

When Craven enters, the masks are flung back on. Julia rushes to him, crying "Daddy!" (*Philanderer*, 52). Since Charteris, now rejected by Grace, is not as attractive to Julia as he had been, she soon rushes off to Paramore's house, where all will gather for the last act, while Charteris tries to delay their arrival in the hope that Paramore will have enough time to propose to Julia. Though we get further insight into the characters in Act IV, especially Julia and Charteris, the key to sustaining the action here is suspense: the suspense of waiting for the answer to the question "How is the play going to end?" or "Who will marry whom?" And this is by no means certain at the end of Act III. Grace seems to be out of the picture as a mate for Charteris, which somewhat increases Julia's chances, but Paramore is suddenly much more attractive to Julia now that Grace has shown an interest in him. Moreover, it is not at all certain that Grace will not change her mind about Charteris's proposal, and she insists at the end of Act III that she, too, is going to Paramore's house to see what will happen in the end.

In the course of Act IV, Julia has a dramatic anagnorisis, as we see from the following exchange:

> PARAMORE. As it is, I can only admire you, and feel how pleasant it is to have you here.
> JULIA (*bitterly*). And pet me, and say pretty things to me! I wonder you dont offer me a saucer of milk at once. . . . you seem to regard me very much as if I were a Persian cat. . . . You are all alike, every one of you. Even my father only makes a pet of me. (*Philanderer*, 55)

This is not an act on Julia's part, even though she is toying with the idea of marrying Paramore; she is having an extended recognition. As Act IV progresses, she realizes that what Charteris says of her is true, that she is a slave to her feelings or passions, and this is not a noble or wonderful thing to be. Julia has a recognition comparable to Nora's, but she undergoes the further recognition that she can do nothing about it.

Paramore himself talks his way through every cliché of romantic love—in each of which, unlike Charteris, he fervently believes. But his words only further Julia's recognition of how foolish she is when she gives herself over to her own emotions: "(*earnestly*). Believe me: it is not merely your beauty that attracts me: I know other beautiful women. It is your heart, your sincerity, your sterling reality, your great gifts of character . . ." (*Philanderer*, 55). With the arrival of Craven, Paramore hustles his future father-in-law offstage to formally ask for his daughter's hand, while Charteris and Julia are left alone for their last confrontation. And here, all the themes of the play converge:

> JULIA (*earnestly*). It is you who are the vivisector—a far crueller, more wanton vivisector than he.
> CHARTERIS. Yes; but then I learn so much more from my experiments than he does! And the victims learn as much as I do. Thats where my moral superiority comes in. (*Philanderer*, 57)

Charteris is right, and he is helping here to solidify Julia's anagnorisis.

Ultimately, our understanding of Charteris is an ironic one. We wonder if his uncompromising refusal to sink to Julia's level has in fact made him sink just as low, if his advanced ideas have become just another set of Ideals. As a result, the ending of *The Philanderer* is very serious, indeed:

JULIA (*exhausted, allowing herself to take it*). You are right. I am a worthless woman.
CHARTERIS (*triumphant, and gaily remonstrating*). Oh, why?
JULIA. Because I am not brave enough to kill you.
GRACE (*taking her in her arms as she sinks, almost fainting, away from him*). Oh, no. Never make a hero of a philanderer. (*Charteris, amused and untouched, shakes his head laughingly. The rest look at Julia with concern, and even a little awe, feeling for the first time the presence of a keen sorrow.*) [*Philanderer*, 61]

This conclusion is close to tragic. It is the equivalent, from a reverse angle, of Nora's returning to Torvald, not out of a concession to audience taste and Idealism, but because she realizes that her romantic sentimentality is not an illusion or something that she can disown but what she is at the very core of her being, and that, although it would be theoretically wonderful to be liberated and independent, she cannot live without an equally sentimental Torvald—just as Julia requires a Paramore for her own emotional survival. For his part, the advanced Ibsenite philosopher, Leonard Charteris—Shaw's Gregers Werle, a distant cousin of Brand and Rubek—has actually not progressed one step from Jack Horner or any other Restoration rake. As for the New Woman, Grace Tranfield is hardly a flattering portrait, especially when, toward the end of the play, she approaches self-loathing. A glimmer of hope seems to be presented in the uncorrupted Sylvia, but that may be only because she has not yet been tainted by the cyncisim of worldly experience.

The Ideal and the Real, or Comedy and Tragedy

"Technically, I do not find myself able to proceed otherwise than as former playwrights have done. . . . My stories are the old stories; my characters are the familiar harlequin and columbine, clown and pantaloon . . .; my jests are the ones in vogue when I was a boy, by which time my grandfather was tired of them." —Bernard Shaw, Preface to *Three Plays for Puritans* (1901): xxxv.

It has long been assumed that the basis of Shaw's method, in *The Philanderer* as in other plays of his, was the shattering or at least the disregard of popular theatrical conventions of his time. Actually, the opposite is true: Shaw's major plays are the very apotheosis of nineteenth-century dramatic technique and the popular performance tradition. Just as surely as the effectiveness onstage of *Black-Ey'd Susan* (1829), *The Colleen Bawn* (1860), and *The Ticket-of-Leave Man* (1863) depended upon a set assumptions and conventions implicitly accepted by the audience, just so do *Mrs. Warren's Profession*, *Candida*, *Caesar and Cleopatra* (1898), and *Major Barbara* depend almost entirely for their theatrical effectiveness on this exact same set of conventions and assumptions. By injecting into his plays challenging intellectual content, by clouding and thus complicating the moral perspective (i.e., by making the immoral, or even the moral, amoral), and by feeding on the irony between real life and the theater's idealized version of it, Shaw was able to employ the mechanics of the well-made play and the time-tested structural pattern of melodrama with freedom and dexterity.

A simple summary of the action in *Arms and the Man, You Never Can Tell,* or *Man and Superman* (minus the third act) would show Shaw's skill in plot construction. He did not reject the traditions of the *pièce à thèse*, the *pièce bien-faite*, or popular melodrama, but instead employed them in their most extreme and radical forms. He was thus dead serious when he declared, "A really good Adelphi [Theatre] melodrama is of first-rate literary importance, because it only needs elaboration to become a masterpiece" (*Dramatic Opinions and Essays*, 72). It's true that Shaw often seems to be parodying the popular theater or contravening melodrama, but in fact he is shamelessly exploiting every theatrical trick and melodramatic convention known.

The basic situation of *The Philanderer*, for example, was familiar to any nineteenth-century theater audience: A. (Julia) loves and wants to marry B. (Charteris), who loves and wants to marry C. (Grace), while D. (Paramore) loves and wants to marry A. This initial dramatic premise is the springboard for the action of the play, and that action achieves its fruition in the conflicts between the various characters. But the outcome of the play is determined by the beliefs and ideas of those characters, not by the providential design of melodrama. For in melodrama characters are slaves to their moral classification; in Shaw, as Brecht pointed out, "The opinions of his characters constitute their fates" ("Three Cheers for Shaw", 11). If *The Philanderer* were true to classic comic form, its "fate" would be to end with a pair of marriages (Julia-Charteris and Grace-Paramore). But there is no such reconciliation or synthesis in the play, as there is, say, in *Major Barbara*. True, there is a marriage agreed upon at the end, but it is only one that ironically fulfills the dialectical thrust of the drama.

Shaw's plays are all structured dialectically. A thesis is stated; counter to this thesis is presented another one, an obstacle to and contradiction of the original thesis. *The Philanderer* posits two antithetical approaches to the modern institution of marriage: marriage with love and marriage without love. Each thesis produces unpleasant or even diasterous consequences, and both are found insufficient. *The Philanderer* therefore does not produce a reconciliation in the end, and this play, like *Mrs. Warren's Profession, Caesar and Cleopatra, The Doctor's Dilemma, Pygmalion* (1913), *Heartbreak House*, and *Saint Joan*, is not structurally a comedy. It does not bring order out of chaos or reconcile two opposites; the synthesis must be provided by the audience. The original (and rejected) final act of the play did provide the only possible synthesis—love without marriage.

Charteris and Julia, of course, are the two characters who represent the dialectical extremes, in this case of human personality: Charteris feels only intellectually and Julia thinks only feelingly. The dynamic that these two figures represent could be expressed in a number of different ways: the tension between Apollo and Dionysus, Logos in conflict with Eros, the Ethical Man versus the Aesthetic Man, the struggle between the Ego and the Id. Any one of these approaches could be fruitful if applied to *The Philanderer*—when all is said and done, one dialectic is as good as another. But a good way in which to approach the play is to use the vocabulary that Shaw himself employed (and employed, as well, in part II of this essay) in *The Quintessence of Ibsenism* to describe these two types of personality: Realism versus Idealism.

An Idealist is one who cannot look life in the face, and instead puts a mask (an Ideal) over every potentially unpleasant reality. Thus marriage, in reality a simple property relationship originally devised as a means of effectively propagating the species, to the Idealist becomes a sacred or holy institution through which man and woman find their ultimate fulfillment as human beings. Similarly, because it was unpleasant or even terrifying to face the inevitable reality of death, the Idealists invented the notion of an afterlife, and so on and so forth. The rare person, Shaw's one in a thousand, is the Realist, the man or woman who dares to rip the mask away, look reality squarely in the face, and call things by their proper names. A Realist is by nature an Ironist. The ultimate, true Realist is incapable of not seeing anything unironically—indeed, this is the tragedy of the Ironist. The true Realist must be able to preserve an ironic understanding of even his own sense of irony. Indeed, he can turn even it into yet another Ideal, which truly makes him one man in a thousand. Idealists, by contrast, are incapable of an ironic understanding of life. An Idealist will therefore wage wars to end wars and build bombs to preserve the peace.

It is important not to view these categories as permanent classifications or static conditions. Shaw is presenting an evolutionary principle of human society wherein Realists and Idealists are not so much opposites as ideologies that are at different levels of development. Most important of all, we must realize that the Realist, after ripping away the mask from a given Ideal, will eventually substitute another Ideal for the one he has destroyed. Progress does obtain, however, because, as Shaw writes in *The Quintessence of Ibsenism*, "every new ideal is less of an illusion than the one it has supplanted" (45). Now this model of Realism versus Idealism fits certain plays by Ibsen very well and others not at all, but *The Quintessence of Ibsenism* is much more valuable for understanding Shaw than it is in understanding Ibsen.

On a very basic level, the cast of characters in *The Philanderer* can be broken down as follows: Realists—Charteris, Grace, Sylvia; Idealists—Julia, Paramore, Cuthbertson, Craven. Cuthbertson and Craven are modeled on the portrait of the Idealist in *The Quintessence of Ibsenism*. Cuthbertson has had an absolutely wretched failure of a marriage and is now separated, but still he would defend marriage to the death as an institution. Craven, who was in love with the woman whom Cuthbertson married, gave her up, thereby sacrificing what he considered his happiness for the romantic ideal of doing what was best for her; eventually he married, not for love, but for money. Grace, a widow, was an Idealist when she married, but the experience of marriage made her a Realist; like Charteris, she has torn the mask off the institution and now sees marriage not as the ultimate fulfillment of the human personality, through love, but as a conventional social arrangement and property relationship—not at all the correct arrangement or relationship for one person who loves another, because it will degrade them both as human beings. Julia herself believes fervently in the romantic ideal of marriage and the sentimental ideal of deep, intense feeling as the ultimate proof of a sincere, noble, and higher form of being.

The proper mode for the Idealist is comedy, for the Realist tragedy. And the Realist-Idealist extremes of character that are yoked to the central action of this play may partially explain the seeming incongruity of its structure. To wit: *The Philanderer* seems like a different play when Charteris and Grace (two Realists) are onstage together, as opposed to when Charteris and Julia (Realist and Idealist) are together onstage. The conflict in *The Philanderer*, in fact, is precisely the one between Idealist and Realist, and it takes the specific form of a struggle between passion and intellect. The action of the play is an attempt to reconcile this opposition. The plot forces the characters into a series of choices—Charteris decides to reject Julia, Grace decides to reject Charteris, Julia decides to reject Charteris, Julia decides to marry Paramore. Each choice centers around circumstances reflecting the opposition between passion and intellect and the characters' understanding of those circumstances. Since each decision made alters the previous set of circumstances and the characters' understanding of them, it further complicates the next decision that has to be made, and in this way each decision becomes more complex and more important. For example, Julia's final decision to marry Paramore is determined by a causal chain of prior decisive actions in the play—Charteris has rejected her once, Grace has rejected Charteris, Charteris has rejected Julia again, Paramore has shown an interest in her, Grace is showing an interest in Paramore, then Paramore declares his love and asks Julia to marry him.

The "given" of the play is that marriage is an outmoded institution. The hypothesis of *The Philanderer* is that educated, modern, enlightened people can nevertheless find fulfillment through the existing institution of marriage. As each possible match is suggested and debated and each decision made, various aspects of the hypothesis are explored and tested until the play ultimately proves the hypothesis false. Intelligent, advanced, civilized human beings cannot marry and at the same time remain intelligent, advanced, civilized human beings.

The Philanderer's ending is by far its most challenging moment, and it should not be pushed aside or allowed to "take care of itself" in any production. It demands clear choices by the actors and a distinct point of view on the part of the director. The audience must take this conclusion seriously and not just as mere Shavian perversity or paradox. To be part of a satisfying theatrical experience, it must present a clear challenge to audience members, and one that they will actually confront once they are outside the theater. The ending is neither happy nor funny, neither a paradox nor a "cop-out" on Shaw's part. It would have been much easier to unite the pairs of lovers at the end, as Shaw would later often do, and as traditional comic form demands. As it stands, the play's rhythm modulates between an idealized vision of life (comedy) and an ironic vision of life (tragedy). Then it ends on a tragic note.

In *The Philanderer*, then, Shaw would allow himself to explore the basis of his understanding of life and human relationships much more honestly than he would in his later plays, when his ideas about Creative Evolution had ossified into an orthodoxy. It is itself a human, or dramatic, tragedy to see Shaw, the great iconoclast, the great Realist, thus transform himself into as much of an Idealist as any such character in his plays. Nietzsche is reputed to have said, "Save me from my disciples!" and Shaw could well have taken this as a bit of advice, because he became his own worst disciple. At a certain point, in fact, Shaw's ideas become empty and mean nothing, because he invests nothing of himself in his work. His devastating wit and incredible intellect become an insulation. And they ultimately turn against him when we begin to realize that Shaw is clever enough to build convincing arguments for absolutely anything. Shaw's saint and soldier, Greek professor, and munitions maker can all convince us with equal dexterity that their vision of the world is right. As Don Juan himself admits in a Shaw play, "Yes, it is mere talk . . . nothing but words which I or anyone else can turn inside out like a glove" (III.ii [*Don Juan in Hell*], *Man and Superman*: 386).

Part of Shaw's displeasure with *The Philanderer* in his later years was surely that it did not neatly fit into his theory of Creative Evolution in the way that, say, *Man and Superman* did. In the earlier play, Shaw was "shooting from the hip," if you will, for he had not yet developed the vocabulary of Creative Evolution and the *Übermensch*. The confessedly autobiographical nature of *The Philanderer* was also an embarrassment to him. Those who claim that the play is a self-flattering vindication of Shaw's own philandering have not read it very closely. The character of Charteris is a severe self-criticism, whether it was conscious or not. The play remains dark and unpleasant for all its wit and humor; it strenuously questions the possibility of progressive human evolution in a way that reminds me of the following words by Ibsen: "Everyone wants their own special revolutions, always in external things. What is really needed is a revolution of the human spirit" (Letter to Georg Brandes, December 20, 1870, in *Letters and Speeches*, 106-107).

When *The Philanderer* was finally published in 1898, Shaw had already passed the point where he could have written it. The play is alive and attractive precisely because of its roughness, its hardiness, its sincerity; its complex, problematic nature makes it both profound and heartfelt. But, no, this play does not contain the dramatic algebra of *Saint Joan*: Shaw had not yet canonized himself.

Works Cited

Beer, Max. *A History of British Socialism* (1919). Vol. 2. London: Routledge, 2002.

Brecht, Bertolt. "Three Cheers for Shaw" (1926). In *Brecht on Theatre: The Development of an Aesthetic*. Ed. & trans. John Willett. New York: Hill & Wang, 1964. 10-13.

Ervine, St. John. *Bernard Shaw: His Life, Work, and Friends*. New York: Morrow, 1956.

Gahan, Peter. *Shaw Shadows: Rereading the Texts of Bernard Shaw*. Gainesville: University Press of Florida, 2004. 157-188.

Gainor, J. Ellen. *Shaw's Daughters: Dramatic and Narrative Constructions of Gender*. Ann Arbor: University of Michigan Press, 1991. 48-59.

Harris, Frank. *Bernard Shaw*. New York: Simon & Schuster, 1931.

Henderson, Archibald. "George Bernard Shaw Self-Revealed." *Fortnightly Review*, 125 (Apr. 1926): 433-442, 610-618.

Ibsen, Henrik. *Letters and Speeches*. Ed. Evert Sprinchorn. New York: Hill & Wang, 1964.

Kierkegaard, Søren. *Either/Or*. Trans. Alastair Hannay. London: Penguin, 1992.

Murray, J. Review of *The Philanderer*. *The Academy: A Weekly Review of Literature, Science, and Art* (June 4, 1898): 614.

Nietzsche, Friedrich William. *Nietzsche: A Self-Portrait from His Letters*. Ed. & trans. Peter Fuss & Henry Shapiro. Cambridge, Mass.: Harvard University Press, 1971.

Pearson, Hesketh. *George Bernard Shaw*. London: Collins, 1942.

Shaw, George Bernard, ed. *Fabian Essays in Socialism*. London: Fabian Society, 1889.

----------. "The Author's Apology." In Shaw's *Mrs. Warren's Profession*. London: Constable, 1906.

----------. *Dramatic Opinions and Essays*, Vol. 1. New York: Brentano's, 1906.

----------. *Man and Superman*. In *The Complete Plays of Bernard Shaw*. London: Constable, 1931.

----------. *The Philanderer*. In *The Complete Plays of Bernard Shaw*. London: Constable, 1931.

----------. Preface to *Three Plays for Puritans*. London: Constable, 1931.

----------. *The Quintessence of Ibsenism* (1891). In *The Collected Works of Bernard Shaw*. Vol. 19. New York: Brentano's, 1931.

----------. *The Bodley Head Bernard Shaw: Collected Plays with Their Prefaces*. 7 vols. London: Bodley Head, 1970-74.

St. John, Christopher, ed. *Ellen Terry and Bernard Shaw: A Correspondence*. New York:
Putnam, 1932.

Valency, Maurice. *The Cart and the Trumpet: The Plays of Bernard Shaw*. New York: Oxford University Press, 1973.

Wilson, Colin. *Bernard Shaw: A Reassessment*. London: Hutchinson, 1969.

"Bertolt Brecht: The Naturalist, the Theatricalist, and the Dramatist-as-Director; Notes, Mostly on *Mother Courage and Her Children, The Caucasian Chalk Circle*, and *Life of Galileo*"

Introducing Brecht

"Monstrously delicate" is how Brecht described his poetry (as recalled by Eric Bentley in his "Brecht Memoir," 8). The same might be said of Brecht's plays—and of the task of staging them. In the United States particularly, directing Brecht is a process that never seems to go right; one reads or hears of rather frequent Brecht productions in the network of university and regional theaters, but seldom do they spur much enthusiasm, seldom is a real Brechtian satisfied. The cliché persists with few rebuttals: American artists don't seem to know what to do with Brecht's plays.

Given the elusiveness of the Echt, or "pure," Brecht (in production or in production style), one is naturally tempted to idealize Brecht's own stagings at the Berliner Ensemble. Those stagings, now legendary, have browbeaten a generation of theater artists and set a standard that is ineradicable, yet indecipherable: for we sense the superiority of the original stagings without being able to reproduce it. Dutiful imitation is the height of our achievement, and it is poor imitation at that: we manage to bypass the famous power, clarity, and humanity of the original, and reproduce only the grayness, the monotony, of the Berliner Ensemble *Modellbücher* (*Model-Books*) photos in dispiritingly familiar, derivative, and hollow revivals.

Clearly, we have fallen into a trap, albeit one set by Brecht himself. We idealize his stage direction uncritically, failing to discriminate between letter and spirit in the "law" of the *Modellbücher*. Further, because a theatrical style is the most fragile and impermanent of artistic codes, we court the clear and present danger of confining Brecht's plays in what are now overfamiliar and dated theatrical practices—practices that have fossilized at the Berliner Ensemble itself since the playwright's death a generation ago. On the other hand, one cannot ignore the international acclaim for Brecht's own productions when they were first seen, nor avoid the impression that those plays became something greater under the playwright's direction. This wayward genius's eccentric, elusive way with actors and with *mise-en-scène* seems to have added new ranges of signification, a new fullness of import and meaning, to his texts. For this reason, there can be no complete understanding of the plays that does not consider these celebrated productions.

This section of my essay is intended as a beginning effort in a much-needed analysis of Brecht's directing style—both as a dramaturgy of texts and a "theaterturgy" of stagings, aimed at discovering some of the principles which underlie the distracting plenitude of discussable details that Brecht crowded onto Berlin's Schiffbauerdamm stage. It is an axiom of this study that Brecht's direction tapped the power of his own scripts through a precise, organic connection between play and production. If this is true, analysis of the plays and of their stagings must interpenetrate: the play as written becomes a guide to understanding Brecht's staging, and the staging reveals the play. One hopes that, when this project is finally and fully addressed (as can only be done tentatively and in the way of foundations here), it will facilitate new productions that can incorporate new theatrical environments, vocabularies, and conventions without betraying a Brecht play's own structure, techniques, and dramatic identity.

Before turning to Brecht's directing, let me say that his criticism itself must be read critically; only then can it help to deepen our understanding of his dramaturgical procedures. This is particularly true of his persistent inveighing against the tradition of naturalism, and of his sometimes hyperbolic claims for having utterly rejected its techniques. In fact, if one were to say outright that Brecht was a naturalistic director, the error would be only partial. For the textural aspects of naturalism appealed to Brecht's taste a great deal. His careful attention to realistic stage "business," the use of real objects bought in markets rather than stage property simulations, the love of the unadorned textures of real wood, metal, leather, and fabric—all these manifest a personal, visual, and tactile sensitivity that brought a number of naturalistic surfaces onto Brecht's stage, and in so doing insured an appearance of realism, a particular kind of verisimilitude.

Of course, aside from its sensual value, verisimilitude was tonally and ideationally important to Brecht, since it manifested his yearning for a proletarian authenticity. That is why, although he was a great (and self-promoting) theatrical stylist, Brecht was nevertheless suspicious of the impulse toward style. (I am consciously using the word in the customary, if somewhat imprecise way that comes readily to hand in a mimetic age: "style" as anything—including photographic realism—that differs from undifferentiated reality.) He wanted to encourage an audience to peer beneath familiar surfaces so as to discover the political and moral truths that are often undetected in daily living—yet he wanted to leave those surfaces, those outward appearances and manifestations of reality, as undisturbed and undistorted as possible. This, of course, constitutes a fundamental ambiguity: a naturalistic impulse and an anti-naturalistic one mated.

This opposition of impulses yields a kind of Brechtian hermeneutics, in which the audience is impelled to recognize—and more, to penetrate and pass through—familiar appearances in order to seek out a truth that is implied but never explicitly stated. Audience members proceed imaginatively from their own time and space through a fictional realm of more or less realistically rendered events, until they come to a plane of partially defined sources of insight, a plane beyond common appearances, beyond customary ways of seeing. This implicit progression changes the nature of the natural, making it both an oracle and a veil. Thus the term "naturalism" will not do here. Brecht opposed the "natural" ways of seeing that the word implies. He tried to appropriate the word "realism" from the socialist realists, but this term, too, has the wrong connotations. For this essay, I shall call Brecht's peculiar verisimilitude "the lifelike," insofar as the word can imply both a similarity to and a difference from the "life" of objective reality. To study Brecht's dramaturgy and staging must necessarily be to study the lifelike—and the half-disguised, half-exposed techniques with which Brecht violated lifelikeness, shaping experience to his ideas without too severely disturbing its familiar appearance.

For all its incorporation of lifelike elements, however, Brecht's practice clearly differed from any strictly mimetic drama, and Brecht liked to make much of that difference. Unfortunately, he tended to state the matter in somewhat confusing terms, centering on the loosely deployed word *Verfremdung*. In the larger sense, *Verfremdung* is the key concept in Brecht's aesthetic, the umbrella term that covers all his methods of alerting the audience to a special critical awareness of the dramatic action. In this full sense, the term covers a great many different features of Brecht's work: the exotic settings, for example; the use of verse or song to heighten a point in the dramatic argument; an instance of dramaturgical juxtaposition in which a character's most earnest statement is made ironic by an unexpected context.

This is *Verfremdung*, then, as a general or categorical term, covering a number of dramatic and theatrical devices—but only when those devices are used for the specific purpose of surprising the audience into a higher, and more critical, awareness. No device is inherently a *Verfremdungseffekt*. And it was on this point that Brecht himself created confusion, by applying the general term to a smaller and more specific instance of itself, thus blurring principle and example. That is, Brecht came to use the general term *Verfremdung* as a synonym for what a theater historian would more rightly call theatricalism—meaning nothing more than the use of frankly theatrical devices, such as masks, non-illusionary settings, visible scene changes, and the like. Brecht assumed that dressing the *mise-en-scène* with theatricalist elements—which in a loose sense could mean anything non-mimetic—would naturally lead the audience to the elusive wakefulness of *Verfremdung*.

This is, inferably, related to Brecht's misreading of Viktor Shklovsky, whose *ostranenie* was a direct ancestor of Brecht's neologistic *Verfremdung*: where Shklovsky proposed an artistic practice that made one aware of the artist's materials, Brecht added an assumption that this attention to the artistic medium would necessarily draw an audience into contemplating the larger outlines of the dramatic argument. Any good Prague semiologist could have shown Brecht that theatricalism doesn't always work that way; many august Brechtians have made the same argument; and Brecht himself acknowledged the problem, as if on the sly, in the *Short Organum* (1949; *Brecht on Theatre*, 191-192). Yet Brecht continued to function as if on faith, on a willed belief that with the use of theatricalist decoration, he could solve the extremely subtle problem of controlling his audience's sympathy with push-button ease. It became a kind of never-ending refrain in Brecht's self-explanations: every sharply defined stylistic touch became not itself but another *Verfremdungseffekt*, and the *Verfremdung* was supposed to suit and explain virtually everything Brecht did.

The result is an imprecise and reductive vision of Brecht's writing and staging, although a vision that Brecht himself engineered. It suggests that every non-mimetic device in Brecht's extremely heterogeneous staging style is equivalent to every other in intention and effect; worse, it fosters the belief that theatricalist mannerisms are what make Brecht—so that any production, of any kind of play, which uses a visible scene-change is suddenly understood to be "Brechtian." Words like "Brechtian" and "defamiliarization" (or its less adequate synonym "alienation") are drained of meaning in this way, and any precise perceiving of Brecht's work and methods dissolves into a blurred understanding.

If we were to reverse this distorted vision, we would come closer to the truth. Brecht's non-realistic passages and elements are not synonymous and uniform, but diverse, and they are directed toward discrete, separable effects. (Thus, an exposed lighting instrument is not the equivalent of a mask, and an ironic song is not a non-realistic setting.) Moreover, theatricalism in itself is not some Quintessence of Brechtianism. On the contrary, some of Brecht's theatricalist habits are inessential and decorative, while others are indispensable manifestations of central traits in his playwriting. Such distinctions have to be made before the relations among play, production, and theoretical criticism can yield a useful understanding.

The following notes will offer initial explanations of a number of the non-realistic elements in Brecht's stagings, attempting a kind of anatomy or phenomenology of style. That these are what I shall call "first principles" is true in a double sense: in that this analysis is only a beginning that will leave a great deal still to be explored, and in that these principles operate on a primary level, one of deep structure, giving order and predicating dramaturgical patterns. It is important that the incompleteness of these notes be kept in mind, for there is a risk of falling into Brecht's own trap of analyzing his work too narrowly, or of presumptively categorizing every element of the Brecht stage as if it were only another interchangeable element in an abstruse intellectual design. Brecht's work is only partly susceptible to systematic analysis; there is an impulsive, improvisational quality to his writing and staging, and an eccentric beauty to both, that, while important, can only be peripherally addressed here, since my investigation is aimed at what I have called the "hermeneutics"—the significations—of the Brecht stage.

Principles of Directed Attention, or the Heightening of Detail

Stage naturalism—in theory—presumes an accidental quality, a sense of dispersed focus and a prizing of each available locus for the viewer's attention. There is in it at least a pretense of a minimal distortion of experience, a renouncing of manipulation and artifice. (That theatrical naturalism promised this, yet tended to include frankly melodramatic contrivances, was part of what spurred Brecht's disgust for the style—and his preference for relaxed tonalities and disjointed structures.) Brecht's distinctive staging style begins with a rejection of dispersed focus: he specialized in subtly directing his audience's attention so as to arouse a special, penetrating awareness that might withstand distraction.

Characteristically, Brecht loved to direct his audience's attention to the suggestive detail, the small, barely noticeable gesture that bears a huge meaning. This is the vision that sees importance in a general's handling of a bar of soap, draws proud attention to Helene Weigel's way of biting a coin, finds an important hidden meaning in Weigel's accentuation of a single word in Courage's lullaby to the dead Kattrin, and insists that a fugitive aristocrat in *The Caucasian Chalk Circle* (1945) would be unable to copy a poor man's way of eating.

Accordingly, staging methods for Brecht's plays need to include a way of drawing the audience's attention to selected, significant details. This is a principle that shapes not only the performance, but the writing of the plays as well. For instance, characterization tends to be built through selective emphasis. With most of his secondary characters, there are only a few traits that are important to Brecht, and, accordingly, he highlights them. Consider the photographs of the masks for *Mr. Puntila and His Man Matti* (1948) in *Theaterarbeit* (*Theater Work*, 1952), where one can see the "typicality" of characters—the absurdity and obtuseness of the judge, the strangely cold and almost brutal quality Brecht sought to bring out in Puntila. We learn about these characters only what we need to know so that they can fill their place in the drama, but we learn it in a striking, theatrical way.

Significantly, these masks are only very subtly distortive. It would be possible to glance at these figures and see them not as masked "types," but only as unusually vivid characterizations in costume, bearing, and make-up. Always reluctant to stretch the lifelike too far, Brecht saw to it that such physical distortion remained subtle, a matter of stressed detail that moves us immediately into the realm of his idiosyncratic, mannerist realism. With somewhat less subtlety, but by means of a similar process, characters are simplified into an exaggerated essence by the cruder and more obviously theatrical masks of *The Caucasian Chalk Circle*. Even without masks, one can see traces of the same thing in the clearly defined postures of the actors in each of their many characterizations as they are shown in *Theaterarbeit*; and perhaps this was the essence of the doctrine of "gestic" acting—a distinctive, if slight, exaggeration of bodily gesture that makes the essential (and for Brecht that means social) traits of the character unusually readable and clear.

The same kind of selectivity and reliance on detail can be found in Brecht's language. One example might be a phrase in the rubric to the first scene of *Mother Courage and Her Children* (1941), which is usually translated "Mother Courage loses a son," but more precisely would be "Mother Courage comes to lose a son"—a subtle difference that makes a point, since Brecht's effort with this linguistic detail seems to be to draw our attention, not to the fact that Courage loses Eilif, but to the way (that is, the reason) that she comes to lose him, which is the essence of the play in miniature.

In short, Brecht's "realism" is colored and subtly reshaped into something cryptic, suggestive, delicately distorted—a quietly formalized version of reality not unlike the Ernst Barlach sculptures that Brecht admired. Brecht wanted to essentialize experience by carefully directing his viewer's eye, without, perhaps, seeming to do so.

Selective Abstraction

The second principle of focusing the audience's attention is nearly inseparable from the first: that the carefully selected details to which Brecht draws attention are displayed against a ground of great spareness. Conciseness and concentration are the signal virtues of Brecht's poetry; and this is the same quality in theatrical terms: precisely realized details on a nearly blank stage. This principle has proved a major stumbling block for many American designers and directors of Brecht's plays. For those who choose to find some route other than simple imitation of the Caspar Neher or Teo Otto designs, the invitation to use theatricalist techniques often provokes a blinding flurry of mad "creativity," endless elaborations of simple ideas, sheer luxuriation in unnecessary invention. What these enthusiasts fail to realize is that Brecht's technique is one of precisely calculated abstraction in which all unnecessary matters are expunged.

This is most clearly exercised in the design of the settings that Brecht supervised and later glossed in his notes. He adored the spareness of Neher's designs for *Mother Courage and Her Children*, for example: their functional quality of providing the actors with exactly the objects needed to carry out their theatrical tasks, but beyond that only the sketchiest indications of place and physical conditions. Rough screens and a flat stage floor were for Brecht instances of a beautiful aesthetic economy; he exulted in the refusal to fill in the empty spaces, preferring the fragmentary, suggestive, brisk look of a quick sketch.

The same spareness is present in Brecht's distinctive control of stage movement. The movements of actors under Brecht's direction have been described as bold, purposeful, never random, never indecisive or hesitant, but ever organized, clear, and uncluttered. Clearly, Brecht's habit of working from Neher's sketches to create the "grouping" of actors created a continuity of technique from scenic design to *mise-en-scène*; but more important, Brecht and Neher shared an exclusive and spare compositional style that linked not only groupings to scenic design, but all the visual elements to the writing itself.

The same principle thus enters Brecht's writing in a number of ways. It is there in the conflation of time in *The Caucasian Chalk Circle*, when, with a narrator's help, a few minutes' pantomime enacts Grusche's night-long vigil over the child in the first act; or when, without any intrusive devices, a single unbroken conversation stretches from midwinter through the spring thaw in the shed at Lavrenti's farm. Perhaps most important, this radical selectivity affected Brecht's way of writing characters, for he did not write psychologized personalities, but instead cautionary figures whose psyches were dictated and shaped by their given social roles. Brecht politicized the self and expunged purely psychological motivations: there is no libidinous subtext, there are no hidden obsessions. Even when, in *The Tutor* (1950), Gustchen copulates with Lauffer as a substitute for her absent fiancé, the substitution is more or less conscious and excites no horror in the girl. Her motivations are not a Freudian tangle of unbidden urges; for Brecht, desire is concrete and unmysterious.

The real mystery that shapes Brecht's dramaturgy is not that of unconscious desires, but of irreconcilable roles, contradictory social pulls acting on a single character. Inner conflict comes from without. In accordance with Brecht's methods of abstraction, these conflicting needs are generalized, assumed, freed from biographical particularization: there is no point at which Mother Courage came to love her bastard brood, because her loyalty to them is a given; similarly, Shen Te's affection for her flier arrives at an appropriate point in the dramatic action and is not particularized—Brecht is not Marivaux. He was interested in the results of a generous impulse, and typically drew attention away from that impulse's wellsprings or its character-bound idiosyncrasies. Brecht's characters are all to some degree ideational emblems; they are all stylized.

Just as designers are tempted to fill in the Brechtian blanks—those areas of the stage that he deliberately left in rough outline—actors will be tempted to fill in the characters' broadly outlined motivations with psychological additives that shift us onto the wrong sort of dramatic ground. Brecht put certain characters in masks for a reason—their roles were masks, simplified, essentialized, sharply defined theatrical beings that must be played by imaginative actors who can match the thrust and precision of the minor characters' incarnations (as well as those of the more specifically realized central characters), while still keeping the performance "clean," or free of extraneous additions that only muddle the characterizations Brecht devised.

This means that actors and directors in his plays must be critical of their own impulses, able to select from their random impressions those elements that accord with what Brecht has given. He wanted richly detailed acting in his plays: he could wax rhapsodic over the minutiae of a good actor's performance, but those elements that he praised were all relevant to the Brechtian world—the bitten coin, the increasingly servile bow of a frustrated student out of work, the lust of a prostitute's protector—are all what Brecht called "social gests," small, realistic actions that reveal the underlying social and economic relations of the characters involved. The psychological and the quaint are irrelevant here and are best excluded; beneath all its theatrical richness and subtlety, then, Brecht's is a rigorous aesthetic.

The Principle of Visual Contrast

Brecht's dramaturgy is founded on carefully designed contradictions. He stated that explicitly in any number of his working notes. Here follow some of the ways that this ground of calculated contradictions found expression on Brecht's stage.

The clearest example of "contrast over time" is Brecht's immediate juxtaposition, between Scenes 6 and 7, of Mother Courage's "God damn the war!" with her fierce defense of that war ("Stop running down the war. I won't have it" [*Collected Plays*, Vol. 5 (1980): 185])—an opposition that clarifies this "merchant-mother's" contradictory roles and displays her moral discontinuity. By the starkness of the contrast, eliminating all gradation between her opposed positions, Brecht clarifies a striking incongruity that impels his audience toward a critical view of the character.

More common to Brecht's dramaturgy, and less obvious, were the more gradual reversals that shape his construction of scenes. Brecht described this principle—a fundamental structural principle for him—in his treatise *The Messingkauf Dialogues* (1939-42):

> Suppose you've a play where the first scene shows A bringing B to justice, then the process is reversed in the last scene and, after all kinds of incidents have been shown, B brings A to justice, so that there's one and the same process (bringing to justice) with A and B exchanging their

> respective roles (executioner and victim). In such a case you'll undoubtedly arrange the first scene so as to give the maximum possible effectiveness to the last. You'll ensure that on seeing the last scene the audience will immediately be reminded of the first; that the similarity will be striking; and at the same time that the differences will not be overlooked. (78-79)

It was this principle of writing that determined a naturally corresponding principle of staging: reversal of the *mise-en-scène* in the course of a scene, so that the final stage image altered and commented on the first. Thus the famous scene in *Life of Galileo* (1939) of the Pope, whose attitudes toward Galileo change with his social role—with the donning, that is, of his clerical robes. Like Saint Joan's change of costume after her confession in *The Trial of Joan of Arc at Rouen, 1431* (1934/1952), the Pope's scene gives theatrical expression to a change of political roles and its accompanying attitudinal reversal. One man exits, and—both externally and internally—another enters, a transformation of the first.

These examples function within a single scene. Others function over a span of scenes as a progression in the plot and in the *mise-en-scène*. For example, the changes in Courage's financial status are linked to her choices of action; thus, the changing appearance of her wagon and wares and the decreasing number of her family and followers are calculated, theatrically expressed criticisms of her decisions. Shen Te's self-division into generous and selfish halves becomes a sequence of costume changes—a division that is echoed in a similar, but more gradually and realistically rendered, change in her lover, who begins as a careless but visionary pilot, only to become a vicious capitalist lackey.

The same principle can extend across whole plays from beginning to end. In this way, the final image of Mother Courage dragging her own wagon is made more outrageous and telling by our memory of her first entrance with three children and with her own greater youth and strength. Similar are the closing scenes in *Life of Galileo*, when Galileo's lifelong student leaves him to his food. Or the gods' unheeding exit at the end of *The Good Person of Setzuan* (1940), amid cries for help—the exact obverse of their richly anticipated arrival in the first scene. The concluding posture of *The Mother* (1932), with the titular character marching, flag in hand and part of a revolutionary band, itself is strengthened by our memory of her initial appearance alone, homebound, and helpless. In each case the stage picture clarifies the single "ground-reversal" upon which Brecht structured every one of his mature plays.

Brecht loved stage settings simultaneously divided into two adjoining sections, or a "contrast across space": he wrote them into *The Mother, Mother Courage and Her Children, The Caucasian Chalk Circle*, and *Life of Galileo*, either for the sake of allowing one half of the stage to comment on the other (as when Courage sings "The Wise Woman and the Soldier" to disrupt Eilif's dance in the next tent), or else simply because he so enjoyed juxtaposition that he would put dissimilar things next to each other onstage simply for the sake of gratifying his own taste, no more—as in the wedding scene in *The Caucasian Chalk Circle*. But at his best, Brecht could combine this taste for laterally registered contrasts with an eye to clarifying the ideational contradictions in a scene.

Often he would make his points simply by movement and positioning, that is, by "blocking" patterns within the *mise-en-scène*: for example, in the scene outside the devastated village, Mother Courage's acquiring a coat is visually contrasted to Kattrin's rescue of a baby; at the end of the scene, each raises her own booty into the air, and the audience is tacitly encouraged to compare the two kinds of acquisition. Later, during the "drum scene," Kattrin climbs a roof and risks her life to sound a warning of an impending attack to nearby villagers; on the opposite side of the stage, an old peasant woman, helplessly and unhelpfully, kneels and prays for the village's deliverance.

Brecht had a way of using this lateral opposition to suggest moral opposites and temptations: there is scarcely a scene in *Life of Galileo* in which the representatives of Church and science do not position themselves on opposite sides of Galileo in order to sway him each to his or her own side. This is particularly true of the last scene between Andrea, Virginia, and Galileo, but works throughout the drama in an unusually direct way, almost as if Brecht were recalling the good and bad angels arguing with Faustus. Similarly, the playwright specified in his notes the meaning of a tableau in *The Tutor*: "It is here, at the university, that the young store up experiences, both on the intellectual and the physical plane. We see our man Fritz von Berg poised between sacred and profane lovers, between Patus and Bollwerk" (*Collected Plays*, Vol. 9 [1973]: 334). When Courage loses Eilif, she is divided in space between a soldier, who tries to distract her, and Kattrin, who tries to alert her to the danger. Courage's choice, and her priorities, are thereby made into something physical, kinetic—both realistically credible and symbolic at a high level of abstraction.

This intellectual progression from the imagined reality of fictional characters to the issues that their existence implies—what I have called Brechtian hermeneutics—is a journey through three realms of thought. Tacitly Brecht's audience is addressed on three different levels: in terms of its own historical time and place, in terms of a fictional world (a different, conventionally given time and place), and in terms of an awareness of the issues that unite the fictional and contemporary worlds. In a theatrical realization, these three steps of an intellectual process become spaces on the stage, each keyed to a different mode in Brecht's writing. Brecht's theatrical practice and his dramaturgical techniques can thus be said to coalesce into a general pattern: the composite Brecht stage, an ideal division of theatrical space that theoretically houses the fullness of Brecht's theatrical discourse by separating it into its constituent elements.

Of Brecht's three realms of dramatic-cum-theatrical expression, we can begin with the one that Brecht's drama shares with any other dramatic form: the fictional realm of depicted action, what Susanne K. Langer calls "virtual space" (Langer, 102)—the principal stage space behind the proscenium arch, where actors represent characters, and the stage represents a place and time outside itself. What distinguishes Brecht's treatment of the enacted events in this fictionalized space is his desire to endow them with a special, implicative significance. As noted above, Brecht organizes the fictional events through carefully planned juxtapositions in the *mise-en-scène*, and through stylistic heightening of selected details and the de-emphasizing of extraneous matters: he attempts in these more or less subtle ways to clarify patterns and significances within the dramatic action. He also has recourse to other ways of attacking the audience's customary, possibly uncritical, ways of seeing.

Two other realms of thought are recruited by Brecht and physically attached to the action, so that the surrounding stage becomes a commentator on the conventional dramatic sphere. The first of these extensional realms is one that expressly mediates between the fictional world of the drama and the time and space occupied by the audience: it is a sphere of explanation and exhortation, a perlocutionary element in Brecht's writing. In the texts, it is the realm of the prologues that are always addressed expressly to the audience and suggest an understanding of the play in terms of the audience's own current concerns. In the theater, this is a space located just downstage of the famous half-curtain—a space literally between the fictional action and the audience, figuratively joining the same time and space as the audience itself.

It is the place for the prologue to *Antigone* (1948), which relates Sophocles' story precisely to postwar Berlin's situation; it is the realm of the scene-titles for *The Resistible Rise of Arturo Ui* (1941), citing the precise events in German history that the "parable" was to illustrate by analogy. The prologue to *The Caucasian Chalk Circle* is similar in principle, explicitly connecting the ancient myth that is about to be enacted to the problems of postwar reconstruction under socialist principles; and *Mr. Puntila and His Man Matti* and *The Tutor* both have verse prologues that delineate the present usefulness of their stories. The function of this realm is almost anti-imaginative, anti-fictional; if the relation between the fictional realm and the audience's circumstances is one of analogy (as it always is with Brecht), then the intervening realm of the prologue demystifies that analogy by explaining it.

Even when this element of Brecht's thought is not used in so blunt a way, the same impulse can be felt in his writing. This is the impulse to address contemporary concerns through scarcely concealed references in the fictional action and dialogue: for example, Galileo's attention-getting observations on the need to hide the truth while traveling through Germany, or the rather sentimental remarks he makes about the skeptical intelligence of the proletariat, are clearly directed to a particular audience's self-awareness. When Brecht's dialogue strains for this kind of undisguised relevance (in the middle of a fictionalized, "defamiliarized" action), it is language straining to break out into this downstage sphere of discourse, this direct mode of address.

The third realm of expression in Brecht's plays is the physical and tactical opposite of the prologues and similar references to the audience's immediate circumstances. This is the quintessentially Brechtian realm of obscured realities, of the invisible causes of the dramatic situation. If Brecht's direct address to the audience is comparatively crude, this third sphere is refined enough to be difficult to express in any concrete theatrical way. It is a sphere of implications, of what lies "behind" the enacted events—and its stage space is that of the backdrop or even the backstage upstage of the drop, literally "behind" the fictional action.

For this reason, it is fitting that the final chorus of soldiers that comes closest to stating the playwright's "message" in *Mother Courage and Her Children* is heard singing behind the scene. The enormous political forces that govern the action of *The Mother* are embodied in the huge, hovering political portraits projected on the backdrop and peering down at the fictional action. And the reality of *Mr. Puntila and His Man Matti* is shaped by a hermetically sealed bourgeois family situation that cannot tolerate the presence of the proletariat—so Brecht has a portrait of the family and friends, smiling and undisturbed, placed upstage to clarify the tensions that take over when the chauffeur Matti enters; the assumption of bourgeois hegemony is embodied on the backdrop, the better to be put into question by the contrasting tableau beneath it. The stage directions of *Life of Galileo* themselves suggest a frankly symbolic use of light—including a pair of astronomical projections on the backdrop that openly symbolize the allure and challenge of the truth and give a motif-bound unity to a long, complex dramatic action.

Even when it is not manifested as a literal backdrop, the same impulse to imply or to express in symbols the larger social issues "behind" the dramatic action can be detected. In one scene from *Life of Galileo*, when the conflict between the state and the new science is most clearly introduced, the formal cordialities of Galileo and the elder statesman are juxtaposed against the image of Galileo's pupil and the young duke grappling and, in the process, breaking a Ptolemaic model of the universe: the symbolism could hardly be more obvious, but is effectively displayed, like the backdrop projections, as a simultaneous illustration of the underlying tension in the accompanying, lifelike scene.

This assemblage of impulses, which I am calling "The Composite Brecht Stage," is another example of Brecht's way of balancing an unblinkingly specific realism with calculated abstraction: the drama moves from direct audience-address in the most specific terms through a more or less realistically rendered story set in a more remote reality, and from there into a shadowy, symbolically rendered, incomplete and implicative sphere of inquiry—inquiry into implied causes, into the very assumptions of social life that must be addressed and changed. As one imaginatively moves away from the audience into the back reaches of the stage, one traverses fissures in Brecht's language and rhetoric, moving from the almost importunately concrete to the teasingly unexpressed. Working in tandem, Brecht's three modes of address form a complex, suggestive totality. They also create an unusually rich, original use of the stage's opportunities for, and means of, expression.

The Poetic Principle

I want to mention briefly here a matter that is extremely important in an appreciation of Brecht, but one that has been given only scattered attention. This is Brecht's theatrical poetry, his poetry of the theater, in Francis Fergusson's phrase (590 *et passim*), a poetry of theatrical elements and effects rather than words. Beyond the symbolic use of *mise-en-scène*, there are symbolic tropes and patterns of reference, some of which echo from one play to the next and reinforce each other's meaning. There are, for example, the recurring images of the cross and crucifixion in *Mother Courage and Her Children*; the image returns in the flier's scene in *The Good Person of Setzuan* and in the Christ imagery that surrounds the beaten and bloody Azdak in the final scene of *The Caucasian Chalk Circle*, giving Brecht access to received images of martyrdom, which he can then deploy in unexpected and partly ironic ways. In fact, Christian images abound in Brecht, not least in the holy-family echoes in the latter play and in its baptismal scene of Grusche's washing and dressing the child; Brecht's fascination with maternal instinct is thereby colored with a displaced religious reverence.

Not all these motifs can be said to have a precise denotation; some operate affectively and by intuition. There is, for example, the ominous motif of white faces, the origin of which (a suggestion by Karl Valentin) has been frequently repeated; it appears in Begbick's cosmetics in *Rise and Fall of the City of Mahagonny* (1930), in the faces of the soldiers in the prologue scenes of *The Good Soldier Schweik* (1943), in *Coriolanus* (1953), and elsewhere, as well as in Brecht's early poetry, where it is always associated with decay and death. Moreover, some of the symbols, or motifs, seem to change meaning from one play to another: milk and cheese are reminders of Galileo's unidealistic materiality, an aspect of his moral decline, yet the same products signify nurturing and protection in *The Caucasian Chalk Circle*—a play that dwells much on recurring images of milk, blood, and water: a maternalized poetic vocabulary for a play about maternalism. *Life of Galileo*, too, claims its own symbolic tropes, appropriate to its subject: the sun and all other sources of light are used throughout as precise symbols of truth. Galileo's daughter—who at one point carries a shaded candle—faints at the sight of the sun when it is optically magnified and projected on a wall; and Galileo himself symbolically loses his capacity to see the light after his recantation.

One symbol that is put to exquisite use through intertextuality is that of snow. In *The Tutor*, it serves as an explicit sign of the desire to let problems be covered up, concealed, and left uncorrected—an image of vicious complacency. Always, snow has a threatening quality. It is a symbolic (as well as a physical) opponent to the hero in *The Good Soldier Schweik*, as is the wintry chill of *Mother Courage and Her Children*. Only once does snow become an affirmative presence—at the moment in *The Caucasian Chalk Circle* when Grusche, having rescued the child and fully realized its importance to her, describes the world with the eyes of one who has become newly maternal, and entirely generous:

> GRUSCHE (*looking around at Michael*). Never be afraid of the wind, it's only a
> poor devil like us. His job is pushing the clouds and he gets colder than anybody. (*Snow begins to fall.*) The snow isn't so bad either, Michael. Its job is covering the little fir trees so the winter won't kill them. And now I'll sing a song for you. Listen! (*Sings.*)
>
> > Your father is a bandit
> > And your mother is a whore
> > Every nobleman and honest

Will bow as you pass
The tiger's son will
Feed the little foals his brothers
The child of the serpent
Bring milk to the mothers. (*Collected Plays*, Vol. 7 [1971]: 177)

With this peculiar, unaccompanied song, Brecht shows a miracle beginning: imaginatively, Grusche's love transforms the world's evil into a momentary, idyllic vision, in a brilliantly composed and affecting image—made more powerful by its compression and by its subtle reference to related figures in other Brecht plays. In fact, a fuller understanding of Brecht's stage will demand that we see it as a fully symbolized sphere, in which any routine element may unexpectedly take on special meaning, such as Mother Courage's non-progress on the moving turntable floor, or Galileo's Pope exiting into darkness. Like Ibsen, Brecht moved from a boldly poeticized language in his early plays to an apparent realism that nevertheless functions as a transmogrified poetry, a seemingly conventional dramaturgy internally polarized by ideational schemes and complex revelations of an "inner" meaning. For Ibsen, a spiritual meaning is evoked, whereas for Brecht it is more a vision of concrete social facts, but each is reached through a subtle and complex theatrical poetry that has been too long ignored.

It would be wrong to claim that ignorance or violation of the above principles is the sole cause of our difficulties in staging Brecht. But insofar as these principles permit a clearer and more precise vision of the correspondences between Brecht's writing and directing, they may provide a basic understanding through which Brecht's directorial example can be put to better use. I would tell directors who want to undertake Brecht's plays to use these principles, to look for the significant patternings Brecht has put into the action: patterns of spatial juxtaposition and reversal of symbolic images across time, patterns of symbolic reference, patterns of shifting and complementary tones as the work moves from the explicit to the suggestive realms of Brecht's complex discourse. Always, I would advise a director to approach the work with playfulness and sensuality, while honoring a Brechtian tightness of focus.

Just Say No

But perhaps most important, I would encourage a director of Brecht to learn to say no—to make distinctions among the various elements of Brecht's *Modellbuch* legacies, to discover the difference between the decorative and the fundamental, the temporally bound solutions and the still powerful ones to the challenges of the dramatic texts. I would encourage clearing out everything that has grown customary in Brecht stagings and reaching for a new vision, but a vision strengthened by a firm understanding of the dramaturgic structures and strategies that must shape any vivid retelling of these plays.

Saying no is an aspect of any criticism, and it has operated somewhat tacitly in my own analysis. While sorting out these few essential principles of staging, I have deliberately ignored those principles or elements that I find inessential. Since this list of calculated omissions includes some of Brecht's most famous and most imitated habits, some of which are still seen as quintessentially Brechtian, I may be on controversial ground here. But every great director, Brecht included, has quirks that somehow prove lively in his hands but only secondhand in others'. Brecht was perhaps unusually liable to develop such idiosyncratic personal codes in his stagings: he had a decidedly eccentric visual taste (which colors every page of his diaries and nearly every other page of *Theaterarbeit*), and he loved to play with certain historically rooted theatrical devices and with the frisson of then-recent developments, like revolving stages and projections, or, arguably, the scene titles that he seemingly borrowed from silent movies.

Some of the qualities that I relegate to the status of "quirks" (or what a semiotician might call "idiolects") include: the exposed lighting instruments and scaffolding, the ungelled and unmodulated white light, the half-curtain, the revolving stage, the monochromatic color schemes, the generally utilitarian look, and the affectionately (one could almost say sentimentally) detailed attention to whatever routine labor the characters perform during their onstage action. Undoubtedly, each of these elements can be justified in terms of Brecht's themes and his desire for an earthy (proletarian) tone; certainly they have proven effective in Brecht's own hands (and in his theater, his culture, his historical moment).

But by now, all these devices have become the common clichés of mounting a Brecht classic, the calling cards of obedient acolytes, and a sure signal of a kind of sentimental unoriginality; they are almost unvaryingly used instead of deeper and more original insights. If Brecht is a living poet, something not unlike a living prophet, then these superficial stage dressings have become his whited—or dutifully grayed—sepulcher. What is needed is a new practice of staging Brecht that either replaces them or finds a way to render them fresh. For now, I would argue polemically to begin all new Brecht productions by violating one of these less essential stylistic rules. Why not Brecht with colored light, so long as it is used to illumine the play? Why not a masked Grusche and an unmasked, naturalistic Natella Abashwili, in a production that tacitly assumes the normalcy of Natella and the strangeness of Grusche's selflessness? Why not a circus-clown *Good Person of Setzuan*, a *Mother Courage and Her Children* performed outdoors, or a brassy, brightly colored *Mr. Puntila and His Man Matti*?

Jettisoning the Lifelike

If Brecht is to be re-connected to contemporary theatrical practices and experiment, one element in his staging practice must necessarily be challenged, although that challenge could disorient many of our most fundamental assumptions about Brechtian drama. That is the element of the lifelike itself: mimesis in acting, properties, and set—the limited, abstract mimesis around which Brecht organized his productions. There is a risk involved here, for Brecht's naturalism is more than a superficial affectation; it is written into his language and is planned as a grounding element in his visual style. Brecht not only chose to include a dash of naturalism; he gave it a privileged position within his array of styles.

Consider the issue of characterization. Brecht's characters are depicted in a range of abstraction from essentialized political types to detailed individuals whose conflicting social roles produce profound inner disorientation. In staging, Brecht actualized this range of abstraction by using a range of theatrical devices, including facial masks, extreme postures, and caricatured vocal patterns, on the one hand, for the more "essentialized" characters; and unadorned, precisely imitated naturalistic behavior, on the other, for his protagonists. Thus, he grounded his productions in a kind of histrionic naturalism, defining the central characters in lifelike performances so that the peripheral or emblematic (and usually antagonistic) characters displayed their difference through their stylistic distance from verisimilitude. Despite Brecht's demonstrative discrediting of naturalism as a delimited theatrical idiom, it is still the natural, the lifelike, that grounds his performance style.

But surely such a dependence on verisimilitude is partly determined by theatrical history. It is important to remember that Brecht's lifelikeness was a breakthrough in its time, a startling move into a recognizable reality in the face of the hysterical rantings of the Nazi theater. Later, the lifelike quality became the saving grace of Brecht's work under the dicta of socialist realism. But now, in America for one place, the same resemblance to quotidian reality is the common assumption of our least challenging entertainments; Brecht's subtle experimentation is thus absorbed into our customary ways of seeing. That is why, on American stages, Brecht tends to read as a somewhat mannered realist, and not much more.

But Brecht was not naïve. To an extent, he anticipated this problem. When, in the preface to *Roundheads and Peakheads* (1936), he made some very early stabs at defining his own staging style, his suspicion and encouragement of non-realistic impulses are revealed at the same time: he was interested in placing a phonograph onstage to accompany the songs in the play, but retreated from the idea for fear that it would "shock the audience unduly or give too much cause for amusement" (*Brecht on Theatre*, 103). A concern for his audience's level of theatrical experience and flexibility thus imposed limits on his stylistic excursion. Perhaps the time has come to try the phonograph onstage without fear of disorienting the audience. In the age of rock concerts and performance artists and God-knows-what else, the audience is less likely to laugh at a little visible musical equipment; in the age of Serban, Sellars, Ciulei, and Foreman (1970s-1980s)—let alone today—little that Brecht ever dreamed of would have seemed too unorthodox to try.

What would happen, then, if we were to jettison the lifelike, that one seemingly central element of Brechtian staging? After discarding the monochromatic color and lighting schemes, the revolving stage, and the peculiarities of Eisler's or Dessau's music, what might be the result if the naturalistic borrowings were discarded, too? None of the principles I have listed depend upon verisimilitude; in fact, they tend to defy it. What, then, if the defiance were taken further—if Grusche's internal conflicts were enacted by more than one actress at a time, or if Mother Courage's moments of "bargaining too long" were somehow reduced to a single, repeated gestural motif in a production that eschewed lifelike movement for choreographic extremity? What if Brecht's plays were theatrically reconceived as boldly as Shakespeare's, Chekhov's, Ibsen's, Calderón's, or Wagner's have been over the past few decades?

There is no guarantee of any sort of success in all this; I raise these questions fully aware of that. After all, Brecht wrote the naturalistic element into the plays painstakingly, and the loving care with which he did so is one of the signal traits of his achievement. But where there might be losses, there also might be significant gains: Brecht himself recognized and feared the danger of even seeming to belong to or resemble the realistic commercial theater. (That is why, in his final period, he put such stress on the "poetic" qualities of his work, as he did in his notes to *The Tutor*: for he feared that these qualities would be ignored, that his work would not stand out against the stultifying customs—and overwhelming presence—of conventional theater.) To divest these plays of their lifelike pretensions might forcibly awaken us to Brecht as a theatrical poet with a passionate and visionary consciousness, and unseat the somewhat mannered, socialist Zola that he has tended to become on American stages.

In the United States, not so long ago, there were some hints of this kind of liberating experiment. Having seen none of them, I can only surmise about how well they illuminated the plays (or, for that matter, whether they embodied any of the "first principles" noted above). But they have been described vividly enough for one to sense in them the validity of passionate experiment. Productions like the Living Theatre's *Antigone* in 1967, the San Francisco Mime Troupe's *Turandot* (1954) in 1969, and Travis Preston's *Good Person of Setzuan* in 1984 (at Indiana University, Bloomington) seem to have been thoughtful, poetic re-creations of Brecht's works. The presence of such stagings grants these plays their thinkability, their richness, their open appeal to the imagination; these stagings seek, in their irreverent way, to restore to Brecht his status as a poet of the theater, again a living and surprising—rather than tiresomely familiar and predictable—presence on our stage.

Works Cited

Bentley, Eric. "The Brecht Memoir." *Theater*, 14.2 (Spring 1983): 4-26.

Brecht, Bertolt. *Theaterarbeit: Sechs Aufführungen des Berliner Ensembles.* Dresden: VEB Dresdner Verlag, 1952.

----------. *Brecht on Theatre: The Development of an Aesthetic.* Trans. & ed. John Willett. New York: Hill & Wang, 1964.

----------. *The Messingkauf Dialogues* (1939-42). Trans. John Willett. London: Methuen, 1965.

----------. *Gesammelte Werke* [*Collected Works*]. 20 vols. Ed. Elisabeth Hauptmann. Frankfurt am Main: Suhrkamp Verlag, 1967.

----------. *Collected Plays.* 9 vols. Ed. Ralph Manheim & John Willett. London: Methuen, 1970-2004.

Fergusson, Francis. "Poetry in the Theatre and Poetry of the Theatre: Cocteau's *Infernal Machine*" (1950). In *Literary Criticism—Idea and Act: The English Institute, 1939-1972; Selected Essays.* Ed. William K. Wimsatt. Berkeley: University of California Press, 1974. 590-601.

Langer, Susanne K. *Feeling and Form: A Theory of Art.* New York: Scribner's, 1953.

7. *Major Barbara*, dir. Gabriel Pascal, 1941

8. Sybil Thorndike, *Saint Joan*, 1924-41

9. Charles Ludlam, *Hedda Gabler*, 1984

10. Elizabeth Robins, *Hedda Gabler*, 1891

INTERLUDE

"Three Cheers for Shaw" (1926), by Bertolt Brecht

Shaw as Terrorist

Shaw's experience and doctrine are that if one is to express oneself freely on any subject, one has first of all to overcome a certain inborn fear: of being conceited. Very early on he secured himself against the possibility of anybody at any time of his life burning incense to him. And he did so without fear of becoming famous. It was clear to him that any decent man's working equipment had to include that vital piece of apparatus, his own trumpet. He proudly refused to bury his pound sterling. Shaw has applied a great part of his talent to intimidating people to a point where it would be an impertinence for them to prostrate themselves before him.

It will have been observed that Shaw is a terrorist. Shaw's brand of terror is an extraordinary one, and he uses an extraordinary weapon, that of humor. This extraordinary man seems to be of the opinion that nothing in the world need be feared so much as the ordinary man's calm and incorruptible eye, but that this must be feared without question. This theory is for him the source of a great natural superiority, and by applying it systematically he has ensured that nobody who comes across him, in print, on the stage, or in the flesh, can conceive for a moment of his undertaking an action or speaking a sentence without being afraid of that incorruptible eye.

Indeed, even the younger generation, whose qualifications lie largely in their aggressiveness, limit their aggressions to a strict minimum when they realize that any attack on one of Shaw's habits, even his habit of wearing peculiar underwear, is likely to end in the disastrous downfall of their own ill-considered garb. If at the same time it is realized that it is he who broke with the unthinking custom of speaking in a whisper, instead of loudly and cheerfully, in anything resembling a place of worship, and that it is he who proved that the right attitude to any really important phenomenon is a casual (contemptuous) one, because it is the only one that permits complete concentration and real alertness—only then will it be understood how high a degree of personal freedom he has achieved.

Shaw's terrorism consists in this: that he claims a right for every man to act in all circumstances with decency, logic, and humor, and sees it as his own duty to do so even when it creates opposition. He knows just how much courage is needed to laugh at what is amusing, and how much seriousness to pick it out. And like all people who have a definite purpose, he knows that there is nothing more time-wasting and distracting than a particular kind of seriousness that is popular in literature but nowhere else.

As a playwright he takes just as naïve a view of writing for the theater as young writers do, and he shows not the least trace of wishing to behave as if he ignored the fact; he makes free use of such naïveté. He gives the theater as much fun as it can stand. Strictly speaking, what makes people go to the theater is nothing but stuff that acts as a vast incubus to the quite real business that really interests the advanced dramatist and constitutes the true value of his plays. The logic of this is that his problems must be such good ones that he can bury them beneath the most wanton transgressions, and it is the transgressions that people will then want to have.

Shaw Defended against His Own Glum Foreboding

I seem to remember a short while ago that Shaw himself formulated his views about the future of the drama. He said that in future people would no longer go to the theater in order to understand something. What he probably meant was that, odd as it may seem, the mere reproduction of reality does not give an impression of truth. If so, the younger generation will not contradict him.

I must point out, however, that the reason why Shaw's own dramatic works dwarf those of his contemporaries is that they so unhesitatingly appealed to reason. His world is one that arises from opinions. The opinions of his characters constitute their fates. Shaw creates a play by inventing a series of complications that give his characters a chance to develop their opinions as fully as possible and to oppose them to our own. Such complications cannot be too hoary and too well-known for Shaw; he has no pretensions about this. A perfectly ordinary usurer is worth his weight in gold to him; a patriotic girl comes into the story; and all he cares is that the girl's story should be as familiar and the usurer's sticky end as natural and desirable as possible, so that he may strip us all the more thoroughly of our old-fashioned opinions about such characters and, even more, about their opinions.

Probably every single feature of all Shaw's characters can be attributed to his delight in dislocating our stock associations. He knows that we have a horrible way of taking all the characteristics of a particular type and lumping them under a single head. We picture a usurer as cowardly, furtive, and brutal. Not for a moment do we think of allowing him to be in any way courageous. Or wistful, or tender-hearted. Shaw does.

As for the hero, Shaw's less gifted successors have developed his refreshing view that heroes are not models of good conduct, and that heroism consists of an impenetrable but exceedingly lively hotchpotch of the most contradictory qualities; they have arrived at the lamentable conclusion that there is no such thing as either heroism or heroes. Probably in Shaw's view this is unimportant. He seems to find less point in living among heroes than among ordinary men.

Shaw's approach to composing his works is completely above-board. He has no hesitation in writing under the incessant supervision of the public. To give extra weight to his judgments he helps to make that supervision easier; he keeps emphasizing his own peculiarities, his individual taste, and even his (minor) weaknesses. For this he must be thanked. Even when his opinions go very much against those of today's younger generation, they will listen to him with pleasure; he is (and what more could be said of anybody?) a good man. Moreover, his is a time that seems to preserve opinions better than it does moods and feelings. And of all that has been laid down in the present period, it looks as if opinions will last the longest.

A Catching Infection: Fun

It is significantly hard to find out anything about what other European writers think. But I take it that where literature, for instance, is concerned, they all share more or less the same view: namely, that writing is a melancholy business. As usual Shaw, whose views about anything under the sun are far from unknown, differs from his colleagues here. It is not his fault, but at most an embarrassment to him, a thorn in his side, if his vast difference of opinion with all other European writers, covering almost every subject in the world, is not thrown into sufficiently clear relief because the others refrain from voicing their views even when they have any.

At any rate, Shaw would at least agree with me on this point: that he likes writing. There is no room for a martyr's halo even outside his head. His literary activities have in no sense cut him off from life. On the contrary. I am not sure if it is the right way to measure his gifts, but I can only say that the effect of this inimitable cheerfulness and infectious good mood is quite exceptional.

Shaw truly is able to give the impression that his mental and physical well-being increases with every sentence that he writes. Reading his works may not induce Bacchic intoxication, but there is no doubt that it is extraordinarily healthy. And his only enemies (if they need be mentioned at all) would need to be the kind of people who don't care all that much about health.

As for Shaw's own ideas, I cannot at the moment recollect a single one that could be called typical of him, though I know of course that he has a lot; but I could name a great deal that he has found to be typical of other people. He himself may well think that his way of viewing things is necessarily more important than his actual views. That says much for a man of his sort.

I get the impression that a lot revolves for him round a particular theory of evolution, which in his view differs widely and decisively from another evolutionary theory of a clearly inferior brand. At any rate, his faith in mankind's infinite capacity for improvement plays an overriding part in his works. It will be understood as equivalent to giving three heartfelt cheers for Shaw if I simply admit that, although I am familiar with neither of these two theories, I blindly and unconditionally support Shaw's. For it seems to me that so keen-witted and fearlessly eloquent a man is wholly to be trusted. Just as it always and in all circumstances seems to me that the force of a statement is more important than its applicability, and that a man's stature is more important than the trend of his activities.

(Translated by John Willett in *Brecht on Theatre*. London: Methuen, 1964. 10-13.)

"The Form that 'Can Longer Paint': Ibsen's *Ghosts* and Osvald"

Osvald in the End

Osvald Alving can be seen as a symbol of paralysis of the mind at the end of *Ghosts* (1881). His literal paralysis of the brain symbolizes the paralysis of mind that affects the society of Ibsen's time, the Norwegian society in which Mrs. Alving, Pastor Manders, and the other characters of the play live, and from which Osvald has been absent since he was sent to live in Paris at the age of seven. Osvald is "dumb" at the end of the play, his mind paralyzed: suddenly, he is stripped of any psychological life of his own. He is pure, in a manner of speaking. He was "pure" in a similar way while abroad: "dumb" in that, for the most part, he was not communicating with his mother (he wrote occasionally and visited even less often); and without a full psychological life of his own, that is, one known to his mother, since she sent him away when he was seven years old and was never really in charge of his upbringing from that point on.

Osvald is not so "impure" during the play, either. He obviously has a full-formed psychological life of his own, but it is largely *his own*, and it is largely in reserve, since he is in a place and around people he does not know well. He complains about the weather a lot, and he criticizes the citizens of his hometown with a vengeance. To emphasize his foreignness to his "hometown," Ibsen even has him stand onstage through his entire first scene in hat and coat! William Archer has said of Osvald: "We cannot be said to know him, individually and intimately, as we know Helmer or Stockmann, Hjalmar Ekdal, or Gregers Werle" (Archer, 203). This is precisely so, as befits a realistic play, because no one onstage could truly be said to know him in this way. Osvald is, then, the perfect figure to serve as symbol: he is almost "pure," and therefore all the more effective as pure symbol, as opposed to symbol sullied by character.

Osvald has in fact been gradually assuming his symbolic role throughout the play as his own paralysis of the brain has been growing, or getting ready to strike, and his function as symbol at the end of *Ghosts* is the key to a fuller, richer interpretation of the play. Ibsen identifies his play with Osvald; that Osvald is an artist who can no longer paint should have tipped critics off to this long ago. Osvald's paralysis does not simply destroy Mrs. Alving's son, some virtual nonentity from abroad, but, Ibsen leads us to believe, *an artist* of great promise. I do not believe that the play is intended primarily as Mrs. Alving's tragedy, and I think that Ibsen made this clear by ending the play the way he did—without having Mrs. Alving poison, or not poison Osvald with morphine and then depicting the aftermath. To my knowledge, no critic has ever asked why specifically Ibsen ended *Ghosts* precisely at Mrs. Alving's moment of decision and did not show what that decision was. Most critics, of course, take the play, for better or for worse, as Helene Alving's tragedy, or as a simple drama of social protest and reform. They ignore, or are simply unaffected by the "formal" meaning of *Ghosts*' ending and concentrate instead on what has led up to it or what, they believe, will, or should have come after it.

Tragedy and Well-Madeness

Francis Fergusson serves as a salient example of such critics, since so many later ones use his discussion as a starting point. He writes in *The Idea of a Theater* that

> the tragic rhythm of Mrs. Alving's quest is not so much completed as brutally truncated, in obedience to the requirements of the thesis and the thriller. Osvald's collapse, before our eyes, with his mother's screaming, makes the intrigue end with a bang, and hammers home the thesis. But from the point of view of Mrs. Alving's tragic quest as we have seen it develop through the rest of the play, this conclusion concludes nothing: it is merely sensational. (Fergusson, 152)

I do not deny for a moment that *Ghosts* resembles the well-made play described above. I am also aware that "in accordance with the principles of the thesis play, *Ghosts* is plotted as a series of debates on conventional morality, between Mrs. Alving and the Pastor, the Pastor and Osvald, and Osvald and his mother" (Fergusson, 150). But something Fergusson says earlier in his essay comes back to haunt him here, and to lead the way beyond Mrs. Alving's "truncated tragedy": "One may see, in *Ghosts*, behind the surfaces of the savage story, a partially realized tragic form of really poetic scope, the result of Ibsen's more serious and disinterested brooding upon the human condition in general" (Fergusson, 150).

Ghosts resembles a well-made thriller, but in its shadow poetry is constantly lurking, and that poetry, that symbol, finally surfaces at the end. *Ghosts* is plotted as a series of debates on conventional morality, but it hardly hammers home a thesis at the end, a single-minded condemnation of the society that spawned the Alvings and their dilemmas. The play is, in reality, a latter-day tragedy on "the human condition in general"—not so much through Helene Alving, as *Oedipus Tyrannos* is a tragedy on the human condition through the example of Oedipus, as along with her. *Oedipus Tyrannos* (430 B.C.) is the tragedy of man, of self, of how the self conceives of its relationship to the Ideal or the Absolute, whereas *Ghosts* is a tragedy of two or more men, of the effect of men's actions on other men though the generations. Mrs. Alving is a part of the whole, in other words, but she does not stand for the whole, and she cannot be made to stand for it.

Let me illustrate this through the example of the very last moments in the play. Had the play continued, emphasis would have fallen on Mrs. Alving's state after the poisoning, or after her avoidance of it. By ending *Ghosts* at Mrs. Alving's moment of decision and by not showing what that decision is, Ibsen places emphasis on the object or symbol to be or not to be poisoned, and on *whether* it will be poisoned, not on the subject who will or will not do the poisoning. This is one of the reasons he has Mrs. Alving "paralyzed with fear" and "in speechless terror" (*Ghosts*, 153) at the end: he nearly equates her condition here with Osvald's, so that, again, emphasis will fall on whether the paralysis is destroyed or lives on. To Mrs. Alving, whether Osvald lives or dies, whether she poisons him with morphine or not, is a matter of real, of real-life importance. It is of such importance to no one else in the play: Pastor Manders, Engstrand, and

Regine have all gone to look out for themselves. But to Ibsen, to us, and to the form of the play, whether Osvald lives or dies is a matter of symbolic, of extra importance, since he is already both alive *and* "dead" in his present vegetative state, and since we clearly cannot feel for him as his mother does, however little she could be said to know him. Ibsen is not so much interested here in Mrs. Alving's reaction to Osvald as in our own reaction to his play as form.

Osvald, Mrs. Alving, and Centrality

The real focus of the play from an aesthetic point of view, then, is Osvald, not Mrs. Alving. She is the "interest" in the play, along with, to a lesser degree, the other characters. At her most neutral, arousing curiosity about herself, it is her job to deflect attention away from Osvald, to absorb our interest, until it is time for her son—literally kept in the shadows for much of the play—to take over as almost pure symbol, as container of the play. Bert O. States would call her part of the verisimilitude or "environment" of the play. His comments on dramatic form in general and verisimilitude's place in it are of special relevance here:

> One might define a good drama . . . as one which produces a maximum reversal with minimum improbability. Thus, in the dynamics of drama, the function of verisimilitude, or (if you will) environment, is to act as a viscous medium which impedes the runaway energies of the reversal mechanism. Reversal is under much the same environmental restraint as the mainspring of a watch: without the escapement mechanism, which forces it to unwind in an orderly way, the spring would spend its energy in a single discharge. Put simply, the principle of escapement is inherent in the total environment of a play (including supporting characters, social structures, accidents, etc.), and what I mean by minimum improbability is simply the resistance which this environment, behaving "according to nature," offers to the reflexive drive aesthetically imposed on the play's world. (States, 576)

Now some would say that, indeed, a maximum reversal does occur in *Ghosts*, and that it occurs through the character of Mrs. Alving, the main character. But this ignores the fact that Ibsen never completes Mrs. Alving's reversal; he does not show her finally at rest with the knowledge of herself and her past that she has attained in the course of the play. Indeed, it is never clear that she accepts this knowledge: she is beside herself with fear and disbelief from the moment Osvald reveals to her that his illness is hereditary and without cure, until the end of the play. Francis Fergusson thinks that this is *Ghosts*' flaw; I think that it is the play's strategy. Ibsen cuts short Mrs. Alving's reversal at the very moment *Osvald's* reversal is complete, and he has been waiting on Osvald's reversal throughout the play. Following the model of the well-made play, Ibsen thus makes Mrs. Alving's reversal really a reversal in her fortunes as opposed to a reversal in her recognition or perception of her situation, since we never *see* this recognition or perception. Osvald's reversal is that of the nightmare or dream, and Osvald's last moments onstage are like a poem to the well-made play that has preceded them. They give us the image of a paralyzed Osvald, and it is on this image that the play closes, in a state of lyric rest as opposed to dramatic unwinding, one could say.

Osvald's reversal—"the reflexive drive aesthetically imposed on the play's world"—is from entrance into the play as the symbol of freedom and enlightened thinking to exit from it as the symbol of paralysis of thought and action. Because this is an extreme reversal, Ibsen keeps Mrs. Alving's reversal in step with Osvald's throughout the play, only to arrest hers at the moment of truth. This is a dramatic strategy, designed to reinforce the function of Osvald and lend it credibility. Mrs. Alving's attainment or falling short of nobility at the end of the play is less important to Ibsen than the point, made through the now symbolic presence of Osvald, that what happened to the Alvings may, or may not, happen again to others. Mrs. Alving may poison Osvald, or she may not. Osvald, now the symbol of the kind of paralysis of the mind—narrowmindedness, stubbornness, plain stupidity in society—that drove his mother to marry Captain Alving (for wealth and position) instead of Pastor Manders in the first place, may live, or he may die. The paralysis may live on in men, or it may die. Ibsen's ambivalence is tantalizing and suggests that it is not entirely up to him, nor entirely up to us. This is not didacticism, not reform, nor is it pessimism or optimism. It bespeaks the intermingling of fate, chance, environment, and free will, of forces both beyond our control and within our control, in the determination of all our lives. The ending of *Ghosts* contains a very delicate balance, but a balance nonetheless.

Osvald's Journey and the Dream

In order to understand the full power of *Ghosts*' poetic structure, let us see exactly how Ibsen gets Osvald to the position he is in by the end of the play. I said above that Osvald's reversal was of the nightmare or dream, whereas Mrs. Alving's was of the well-made play. By this I meant that his reversal from lucidity to imbecility has about it the quality of a dream; it occurs with the suddenness and unpredictability with which images or symbols are produced in dreams. This is so despite all the preparing for this moment Ibsen has done: we simply are never prepared to watch someone go instantly from the normal human state to complete helplessness. If we do witness such an occurrence, we feel as if we are dreaming; we feel suddenly removed from reality. As Osvald is having his final, paralyzing attack, Mrs. Alving says, "This has all been a nightmare, Osvald—just something you've imagined" (*Ghosts*, 152). Day is breaking as she speaks: the nightmare is over. But what is suggested is that Osvald's attack is a nightmare, or dream, that he has been having throughout the play and from which he now "awakens," his brain paralyzed. It is as if the deteriorating Osvald has been having a dream, that is, since everything is so unbelievable to him—the way people live in his hometown, the revelations about his father. I hope it is clear that I am not trying to make a case here for *Ghosts* as a "dream play." Obviously, it is not one. Osvald does not dream the play; rather, the realistic action of the well-made play strikes him with the unreality of a dream.

And it is precisely the well-made play that Ibsen, through Osvald, is trying to transcend in *Ghosts*. Ibsen the artist, the poet, transcends the well-made form, the form that "can no longer paint," if you will, the form that is a reflection of the traditional, "well-made"—"paralyzed"—society he himself inhabited. This is the selfsame society whose attitudes and beliefs paved the way for the destruction of Osvald, and with him of an artist. Ibsen gets the well-made form to participate in its own calling to account, even trumping, through the controlling presence of Osvald and the at once innovative and disingenuous devices of realism. Thus we get the break between well-made form and what I would call the life of poetry and symbol at the end of the play, between Osvald's line, "Thank you, Mother" (*Ghosts*, 152), and the breaking of day. The well-made form deteriorates once Osvald's mind deteriorates.

It is the well-made form, society, that originally produced Osvald, and it is he who lays that form to rest. *This* is the overriding action of the play, what Osvald "does," what Ibsen does for Osvald, how he "loves" him, to borrow Robert B. Heilman's usage of the word (Heilman, 26). Osvald's release is into complete mental paralysis, and the suggestion is that this is preferable to complete mental alertness (or what passes for it) in a "paralyzed" society. The play's release is into mockery of the well-made form's "paralysis": the frozen moment, the tableau ripe with possibility. Osvald, who can no longer paint, becomes a figure in the "painting" that would make way for the "joy of life" (*Ghosts*, 136) he was always talking about. The sunshine is there. And the "glowing happy faces" (*Ghosts*, 136) might at least be our own, just beyond the "frame," if not those of the figures themselves.

There is strong evidence that Ibsen places a well-made play inside a dream structure—or a structure that keeps Osvald "in mind," that has him as its focus or concern—in order to subvert the well-made-play structure even as he uses it and thereby stress Osvald's poetic importance as symbol. Although all the action before the final moments is not seen from Osvald's point of view, as it would be in a dream play, he does provide a kind of frame for the action. It is his presence in the Alving home that motivates all the action and supplies Ibsen's reason for beginning the play when he does. *Ghosts* opens with Osvald asleep upstairs, controlling the volume of Regine and Engstrand's conversation and lending to its incredibility, since none of the three is aware that Regine is actually Osvald's half-sister and that Captain Alving is Regine's real father. *Ghosts* closes with the "death" of Osvald's mind.

Then there is Osvald's presence right outside or around scenes when he is thought to be outside and away, taking a walk or attending the fire at the Orphanage. The characters onstage are unaware of his presence; like a figure in a dream, he may appear to be in two places at once, or he may suddenly appear in one place when he was thought to be in another. It is noteworthy that no one "discovers" Osvald, that no one comes upon him; this is one of the ways in which Ibsen makes him the poetic focus or force of the play. Osvald has four entrances in *Ghosts*, each one *onto* a scene. One time Regine does come upon him and his mother (in Act II; *Ghosts*, 132), but only because Mrs. Alving has rung for her, and Ibsen gives Regine four more quick entrances after this in order to play down the significance of her first entrance. So too does Pastor Manders come upon Osvald, his mother, and Regine, but, significantly, Osvald hears him coming: he is waiting for him. And when Mrs. Alving herself has the chance to come upon Osvald right after he has returned from a supposed walk, she does not do so. Structurally, the play cannot let her. She hears Regine resisting Osvald's advances in the dining room at the end of Act I, and she could go in and break them up (just by her presence) without revealing their true relationship to each other, but her emotional state, and the state of the play, prevent her from acting.

During his supposed walk in Act I, Osvald may be right outside or around the scene between his mother and Pastor Manders. Whereas he had his coat on and his hat in his hand for the entirety of his first scene onstage (right before he leaves for his walk), he returns from his walk without his hat and coat! This may not appear very remarkable on the surface—he could have left a wet hat and coat in another room—but it becomes so when one considers that his entrance with the information that "dinner's nearly ready" (*Ghosts*, 112) is followed immediately by Regine's with the same information and with the parcel of songs for the Orphanage dedication ceremony. Has Osvald been right outside the garden room all along, perhaps with Regine the whole time, and has he decided to break in on Manders and Mrs. Alving because it is nearly dinnertime and he is hungry (Ibsen makes much of Osvald's appetite for his mother's food)? Has he been without hat and coat, inside the house, for as long as he was *with* hat and coat during his first scene, with Manders and his mother? His immediately intimate responses to Regine when she comes in to announce dinner, and his quick advances on her once they are behind a closed door again for a moment, strongly suggest that they are continuing something begun just previously, right outside the garden room. Regine's line, "Osvald!—Are you mad?—Let me go!" (*Ghosts*, 113), especially suggests this. Regine is not resisting Osvald here; she is not expressing a lack of interest in him (only to be ready to go to Paris with him as his wife in Act II). She is telling him that he is crazy to be embracing her now, with his mother and the pastor close by and about to come in to dinner—not so unusual a reaction for a woman of any era.

At the beginning of Act II, Osvald says that he is going out for a walk again. In a brilliant theatrical stroke, Ibsen has him say this from offstage, in the dining room, where, we will learn later, he remains for all of the subsequent conversation between Pastor Manders and Mrs. Alving, and after that between Manders and Engstrand. Regine then answers Mrs. Alving from the same dining room that she will go down to the laundry and help with the wreaths. We do not learn if she does this, but we can guess that, even if she does, she comes back to the dining room to be with Osvald (her next entrance is from the dining room), thus connecting this "walk" of Osvald's with his first one. In other words, during both "walks," he spends at least some of his time offstage, in the house, with Regine.

One other factor connects these two "walks" with each other. When Mrs. Alving discovers, after Manders and Engstrand have left, that Osvald has been in the dining room all along, she asks him why he did not go out for his walk. He replies, "In this kind of weather?" (*Ghosts*, 127). The implication is that if he would not go out "in this kind of weather" after dinner, he would not have gone out in it right before dinner (or he would have gone out only for a moment; he would have gotten just past the door before returning).

Mrs. Alving carries on a conversation of thirteen lines at this point with an Osvald who is offstage. There is a realistic reason for this: Osvald is smoking a cigar, which is not allowed in the garden room. But the conversation goes on for so long—we got our first taste of it at the beginning of the act, remember—that we are left with this haunting image of Osvald just beyond the "frame," overseeing the action. Mrs. Alving senses Osvald's presence in the dining room once she is alone, but, again, she does not come upon him: she does not go into the dining room to see if he is there. She calls out, and he replies.

Mrs. Alving senses Osvald's presence in this way at two other times. She hears him coming upon his first entrance in the play (he has been asleep), and he enters, without comment from her, looking exactly like his father—as one might *be* oneself but look like someone or something else in a dream. Mrs. Alving goes to meet Osvald when he returns from the fire at the Orphanage, and, to judge from Ibsen's stage direction, it is as if she were going to meet him before she had evidence he was coming; it is as if she knew instinctively, as the figures in a dream are wont to do, that he would appear when he did, when the "dream" produced him. Even though Osvald has been at the fire, Mrs. Alving's going to meet him in the way she does thus makes it appear that he has been right outside the garden room, in the garden, all along. When, toward the end of the play, Osvald goes into the offstage hallway outside the garden room in order to lock the door of the Alving home, it is as if he is sealing himself into the nightmare that his life has become—the nightmare from which his only "escape," very shortly, will be complete paralysis of the mind.

Engstrand, Regine, and Manders, or Dreams and Paralysis

Perhaps the most startling evidence for Ibsen's subversion of a well-made-play structure through a dream structure is to be found at moments in the play that other critics have faulted for their unbelievability. I am thinking particularly of Pastor Manders' failure early in Act III to ask Engstrand why, if he saw the beginnings of a fire at the Orphanage, he did not do something immediately, and of Osvald's and Regine's instantaneous assimilation of the fact that they—two people who might have married—are half-brother and half-sister, also in Act III.

Many have faulted *Ghosts* for letting Engstrand, Regine, and Pastor Manders "get away," for not including these characters more in *Mrs. Alving's* tragedy. It is said that they are disposed of too quickly and easily as excess baggage in this well-made play's headlong drive to completion. But a close reading of the text shows that the three of them are very much included in the poetic structure that makes *Ghosts* a tragedy of "two or more men." Just as Osvald is the symbol of paralysis that Mrs. Alving will destroy or not destroy, so too is "Captain Alving's Haven" (*Ghosts*, 142)—Engstrand's proposed "home for poor seamen" (*Ghosts*, 142) that will be nothing more than a brothel—a symbol of the same kind of paralysis infecting the Norwegian society of the time, and likewise a symbol that Engstrand, Regine, and Manders will destroy or not destroy. Ibsen has planted the clues, and they fairly leap out at us once the grand strategy of the play is discerned.

Osvald is linked with Captain Alving's Haven as symbol on three counts. First, Osvald has come home in time for the ceremony celebrating the completion of the Orphanage to Captain Alving's memory (significantly, Osvald has also come home to Norway in the first place to suffer the [second] attack of paresis that will result in the paralysis of his brain. He tells his mother late in Act III), and the Haven is Engstrand's answer to the Orphanage that he himself burns down. Second, it was Captain Alving's whoring—"the sins of the father"—that led in the first place to Osvald's contracting of paresis (a disease of the brain caused by syphilis of the central nervous system and characterized by inflammation of the meninges, dementia, and paralytic attacks), and in Captain Alving's memory, appropriately, a brothel is going to be erected, where future Captain Alvings will become diseased and produce their own diseased Osvalds. Third, Regine is the offspring of the Captain's sexual relations with Johanna, his servant and Engstrand's future wife. That is, Regine is as much the product of the Captain's whoring, she is as much associated in our minds with the disease, as she is Osvald's true half-sister. In fact, she has some of the whore in her, too, as she herself says: "I take after my mother, I suppose" (*Ghosts*, 146); she might have added that she may be taking up work in Engstrand's brothel soon.

It is easy to assume that "after" *Ghosts*, Engstrand gets his brothel, Manders keeps his reputation untarnished, and Regine begins her descent into a life of prostitution. In a word, that Ibsen loses control over these characters' fates, which then run wild toward their most negative capability. But this assumption is based almost entirely on one piece of evidence and virtually ignores Regine's place in the dealings of Engstrand and Manders. Early in Act III, Engstrand blames the fire at the Orphanage on Manders, saying, "I saw you snuff one of the candles and throw the bit of wick right into a pile of shavings!" (*Ghosts*, 140). Manders takes Engstrand at his word for the moment, even though he swears he "never went *near* the lights" (*Ghosts*, 140) and claims that he is "not in the habit of snuffing candles with [his] fingers" (*Ghosts*, 140) anyway. Engstrand has Manders where he wants him: he offers to take the blame for Manders so that the newspapers won't attack the pastor, and in return Manders will see that Engstrand gets the funds for his "Seamen's Home" (*Ghosts*, 89).

As far as I know, no one has ever disputed that this is exactly what happens. I say above that Manders takes Engstrand at his word *for the moment*, however, because if Manders is in the least questioning and analytical—and he has these traits where his own interests are concerned; he is an intelligent man for all his narrowmindedness—then he is soon going to be asking Engstrand why he didn't say something if he saw the pastor throwing a piece of candlewick into a pile of shavings, or why Engstrand didn't make sure that the shavings would not catch fire. This seems rather obvious to me, yet critics have persisted over the years in pointing to Manders' quick capitulation to Engstrand as a striking flaw in the play (Gray, 65-66; Northam, 112). I prefer to see the capitulation as a mistake (made in the heat of the moment: nothing so improbable) that Manders may, or may not, rectify. (Engstrand, sly dog that he is, may have a very good explanation ready for Manders.) Once again, a symbol of paralysis, here Captain Alving's Haven, may, or may not, be destroyed—that is, lose the funds Manders had promised for its construction.

Even if Manders never thinks to question why Engstrand didn't do anything about the piece of candlewick thrown into the pile of shavings, Regine will be along at any moment to do a bit of questioning and answering herself. She knows now that Captain Alving was her real father, and so does Manders. Engstrand does not know about her real paternity, and Manders does not know that Regine knows about it. Regine has probably figured out by the end of the play that Engstrand himself set the fire at the Orphanage. (Engstrand's aside to her, "We've hooked the old fool now, my girl!", at the start of Act III [*Ghosts*, 139] should have set her to thinking.) Manders doesn't know that Engstrand is the real arsonist. Regine wants some of the money that Manders has said he will find for the construction of Captain Alving's Haven (the money will come from the interest on the capital Mrs. Alving had laid aside for the building and administration of the Orphanage), for she wants to lead the kind of life "suited to a gentleman's daughter" (*Ghosts*, 146). What she will do to get that money is play Engstrand against Manders with the knowledge she has that each man does not have. Regine reveals this in the following exchange with Mrs. Alving just before the former leaves the Alving household for good:

> REGINE. . . .—May I ask, Mrs. Alving, if Mr. Manders knows this? [that Regine is
> really the daughter of Captain Alving and Johanna Engstrand].
> MRS. ALVING. Mr. Manders knows everything.
> REGINE. (*Rapidly putting on her shawl*) Then I'd better try and catch that boat. Mr. Manders is such a kind man, he's sure to help me. It seems to me I have a right to some of that money too—a better right than that filthy old carpenter. (*Ghosts*, 146)

Regine can do a lot to embarrass Pastor Manders if she makes public her true father's name and Manders' knowledge of the illicit relationship between the Captain and Johanna Engstrand (when the pastor received this knowledge will have become beside the point). Regine can, of course, ruin Engstrand if she tells Manders that it was really Engstrand who started the fire at the Orphanage. She can blackmail either man (or both at the same time) to get something of what she wants, and Captain Alving's Haven can still see the light of day. But if she decides to pursue her "better right" to the money—and her line, "What do I care?" (*Ghosts*, 147), in response to Mrs. Alving's warning to be careful, tells us she might go this far—that is, if she decides to expose Engstrand completely at the same time that she holds the truth about her paternity over Manders' head, she may undo herself, Engstrand, and Manders. The reason for this is that even if the money is there to be handed over in full to her, she won't have it for long before the newspapers have her (and Manders). Captain Alving's Haven will never see the light of day in this case. Our symbol of paralysis will have been put to rest. Or it will have been allowed to live. The decision is Regine's. Or it is Pastor Manders'. *Ghosts* is indeed a tragedy of "two or more men," and that tragedy is completed. No one escapes, yet no one has simply been disposed of. Everything hangs in the balance, forever waiting for them, forever waiting for us. This is the charity, and hope, of the play.

All of *Ghosts* can be seen, then, as an attempt by Ibsen to elaborate the right image or symbol for the tragic paralysis of mind in Norwegian society. Captain Alving's Haven and Osvald are highlighted, finally, as twin symbols for that paralysis through Ibsen's subversion of the well-made form by means of a dream structure, and through his arresting of the action before Mrs. Alving, Manders, Regine, and Engstrand experience any reversal in their perception of the overall situation. Thus Manders' failure to ask Engstrand why he did not take action immediately if he saw the beginnings of a fire at the Orphanage, and Osvald's and Regine's instantaneous assimilation of the fact that they are half-brother and half-sister, can be viewed as examples of Ibsen's dream structure at work. Manders', Osvald's, and Regine's actions could occur in a dream and not be thought of by the dreamer as unrealistic or unbelievable, for dreams are not preoccupied with realism or believability. But the well-made play is so preoccupied, and it would be concerned with making the actions of Manders, Osvald, and Regine credible.

Although a case can be made for Manders' behavior on realistic grounds, it could also be argued that Ibsen's lack of concern with making Manders', and Osvald's and Regine's, actions believable was intentional: he wanted to subvert the well-made play; to call attention to his departures from it and thus give its action even more of the very quality of unreality that it has for its primary "dreamer," Osvald; and in this way to direct the spectator to the imminent ascent of poetic symbol in *Ghosts*. Like Manders, Osvald, and Regine, Mrs. Alving herself is included in the dream structure of *Ghosts*: what happens, happens so suddenly and irreversibly that it seems like a dream to her. But we leave Mrs. Alving on the verge of her "awakening." Osvald is "asleep" forever; the woman "sleeping" next to him, however, who has been "asleep" for most of her life, is about to "wake up" and do something. At the end of *Ghosts*, it could be said, Mrs. Alving's life, and the true life of the play, begin.

Ghosts and *Hedda Gabler*

Ghosts owes its permanence, finally, less to realism as a dramatic movement and the analytical method of characterization than to Ibsen's permanent concerns, expressed most cogently through his manipulation of structure to create poetic symbol. Unfortunately, the play has tended to be interpreted along the paths of least resistance: the narrowest path of social drama, or the unchallenging one of failed tragedy. But Ibsen put a lot into *Ghosts*, and it is on the broader, or more abstract, grounds that the play points in so many directions while leading in only one, that it is so highly imaginative while yet so simple, that I am making my case for it as great dramatic art.

And not only for it, of course. What I am saying about *Ghosts* could also be said about *Hedda Gabler* (1890), for example. Osvald must live and Osvald must die at the end of *Ghosts*, the possibility that he may or may not be poisoned must be left open, for the same reason that Hedda must die and Løvborg's manuscript must live at the end of *Hedda Gabler*. Hedda's ideal (to live beautifully, free from the constraints of her socialization) dies with her, but Løvborg's ideal (a book on the future of civilization, in which he frees himself, and potentially others, from the poisonous constraints of society by writing a prescription for that society's health or liberation) lives—it is reconstructed from notes by Tesman and Thea. Hedda kills herself with child; Løvborg and Thea speak of the manuscript as *their* "child." Hedda dies to achieve the ideal she could not achieve in life; Løvborg kills himself (or is killed in a mistaken attempt to retrieve his manuscript from "Mademoiselle Diana's boudoir") because he felt he had achieved, or helped to make possible, the ideal through his book and then senselessly lost the manuscript.

In the same way as Osvald's paralysis of mind could be said to be growing throughout *Ghosts*, to turn him at the end into a symbol of the paralysis of mind of Norwegian society, so too could the notes for Løvborg's book that Thea produces in *Hedda Gabler* be said to have been "growing" throughout the play, to be given birth at the end as a symbol of hope for the future of civilization. Thea and Løvborg had spoken of the manuscript as their "child," as I mention above, and thus it is no accident that Thea "nurtures" these notes in the pocket of her dress throughout the play (she says at one point, "Yes. I took them with me when I left home—they're here in my pocket—" [*Hedda Gabler*, 422]), to produce them at the right moment for reassembly by herself and Tesman.

In the same way that Ibsen leads us to believe that in Osvald an artist of great promise is ultimately destroyed by the paralysis of mind of his society, so too does the playwright lead us to believe that in Hedda a person of potential creativity is destroyed by her upbringing as the daughter of the aristocratic General Gabler. Martin Esslin writes that

> [Hedda's] sense of social superiority prevents her from realizing her genuine superiority as a potential creative personality. If the standards prescribed by the laws of noblesse oblige had not prevented her from breaking out into the freedom of moral and social emancipation, she might have been able to turn her passionate desire for beauty (which is the hallmark of real, spiritual, as distinct from social, aristocracy) to the creation of beauty, living beauty rather than merely a beautiful death. It is the creative energy, frustrated and damned up, that is finally converted into the malice and envy, the destructive rage, the intellectual dishonesty that lead to Hedda Gabler's downfall. (Esslin, 39)

Like Osvald, Hedda is a potential artist. Like Mrs. Alving, she has no true moment of recognition or perception: Ibsen is interested at the end more in whether Løvborg's ideal will be promulgated, to the benefit of future Heddas. Whether he has succeeded—in the cases of Hedda and Osvald, on the one hand, and Norwegian as well as global society, on the other—is an extra-dramatic question that I shall leave the reader to ponder.

Works Cited

Archer, William, intro. *The Collected Works of Henrik Ibsen:* A Doll's House *and* Ghosts. Vol. 7. New York: Scribner's, 1917. xvii-xxvi.

Esslin, Martin. "Ibsen." In Esslin's *Reflections: Essays on Modern Theatre.* Garden City, N.Y.: Doubleday, 1969. 29-48.

Fergusson, Francis *The Idea of a Theater.* Princeton, N.J.: Princeton University Press, 1949.

Gray, Ronald. *Ibsen: A Dissenting View.* Cambridge, U.K.: Cambridge University Press, 1977.

Heilman, Robert. *Tragedy and Melodrama: Versions of Experience.* Seattle: University of Washington Press, 1968.

Ibsen, Henrik. *Ghosts.* In *Six Plays by Henrik Ibsen.* Trans. Eva Le Gallienne. New York: Modern Library, 1957. 87-157.

----------. *Hedda Gabler.* In *Six Plays by Henrik Ibsen.* Trans. Eva Le Gallienne. New York: Modern Library, 1957. 341-428.

Northam, John. *Ibsen: A Critical Study.* Cambridge, U.K.: Cambridge University Press, 1973.

States, Bert O. "The Art of Dreaming." *The Hudson Review,* 31.4 (Winter 1978-79): 571-586.

"To Be or Not to Be . . . a Tragedy: Shaw's *Androcles and the Lion*"

Greek Tragedy

The Greek people who attended ancient tragedies, according to the classical scholar Charles R. Beye,

> contemplated a universe of willful, uncaring, arbitrary, capricious deities whose interest in mankind was exploitative, retaliatory or sportive. The ancient Athenians went to their theatre to confront this fact. And they saw stories which reinforced [the following] central truths . . .: life does not work, death cancels meaning. (Beye, 35)

Indeed, in Greek culture tragic drama satisfied a need that in other cultures is satisfied by religion. Since there was neither a body of theology nor a priestly caste in ancient Greece, the poets were free to contrive the Godhead as they chose. The task fell to them of making meaning out of nature. They did so by protesting, through their art, against the *meaninglessness* of events. Greek tragic drama, then,

> seems to mute the fundamental horror and despair of human existence, and to do this by its very form. . . . The use of well-known stories with established endings sets the tone for viewing subsequent events. . . . The implicit sense of the *déja vu* or *entendu* which the spectator brings with him allays all fears, dulls suspicion, palliates horror and fear by taking the tension from the drama. . . . Ancient Greek tragedy . . . constantly [insists] that whatever is, is, and it must be so. (Beye, 17, 22, 24)

Shavian Tragedy

Bernard Shaw himself was well-informed on the subject of classical tragedy, having lectured at Oxford on the subject and having discussed classical drama with the scholar Gilbert Murray. Shaw's *Major Barbara* (1905), references Murray himself, and is partly indebted to *The Bacchae* (405 B.C.). The plays by Shaw that have the word tragedy, or a variation thereon, in their generic descriptions are *The Doctor's Dilemma: A Tragedy in Four Acts and an Epilogue* (1906); the essentially comic one-acts "Passion, Poison, and Petrifaction, An Indigestible Tragic Romantic Comedy" (1905) and "The Glimpse of Reality, A Tragedietta" (1909); and the fourth play in the *Back to Methuselah* cycle (1921), titled *The Tragedy of an Elderly Gentleman*, which is really a comic spectacle touched with pathos in which the central character is a satirical substitute for self-pity.

As one can tell from several of the above titles, the idea of a Shavian tragedy has caused much critical confusion, and the reason is that Shaw was ideologically committed to comedy, where his focus was less on the psychology of the individual and the empathy of the audience with his protagonists than on the sociology of existence—people molding and being molded by the society of other human beings—and on the audience's objective or critical consideration of that existence. So much was Shaw ideologically committed to comedy that, as Nicole Coonradt proposes, he even conceived of satire as a kind of anti-tragedy. Indeed, formally as well as thematically, Shaw's *Androcles and the Lion* (1912) can be construed as, among other things, an argument against both the possibility of and the need for such tragedy—for any tragedy, modern, Shavian, or otherwise—in the Christian era. (See Meisel for a detailed discussion of *Androcles and the Lion* as a satire on Christian melodrama, *The Sign of the Cross* in particular.)

Androcles, Tragedy, and Christianity

To wit: if death cancelled meaning for the ancient Greeks, it *begins* meaning for Christians: life on earth is for them only a prelude to the afterlife. The Christians in *Androcles* may fear the pain of death at a gladiator's hands or in a lion's jaws, but they welcome death itself. They conceive of God not as an adversary but as their champion, their guide, their example; they conceive of death not as arbitrary punishment but as deliberate reward. (Or they conceive of death as deliberate punishment in the case of an unrepentant sinner, such as Spintho in the play. Right after he decides to sacrifice to the Roman gods in order to avoid death in the arena, he is eaten by a lion.) Ideal Christians view other men not as potential adversaries or enemies but as potential brothers; when struck, figuratively or literally, they turn the other cheek. Thus Androcles is very patient with his wife, Megaera, ignoring her taunts and encouraging her to make the best of their bad situation in the jungle; and Ferrovius, at least until he resumes his devotion to Mars, the god of war, struggles to control his temper, to refrain from smiting all who challenge him. In such circumstances there can be no tragic drama, because God is moving man *not* to conflict with his fellow men. One need look only to Aeschylus's *Oresteia* (458 B.C.) for an opposite instance, a tragedy of the highest order founded on revenge.

Although *Androcles and the Lion* argues against the possibility of classical tragedy in the Christian era, it does not argue for Christianity *per se*. The history of this religion is a violent one, Shaw obviously knew, and he chose to write a play perched on the cusp between pagan and Christian eras, I think, because he wanted to point up the impossibility of pure tragedy after the birth of Christ, yet at the same time to suggest the reality of Christianity's bloody ("tragic," in the vulgate) history, a reality clearly contrary to its ideal of "the other cheek." Shaw's point was that this history was *not* tragic, inevitable, divinely caused; it was man-made, avoidable, and reprehensible. His Ferrovius converts back to belief in Mars after going berserk and slaying six gladiators, partly because this is not what Christian soldiers did in the years to come: they slew infidels in the *name* of Christ.

Androcles and Creative Evolution

Ferrovius's faith in Mars is at one with Shaw's universal faith, Creative Evolution, which he called "the religion of the twentieth century, newly arisen from the ashes of pseudo-Christianity, of mere skepticism, and of the soulless affirmations and blind negations of the Mechanists and Neo-Darwinians" (Preface, *Back to Methuselah*: lxxviii). Shaw believed that the drive of the will was toward ultimate good. Thus any sincere manifestation of it, even if it appeared evil on the surface (as does Ferrovius's devotion to the god of war), would contribute to the improvement of the human condition. Creative Evolution is an argument both for sincerity and plurality of belief. As Susan Stone-Blackburn says of *Androcles and the Lion*,

> Shaw's moral is that he . . . who believes in himself, is saved. Spintho does not have the necessary faith in himself and his religion. . . . Androcles, Lavinia, and Ferrovius all believe in themselves; each chooses a different road to salvation, but none obstructs the others in their choices, and each seems to have chosen rightly for himself. (Stone-Blackburn, 97-98)

Lavinia's "different road" is to question the literal truth of the Christian stories but to retain her faith, even though she decides that the stories might not be true. Androcles' "different road" is to believe, contrary to Christian doctrine, that animals have souls and go to heaven, just like men. Even the Roman Emperor follows his own peculiar path: because of Ferrovius's fighting ability, the Emperor declares that the persecution of Christians shall cease and that (neat Shavian paradox) none but Christians will be his gladiators from now on.

Pathos and Dramatic Tension

Although there is no attempt at tragic conflict in *Androcles and the Lion*, classical or otherwise, there *is* dramatic tension: we wonder, for example, when Ferrovius's violent temper will finally erupt. He expresses it in a controlled manner in his dealings with Lentulus; almost loses it when he is challenged by the Editor; and finally gives it full vent after he is whipped in the arena. In despair, Ferrovius asks to be put to death at once for betraying God, so that he will go straight to Hell. But Lavinia and the rest of the Christians refuse to raise a sword against him, and the exultant Emperor, instead of immediately slaughtering Ferrovius and his friends for the former's killing of six gladiators, makes the giant a member of the elite Pretorian Guard. We conclude by being happy for Ferrovius instead of lamenting his condition.

Another dramatic tension in *Androcles and the Lion* concerns Spintho: we await the moment when he will sacrifice on the altar of the Roman gods in order to save his life. He is both a comic and a pathetic figure as he makes his decision:

> I can't bear it. Where's the altar? I'll sacrifice. I'll repent afterwards. I fully mean to die in the arena: I'll die a martyr and go to heaven; but not this time, not now, not until my nerves are better. Besides, I'm too young: I want to have just one more good time. Oh, will no one tell me where the altar is? (*Androcles*, 455)

Spintho's name may have its roots in either Greek or Italian. The Greek noun *spinther* means "spark", and the past participle *spinto* comes from the Italian verb *spingere*, "to push, spur on, spark". Spintho, like the sparks of Restoration comedy, is a debauchee. Unlike a true spark, he has attempted to repent; unlike a true Christian, he is afraid to die for his beliefs. He leaves the stage uncertain where he is going, just as he has been uncertain about which way of life to give his complete allegiance to. Caught between the two extremes, let us say, of Restoration comedy and Christian pathos, Spintho exchanges his uncertainty of identity for the certainty of death. His death is comically appropriate—he whose practice it has been to indulge his sensual appetites in a nearly bestial fashion, indulges the appetite of a wild beast; and his death is pathetically apt—in return for betraying his faith, he goes straight to Hell.

Spintho is a pathetic figure at whom we laugh; the rest of the Christians, on the other hand, are pathetic figures *with* whom we laugh. Their faith gives them the strength to find comedy in their situation; Spintho's lack of faith makes him so weak as to be the target of the other characters' derision. There is little dramatic tension in the Christians' life-and-death situation because we know that, with the exception of Ferrovius, not one of them has the power to resist his captors. There is *comic* tension in their situation, however, because we never know when they are going to make another joke out of something that the Centurion in charge of them or the Captain says. Neither does the Centurion know when they are going to make their next joke, and ironically, this makes him more uneasy before the Captain than the Christians are before death. The Centurion and every other Roman soldier must obey their superior officers, never their own whims, but the Christians are in a sense authors of their own situation because they have chosen their deaths and can afford to say what they wish along the way. (What punishment worse than death could they be given?) Thus when the Centurion speaks of them as the lion's dinner at the end of Act I, several Christians scandalize him by imagining which portion of the meal they will be:

> LAVINIA (*marching*). Come along, the rest of the dinner. I shall be the olives
> and anchovies.
> ANOTHER CHRISTIAN (*laughing*). I shall be the soup.
> ANOTHER. I shall be the fish.
> ANOTHER. Ferrovius shall be the roast boar.
> ANDROCLES. I shall be the mince pie. (*Each announcement is received with a louder laugh by all the rest as the joke catches on.*)
> CENTURION. Silence! Have some sense of your situation. Is this the way for martyrs to behave? (*Androcles*, 452)

Androcles and Farce

I have attempted to demonstrate so far how there are drama, comedy, and pathos in *Androcles and the Lion*, but no tragedy; how the plurality of beliefs in the play is reflected by the plurality of forms of which it is composed. It remains for me only to discuss the last form that it embraces or, I should say, that embraces the play, since *Androcles* both opens and closes with farcical episodes. Although there is little dramatic tension in the Christians' life-and-death situation, as I have discussed, there is plenty of dramatic tension (though there are no consequences) in the life-and-death situations at the start and finish of *Androcles*. The stakes are often high in farce, characters often find themselves faced with death, and Androcles, Megaera, and the Emperor are no exceptions. In the Prologue Androcles and his wife come upon the sleeping lion, "Tommy", in the jungle, and much physical comedy ensues as they try to get out of his way. Unlike the comic Christians (whom Androcles will of course later join as a prisoner), the farcical Androcles and Megaera are never aware that they're funny. Also unlike the Christians, they have a direct opportunity to escape death, or at least one of them does. (Androcles elects to serve as decoy while his wife runs away.) The same is true for the Emperor at the end of the play: he has an opportunity to escape being eaten if Androcles will stand between him and the lion. And like Megaera and her husband in the Prologue, the Emperor is never aware that he's being funny as he races frantically to get out of Tommy's way.

If there was any doubt that Shaw intended *Androcles and the Lion* to be viewed in light of or, better, in opposition to ancient Greek tragedy, that doubt should be laid to rest by his naming of Androcles' wife. "Megara" is also the city (about twenty-five to thirty miles from Athens) where, a little after 581 B.C., short mime plays appeared that are believed to have influenced Athenian comedy (Brockett, 22). These mimes (later ones actually, since none from the early period survive) were often satirical treatments of everyday domestic situations, just as the Prologue of *Androcles* is such a treatment for the most part. They could also be burlesqued versions of myths and thus, like some of Aristophanes' plays, satires on Greek tragedy. Even as Megaera looks back longingly to the Greek town from which she and her husband were expelled on account of his Christianity (Megaera is neither a Christian nor a Roman, and for this reason, when in Act I the play moves into the Christian era, so to speak, she disappears from the action entirely), so too does Shaw's Prologue look back to Megaran mime and Athenian comedy. If Shaw was quick to label a play such as *The Doctor's Dilemma* a tragedy, but careful to imitate the tragicomic Ibsen in this drama in the sense that he willfully, almost wantonly, followed his four-act comedy with a one-act tragedy, so too might we label *Androcles and the Lion* a work of comic pathos in which the wishful or whimsical Shaw was careful to *oppose* the tragicomic Ibsen by preceding and following his two-act drama with farcical episodes. To be or not to be, indeed.

Works Cited

Beye, Charles R. "Nature's Mirror or Nature's Distillery: The Proper Metaphor for Ancient Greek Tragedy". In *To Hold a Mirror to Nature: Dramatic Images and Reflections*. Vol. 1 of the University of Florida Department of Classics Comparative Drama Conference Papers. Ed. Karelisa V. Hartigan. Washington, D.C.: University Press of America, 1982. 11-36.

Brockett, Oscar. *History of the Theatre*. 3rd ed. Boston: Allyn & Bacon, 1977.

Coonradt, Nicole. "Shavian Romance in *Saint Joan*: Satire as Antitragedy." *Shaw: The Annual of Bernard Shaw Studies*, 29 (2009): 92-108.

Meisel, Martin. *Shaw and the Nineteenth-Century Theater.* Princeton, N.J.: Princeton University Press, 1963.

Shaw, George Bernard. *Back to Methuselah*. London: Constable, 1921.

----------. *Saint Joan, Major Barbara, Androcles and the Lion*. New York: Modern Library, 1956.

Stone-Blackburn, Susan. "Unity in Diversity: *Androcles and the Lion*." *Shaw Review*, 21.2 (May 1978): 92-99.

"'Right Up into the Skies': Transfiguration and Ascent in Shaw's *Major Barbara*, *Misalliance*, and *Saint Joan*"

Shaw and Christianity

Deeply imbedded in Christian theology is a tension between life in the world and life beyond it. Christ, as the manifestation of God, enters the world in the humblest form imaginable to live among human beings as a teacher and healer; however, underlying the story of his Passion—by far the most dramatic portion of his life—is the impulse to escape this world for another, more satisfying one. The flogging and crucifixion underscore the "man-ness," some would say "mean-ness," of Christ's existence on earth, but the resurrection and ascension point toward deliverance from worldly constraints.

The belief that ascent towards God, in the "other world," is humanity's natural destination finds reflection in the medieval chain of being, which is organized hierarchically from the natural to the supernatural. Man, in imitation of Christ, must operate in the world but at the same time seeks ultimately to leave it, and, cleansed of his sins, his departure is always seen as an ascent—a release from the earth's gravity. The metaphoric ascent of man is most easily seen in the Gothic cathedral, whose flying buttresses make possible the immense, vaulted spaces that hint of freedom from the mundane. Before the Gothic style, architecture had always been limited by problems of stability and weight, and in the end it kept man down to earth; the new style made stone seem weightless: the weightless expression of mankind's spirit.

Bernard Shaw's plays themselves—among them *Major Barbara* (1905), *Misalliance* (1910), and *Saint Joan* (1923)—sometimes reflect the tension between gravity and ascent that makes up so much of the legacy of Christian thought. The use of these motifs should not be surprising in the work of a dramatist whom J. Percy Smith has described as "not only a profoundly religious man but a profoundly religious playwright" (Smith, 74). Their presence in his plays, however, also suggests something of the inner conflict of the artist who would transcend his art—become, as it were, his own audience—at the same that he creates it. Comedy requires more detachment from life, or more objectivity toward it, than most forms of art, as many critics have observed, and Shaw's own detachment, his would-be transcendence, results in a comic style that is more remotely contemplative than directly experiential. Even at the height of emotional involvement, his characters are able to pull up short in order to speculate about their own condition or to question the nature of their next action. Not every rhetorical or "set" speech in Shaw's *oeuvre* is an instance of a character's transcendence to a higher realm of the intellect or the spirit, but these speeches nonetheless are often evidence of a schism between a character and the world of his or her play—a schism that deepens as Shaw's theory of Creative Evolution, with its own schism between Darwinism and mystical will, begins to take shape.

My purpose is not to trace Shaw's relationship with Christianity, yet I must emphasize that the theater for Shaw was more than a means toward social progress. It was, Shaw wrote in *Our Theatres in the Nineties*, "a temple of the

Ascent of Man" (vi), a place "where two or three are gathered together" (Preface to *Major Barbara*, 22). In the lay sermon "The New Theology," which he delivered in London on May 16, 1907, Shaw outlined a religious hierarchy of being that has its origins in his own plays:

> If there are three orders of existence—man as we know him, the angels higher than man, and God higher than the angels—why did God first create something lower than himself, the angels, and then actually create something lower than the angels, man? I cannot believe in a God who would do that. If I were God,
>
> I should try to create something higher than myself, and then something higher than that, so that, beginning with a God the higher thing in creation, I should end with a God the lowest thing in creation. ("New Theology," 312)

This is, of course, a radical inversion of other systems of belief, but Shaw's model still retains a vertical quality. Unfortunately, as he writes further in "The New Theology," the "continual struggle to create something higher and higher," to make social as well as spiritual progress, has been marred by "innumerable experiments and innumerable mistakes" (313), such that the tension between gravity and ascent has continued to inhere in human existence.

My interest here is in some of the moments in Shaw's dramaturgy, specifically in *Major Barbara*, when the balance between these two forces cannot be sustained, and the impulse toward escape or release catapults his characters upward into a realm of "otherness." Northrop Frye once discussed the movement in Shakespeare's comedies away from the normal world toward a "green world," in order that a metamorphosis can occur, and then back to the normal world, where order will be restored (Frye, 182). Shaw's plays are not so tightly as this, nor are escapes in them always followed by a return to the status quo. There is also considerable variation in the tone surrounding these ruptures, which ranges from the sublime to the ridiculous. Moreover, the characters who undergo transfiguration in Shaw have a remarkable tendency to be women.

Without pausing to discuss to discuss Shaw's principle of the Divine and its connection with women, I note Barbara Watson's thesis that female characters offer themselves as mouthpieces for his ideas because they are outside the idealist world of male society; and Norbert Greiner's counter argument that woman, "because of the educational processes that she [is] subject to, adopts and realizes men's ideals" (Greiner, 96). In fact, what these female characters have in common is the spirit of rebellion, the original spirit of the Protest-ant (as Shaw insisted it be pronounced) that Warwick describes in *Saint Joan* as "the protest of the individual soul against the interference of priest or peer between the private man and his God" (*Saint Joan*, 108). The operative term here is "private," and it is a moot point whether these women seek privacy via escape from the tentacles of a problematic world because their traditional roles have not allowed them privacy, or whether they seek such privacy because their immersion in male ideology has given them the conviction, and the power, to demand their rights. What remains are women who, with heroic effort, lift themselves out of the morass for sometimes brief, sometimes eternal moments of transcendence.

Since I use the word "transfiguration" in my title, it is necessary now to return to Christian theology in order to define this term more completely. The story of Christ's transfiguration is told in three of the Gospels (Matthew 17:1-9, Mark 9:2-8, and Luke 9:28-36) and varies little from version to version. The chief points worth noting about this event are that it begins in prayer at a high place, on a mountain, and that it grows into an intense religious experience—during which Jesus speaks with Moses and Elijah and is called "Son" by a voice in the sky assumed to be God the Father—only dimly perceived by the apostles Peter, John, and James. The aura of unnatural brilliance that surrounds Christ at the moment of transfiguration (he takes on, in all three Gospels, an "unearthly appearance") foreshadows his appearance as the Messiah after the resurrection. But just as important as the transfiguration itself is the event's context within Christ's tenure on earth. The transfiguration follows directly after the feeding of the multitudes and the healing of the blind man. It is one of the few moments of meditative escape from the constant activity surrounding Christ before his entrance into Jerusalem; as soon as he descends from the mountain, he is again caught up in the sickness of the world as he is called upon to cast out the demon from an epileptic boy.

Two contrasting views of the transfiguration can be found in Fra Angelico's and Raphael's paintings, the one a static presentation of the event, the other a dramatic representation of it. Fra Angelico's Christ stands on sculptured rock, surrounded by an aura of pure white, with his hands outspread in prefiguration of the crucifixion to come. His separation from the kneeling apostles here is complete, except for a downward glance that suggests his continuing attachment to the beings who cower in terror below him. This *Transfiguration* (1438-45)—painted as a fresco for an individual cell in the Monastery of San Marco—presents a single, contemplative subject from which the rest of the world is in retreat. Raphael's *Transfiguration of Christ* (1517), by contrast, depicts both Jesus's glory and his gloom, or the gloom that continues to pervade his life on earth. Christ is in mid-air, his arms and head raised to the heavens as if to greet the divinity above him. But down below, the windswept apostles, in the foreground, impatiently await his return as their confused gesturing envelops the demon-possessed boy and his father. The world beneath Christ in this instance is dark—only half-lit by the radiance of his transfiguration.

Major Barbara, in the Beginning

Raphael's version of the transfiguration, then, more dramatically captures the eruption of the spirit toward privacy or solitude, away from the strictures of the demanding society of men. A similar moment is captured in the last scene of *Major Barbara* as the now enlightened Barbara, stripped both of her uniform and her idealism by her realist father, begins her new mission of saving human souls without the "bribe of bread" (*Major Barbara*, 158). Shaw describes a scene of visual contrast here: "*a platform of concrete, with a firestep, and a parapet which suggests a fortification*" (*Barbara*, 133), overlooks the town of Perivale St.

Andrews, which is spotlessly clean and "*only needs a cathedral to be a heavenly city instead of a hellish one*" (*Barbara*, 133). Included in this otherwise pristine picture are the instruments of war—a huge cannon, sheds for explosives, and dummy soldiers who, "more or less mutilated, with straw protruding from their gashes" and strewn about like grotesque corpses, are constant reminders of the destructive forces controlled by the gigantic "creative" will of which Andrew Undershaft is a part.

Barbara herself stands on the firestep, "*looking over the parapet towards the town*" (*Major Barbara*, 133). Often during the scene she is above the action, and at one point she steps onto the mounted cannon so that her father must reach up to grasp her hand. Shaw's placement of Barbara on the parapet and on the cannon, where she is above the earthly powers at her feet yet still connected to them, suggests the imprisonment (by her father) in a tower of the Christian saint of the same name. And it is no accident that these two Barbaras are linked, for St. Barbara is the patron saint of the hour of death and liberation from the prisonhouse of earth.

Barbara is silent in this scene until Cusins declares the circumstances of his birth, but her presence is noted by Shaw as Undershaft announces the death of 300 soldiers and follows this announcement by "*kicking a prostrate dummy brutally out of his way*" (*Major Barbara*, 135). At this moment Barbara and Cusins exchange glances, and when Cusins sits on the step and buries his face in his hands, "*Barbara gravely lays her hand on his shoulder*" (*Barbara*, 135) in Shaw's stage direction. As Cusins subsequently explains his status as a foundling, Barbara climbs onto the cannon and remains there during most of what has been called "Undershaft's apologia" (Otten, 92). Only when her father takes her hands and demands a definition of power does Barbara finally confess her anxiety—how she waits in "dread and horror" (*Barbara*, 145) for the second shock of the figurative earthquake that has caused her world to reel and crumble around her.

Barbara then reverses herself by erupting with "sudden vehemence" in response to her father's scoffing remark about her "tinpot tragedy" (*Barbara*, 145), and demands that he show her "some light through the darkness of this dreadful place" (*Major Barbara*, 146). Shaw has been careful throughout to present this "dreadful place" as beautiful, blemish-free, and enlightened, both in his stage directions and through Sarah's, Stephen's, Lomax's, and Lady Britomart's surprised and even possessive approval of Perivale St. Andrews. But Barbara, the divine spark in the play (Cusins declares, "I adored what was divine in her, and was therefore a true worshipper" [*Barbara*, 139]), reveals the correct perception of this gleaming factory town. Though it may bask in middle-class morality and the respectability that comes with it, Perivale St. Andrews remains the home of a dreadful factory of death and destruction. By the end of the play, though, it will have become the object of Barbara's energy, the demonic child from which she herself will cast out the devil.

Barbara's relative silence during this scene, in contrast with Undershaft's and Cusins' loquacity, suggests that her focus is turning inward. Her responses become increasingly reflective, seeming to arise out of a sedate, even somber mood—and responses like this from a character who, for the two previous acts, has been vigorously outspoken, rhetorically persuasive, and charmingly humorous. When Lady Britomart demands that they leave, since the father of the family is obviously "wickeder than ever" (*Major Barbara*, 149), Barbara's rejoinder is simple and softspoken: "It's no use running away from wicked people, mamma" (*Barbara*, 149). The word "wicked" is repeated here, though subtly altered, as Shaw contrasts Lady Britomart's superficial objection to Undershaft's social behavior with Barbara's heartfelt insight not only into her father's character, but into the major premise of the play—that "there is no wicked side. Life is all one" (*Barbara*, 157).

In the final scene the trio of Undershaft, Barbara, and Cusins is reduced to a duet, yet Barbara's questions and responses continue to give no hint of what her final action will be. Cusins' own rationalized defense of his decision to join Undershaft grows more and more assertive, until his final cry is characterized by the repeated use of the first person: "Dare I make war on war? I dare. I must. I will" (*Major Barbara*, 152). When he then turns and asks Barbara if their relationship is over, in "*evident dread of her answer*" (according to Shaw's stage direction [*Barbara*, 156]), she replies, "Silly baby Dolly! How could it be!" (*Barbara*, 156). She has answered Cusins' weakness in the only way her nurturing nature will allow, but the "levity" of his response, as Shaw describes it (and which understandably would follow his previous dread) is too indelicate for the intensity of the moment. Accordingly, Barbara reacts by transcending in word and thought the "mereness" of the world: "Oh, if only I could get away from you and from father and from it all! if I could have the wings of a dove and fly away to heaven!" (*Barbara*, 156).

Barbara is thus gradually transfigured, as the pull of her mission raises her above the paltry concerns of her family and lover to reveal the agony of the soul who finally faces evil without illusions, who must endure evil "whether it be sin or suffering" (*Major Barbara*, 157). The second act of this play has removed the "bribe of bread" (*Barbara*, 158), and in her transfiguration in Act III Barbara dismisses the "bribe of heaven" (*Barbara*, 158), for God's work is to be done "for its own sake" (*Barbara*, 158). Moreover, in indirect reference to the quotation above from Shaw's unique "new theology," Barbara vows that she will forgive God—an inversion that places her higher than the Creator, since He will now be in her debt.

Like the apostles in the Raphael painting, Cusins has become a disciple at her feet, and his question, "Then the way of life lies through the factory of death?" (*Major Barbara*, 158) elicits from Barbara the mystical outpouring that has puzzled so many, and that can itself be explained as a gloss on Shaw's new hierarchy of being: "Yes, through the raising of hell to heaven and of man to God, through the unveiling of an eternal light in the Valley of The Shadow" (*Barbara*, 158). Her religious ecstasy here oddly parallels Luke's own at the transfiguration of Christ, when he speaks of clouds, God, man, and revelation:

> . . . a cloud came and overshadowed them; and they were afraid as they entered the cloud. And a voice came out of the cloud, saying, "This is my Son, my Chosen; listen to him!" And when the voice had spoken, Jesus was found alone. (Luke 9:34-36; p. 1258)

Eric Bentley once said of Vivie at the end of *Mrs. Warren's Profession* (1893): "A soul is born" (*Major Barbara*, 107). A description of Barbara at the end of *Major Barbara* might be: A soul is illuminated. Fighting the limitations of the world and seeking escape through meditation, she reaches out in the end toward the eternal, only to find it in herself. Barbara's return from the metaphorical mountain (the parapet of the gun factory) results in marriage to Cusins and not only the start of a new dynasty and the continuation of the Undershaft inheritance, but also the start of new spiritual mission—proof of Shaw's abiding optimism in 1905, before world war would change him, his art, and the world forever.

Misalliance, in the Middle

> Death is for many of us the gate of hell; but we are inside on the way out, not outside on the way in. Therefore let us give up telling one another idle stories, and rejoice in death as we rejoice in birth; for without death we cannot be born again . . . —Bernard Shaw, Preface to *Misalliance*: xi.

When Lina Szczepanowska drops out of the sky into the Tarleton household, her perceptions become the lens through which the antics of these summer folk are judged. Without Lina, *Misalliance* would be a somewhat pointless romp through the fertility rites of an eccentric family. Shaw sets up a tension between the family's inconsequential activities and the foreign Lina's consequential actions—ones taken, that is, at the edge of existence. While they tell one another "idle stories" (*Misallianc*e, xi), Lina rejoices over life lived in flirtation with death. Hypatia herself complains about the continual "talk, talk, talk, talk" (*Misalliance*, 34) of the Tarleton clan and wants to become an "active verb" (*Misalliance*, 39), but her aspirations become mere lip service to a high-sounding ideal when contrasted with Lina's decisiveness, vitality, and bravery.

Lina is more than a means for perspective, however. Like Barbara, who proceeds her, and Joan, who is to follow, Lina contains the divine spark. Her development assumes a different tone from that of the other two heroines, primarily because the disquisitory nature of *Misalliance* does not permit the social drama of *Major Barbara* or the tragic *agon* of *Saint Joan*. Yet certain elements in Lina's character find their counterparts in both Barbara's and Joan's; her contemplative side (to Summerhays's question "What is the Bible for?" she replies, "To quiet my soul" [*Misalliance*, 56]), her compassion for others, and her ego, which enables her to divorce herself from the crowd. Her transfiguration is essentially comic, however, because it arises not out of a crisis of soul, but from outrage and frustration. But it is a transfiguration nonetheless and through its energy propels the play to the bursting point, where the significance of a world that, by its nature, must remain earthbound is placed in question. Her vocation is to defy gravity, as Summerhays describes: "The last time I saw that lady, she did something I should not have thought possible . . . she walked backwards along a taut wire without a balancing pole and turned a somersault in the middle" (*Misalliance*, 53).

Lina's outburst, "I must get out of this into the air: right up into the blue" (*Misalliance*, 101), springs from the same impulse as Barbara's more tormented cry. In only an hour, every male in the house except Percival (who has had his hands full with Hypatia) has made love to Lina. As she says, she has forgiven Tarleton because of his affection for his wife, Lord Summerhays because his position as ambassador demanded such behavior, and Bentley because of his youth and obvious weakness. All this she has borne "in silence" (*Misalliance*, 102), even though she has come to regard the atmosphere of the house as "disgusting" (*Misalliance*, 102) and "not healthy" (*Misalliance*, 102). But it is Johnny Tarleton's proposal—priggish, complacent, condescending—that elicits the fury and scorn of a woman who is accustomed to living in the world as an active agent, and whose privacy and honor have been violated:

> This to me, Lina Szczepanowska! I am an honest woman: I earn my living. I am a free woman: I live in my own house. I am a woman of the world: I have thousands of friends: every night crowds of people applaud me, delight in me, buy my picture, pay hard-earned money to see me. I am strong: I am skillful: I am brave: I am independent: I am unbought: I am all that a woman ought to be . . . (*Misalliance*, 103)

Coming as it does immediately after Hypatia's line "Papa: buy the brute for me" 95, *Misalliance*), Lina's exclamation that no one can buy her becomes a comment on the previous action. Through her eyes the children are seen as spoiled and caddish, and the older generation is regarded as garrulous and pathetic. There is no possibility for redemption for anyone here except the cowering Bentley, who vows to accompany Lina after she exhorts, "You must learn to dare" (*Misalliance*, 105). Lina's transfiguration results, though, not in comic restoration but in her actual ascent—in an airplane. When told there may be a storm coming, she responds, "I'll go: storm or no storm. I must risk my life tomorrow" (*Misalliance*, 106). The figurative storm that lies on the horizon of *Misalliance* suggests Shaw's growing pessimism about any reform of the indolent, vapid upper classes—a pessimism that would culminate in *Heartbreak House* (1919). Lina cannot single-handedly cast the demon out of this society; she can save only the weakest member, then return to her circus of unbought souls.

Saint Joan, in the End

In *Misalliance* and *Major Barbara*, the heroines break out of the confines of society but return to their respective missions: Lina will return to performing in the "otherworldly" circus, where people exhibit bravery and skill every day, and Barbara will save souls at the Undershaft factory. At the end of *Saint Joan* the status quo also returns, as the epilogue emphasizes, but it is a status quo without the heroine. Joan bursts the boundaries of the world and, in doing so, proves herself unwilling and unable to return to the society that has rejected her. The spark that illuminates Shaw's heroines is magnified in Joan to the point where she prefers divine to human company, as she herself declares:

> I see now that the loneliness of God is His strength: what would He be if He listened to your jealous little counsels? Well, my loneliness shall be my strength too: it is better to be alone with God; His friendship will not fail me, nor His counsel, nor His love. In His strength I will dare, and dare, and dare, until I die. (*Saint Joan*, 115)

The first three scenes of Saint Joan mark the ascent of Joan's ideals—nationalism, Protestantism, and individual genius. God's blessing is evident throughout this ascent as the natural world responds in harmony with her actions: hens lay eggs, the wind shifts, and an arrow in her throat cannot prevent Joan from winning the battle at Orléans. The next three scenes mark the decline of her ideals at the hands of the government, the Church, and other pedestrian souls. The natural world becomes crass and threatening, and by the beginning of Scene 6, physical pain is depicted onstage—something Shaw had not done in his previous plays. Joan is weak from imprisonment, ill from bad food, her feet are chained to a block of wood, and the instruments of torture have been shown to her. She suggests that she is a caged bird:

> D'ESTIVET. You tried to escape?
> JOAN. Of course I did; and not for the first time either. If you leave the door of the cage open the bird will fly out. (*Saint Joan*, 122)

This, of course, is an image that fits Barbara and Lina as well as Joan, but it is crueler and more hopeless in Joan's case.

It is the pain of death by fire that confronts Joan, finally. Her flesh naturally shrinks from flame: "I have dared and dared; but only a fool will walk into a fire" (*Joan*, 126). At the moment she signs the recantation, Shaw describes her as "*tormented by the rebellion of her soul against her mind and body*" (*Saint Joan*, 127). The glorious simplicity of Joan as a child of God, pursuing nearly impossible goals with unbroken confidence and through direct communication with her own divinity, is thus destroyed by the scratch of a pen. At the sentence of life in prison, however, her body and mind rejoin her soul. In her moment of transfiguration she rejects the cage and, with it, the world:

> His ways are not your ways. He wills that I go through the fire to His bosom; for I am His child, and you are not fit that I should live among you. That is my last word to you. (*Joan*, 128)

Like Barbara, Joan goes "right up into the skies" (*Major Barbara*, 158), but, unlike the major, her soul's impulse to escape confinement cannot be tempered by love, marriage, and good works. As Lavendu takes the cross from her sight on the lighted pyre, Joan looks up to heaven and utters her final word, to God. Ascent follows, with only her unsinged heart left behind.

Charles Krauthammer has written that "among the purposes of remembrance are pedagogy (for those who were not there) and solace (for those too much there). But the highest aim of remembrance (for us, here) is redemption" (Krauthammer, 90). Christ asked that the Last Supper be held "in remembrance of Me"; and the Eucharist celebrates the redemption of mankind as well as Christ's memory. Shaw's play about the young woman from Lorraine is neither pedagogical, consolatory, nor redemptive. Saint Joan is not so much remembrance as testament that, after hundreds of years of so-called civilization, the world is still trapped in the Dark Ages of misery and persecution. Joan asks, "Must I burn again?" (*Saint Joan*, 137), and Shaw's answer between the two world wars was a profound, despairing "yes."

Maurice Valency has noted that Shaw shares with Strindberg and Ibsen an interest in the tragic dilemma "of the extraordinary individual in a world of ordinary people" (Valency, 381). The cry with which Joan ends the play, "How long, O Lord, how long?" (*Saint Joan*, 138), is at the core of modern tragic thought, for her *agon* results from the disparity she perceives between herself and the world. And the sinking of Joan's heart to the bottom of the river with the rest of Rouen's garbage is a metaphor for Shaw's dark belief that this world is governed by waste. Despite the tendency of the spirit in *Saint Joan*, *Major Barbara*, *Misalliance*, and other plays by Shaw to fight gravity through transfiguration and ascent, to achieve moments of blissful weightlessness, it must finally return, like Raphael's Christ, to a world that crucifies and burns those who would lead it to salvation.

Works Cited

Frye, Northrop. *Anatomy of Criticism*. Princeton, N.J.: Princeton University Press, 1957.

Greiner, Norbert. "Mill, Marx, and Bebel: Early Influences on Shaw's Characterizations of Women." In *Fabian Feminist: Bernard Shaw and Woman*. Ed. Rodelle Weintraub. University Park: Pennsylvania State University Press, 1977. 90-98.

Krauthammer, Charles. "The Bitburg Fiasco." *Time* (Apr. 29, 1985): 90.

The New Oxford Annotated Bible. New York: Oxford University Press, 1977.

Otten, Kurt, & Gerd Rohmann, eds. *George Bernard Shaw*. Darmstadt: Wissenschaftliche Buchgesellschaft, 1978.

Shaw, Bernard. *Misalliance, Fanny's First Play*, and *The Dark Lady of the Sonnets*. New York: Brentano's, 1914.

----------. *Major Barbara*. New York: Brentano's, 1920.

----------. *Our Theatres in the Nineties*. London: Constable, 1932.

----------. *The Bodley Head Bernard Shaw: Collected Plays with Their Prefaces*. 7 volumes. London: Bodley Head, 1970-1974.

----------. "The New Theology" (1907). In *The Portable Bernard Shaw*. Ed. Stanley Weintraub. New York: Penguin, 1977. 304-315.

----------. *Saint Joan*. In *Our Dramatic Heritage*. Vol. 5, Reactions to Realism. Ed. Philip George Hill. Rutherford, N.J.: Fairleigh Dickinson University Press, 1991. 53-138.

Smith, J. Percy. "The New Woman and the Old Goddess: The Shaping of Shaw's Mythology." In *Women in Irish Legend, Life, and Literature*. Ed. S. F. Gallagher. Totowa, N. J.: Barnes & Noble, 1983. 74-90.

Valency, Maurice. *The Cart and the Trumpet: The Plays of George Bernard Shaw*. New York: Schocken Books, 1983.

Watson, Barbara Bellow. *A Shavian Guide to the Intelligent Woman*. New York: Norton, 1964.

"New Drama, New Woman: Reconstructing Ibsen's Realism"

Kewpie Dolls, Real Women, and the Drama

After Nora dances her liberating *tarantella* at the party in *A Doll House* (1879), Torvald Helmer criticizes it for being "a bit too naturalistic—I mean it rather overstepped the proprieties of art" (Fjelde, 180-181). Torvald doesn't mean that he believes his wife had really been bitten by a tarantula and was trying desperately to shake off death (though we know how much her life was at stake, in a manner of speaking). Rather, he's commenting on the indecorousness of her frenzy. Unable to contain her passions in a more genteel form, Nora, we assume, danced at the offstage party with the same abandon we witnessed in her rehearsal a few scenes earlier. Then, stage directions assert, "Nora dances more and more wildly . . . she seems not to hear [Torvald's instructions], her hair loosens and falls over her shoulders; she does not notice, but goes on dancing" (Fjelde, 173-174). Her performance is "naturalistic" not because Torvald mistakes it for the real thing, but because it depicts the deepest, most ineffable experience in a way that breaks past conventions. Alarmingly, Nora has exceeded expectations, just as Henrik Ibsen did—by bursting the seams of the well-made play and perfecting a realistic drama that seethes with inexplicable emotion.

The shocking actions of Ibsen's female heroes parallel his shocking actions as a playwright. And both, in turn, respond to contemporary crises over the representation of women—in affairs of state (would they vote?) and stage (would they remain dainty, decorous, and in distress?). Ibsen investigated both kinds of representation by framing and refiguring contemporary dramatic forms. It wasn't just that the actions of Ibsen's female protagonists crossed the bounds of ladylike conduct. (The conservative critic Clement Scott complained, after *A Doll House* premiered in England in 1889, that Nora is not "the pattern woman we have admired in our mothers and sisters"; Hedda, he charged a few years later, "has glorified an unwomanly woman" [Egan, 114, 127].) At the same time, these characters overstepped dramaturgical bounds, displacing the male protagonist and claiming a central place in the action. Juxtaposed against these women, Ibsen's men, as George Bernard Shaw sadly noted, exposed "the shameful extremity of a weak soul stripped naked before an audience looking to him for heroism" (Matthews, 192).

Ibsen's disruption of dramatic and social conventions challenged contemporary assertions about the inevitability and incontrovertibility of gender roles. Even as the New Woman emerged in *fin-de-siècle* Europe, staking a claim for equality and inclusion in the public sphere, science itself was slamming the door on her exit from the home. Both Sigmund Freud and Havelock Ellis, for all their differences in approach and ideology, promoted the idea that anatomy is destiny, that biology determines gender. Marriage and motherhood had nothing to do with choice or social pressure, they asserted; these functions were hardwired into a woman's body. To resist the roles of wife and mother, then, was to be "abnormal," "psychotic," "monstrous."

Despite the now commonplace notion (first promulgated by the naturalist Émile Zola) that the period's realistic drama lined up with the drive for such scientific "objectivity" (and its corollary, biological determinism), Ibsen's prose plays negotiated these dominant currents, reproducing them, perhaps, but also (maybe even for the purpose of) resisting them. Ibsen's innovative dramatic structures, the new acting style his work demanded, the resonance of his settings, and his invocation as well as rerouting of well-made strategies thus become as important as the stories the plays tell and the characters they represent. And certainly, all of these are more important than anything Ibsen said to defend or contradict the aims of the women's movement. In sum, Ibsen's plays engaged the roiling controversy over gender through their self-scrutinizing dramatic actions, questioning the representation of women by questioning the means of representation itself. From our vantage point today, it's hard to think of realism as a form that oversteps the proprieties of art—indeed, we tend to think of it as doing quite the opposite, as strictly delineating, and then hiding the marks of, those proprieties. That's the first bias that must be overcome in approaching Ibsen's prose plays. Too frequently they're measured according to a standard calibrated by the most debased instances of the genre—the contemporary psychological realism that dominates American drama on stage, film, and television.

Accordingly, we expect an Ibsen production, with precise period costumes and picture-perfect wallpaper, to convince us that it represents nineteenth-century reality—and then we belittle it for failing to sweep us into that world with the illusionistic power of a film, or the "virtual reality" of a computer game. Or, if we're Lacanian-influenced feminist theorists (God forbid), we belittle it for succeeding—thereby objectifying women in a "prison-house of narrativity." Experienced this way, as any stage-struck undergraduate will tell you, Ibsen, compared to, say, Beth Henley or August Wilson, seems stodgy, old-fashioned, and fake. Of course that says less about Ibsen than about how we teach (and, too often, produce) him: as the progenitor of the form that so transports such students in these more "real" and "relevant" contemporary expressions. Indeed, if students learn anything about Ibsen, it's that his plays follow a clear progressive trajectory from overwrought verse dramas to realistic paragons, the prose plays themselves evolving like an ever more fit species, shedding soliloquies, asides, and all the integuments of the well-made play as they creep, then crouch, then culminate in that upright masterpiece from 1890 known as *Hedda Gabler*. (Ibsen's last plays leave proponents of this model speechless. That Aurélien Lugné-Poë seized on them immediately for his symbolist theater counts as an embarrassing reversion, an affront to everything we should most prize in our father of modern drama.)

Ibsenian "Narrative" and Counter-Narrative

This grand narrative, as a number of contemporary Ibsen scholars have suggested, is at best misleading, supporting a handy teleology at the expense of Ibsen's poetic vision. The Hegelian, mythic, or metaphoric readings offered by these critics—among them Brian Johnston, Richard Gilman, Robert Brustein, and Orley Holtan—are not only illuminating; they open Ibsen up to expansive critical approaches usually reserved for William Shakespeare. But instead of pointing out how our own saturation in a tiresome, formulaic realism prevents us from encountering Ibsen's complex, self-referential use of the form, these men dismiss his dramatic style as a sort of necessary evil, as the most convenient conduit to Ibsen's "higher" concerns.

Gilman has written, for example, that "the seeming naturalism of *Hedda Gabler* is . . . a ground for the play's true action: its movement into a realm of existential, or ontological, being and its vision of crucial values at stake and at war." (Although "naturalism" and "realism" are often used synonymously, as Gilman does here [preceded by Zola and even by Ibsen himself], they are not the same. See Cardullo in Works Cited, 307-308.) In *To the Third Empire* Johnston goes further in characterizing Ibsen's dramaturgy as a kind of trick, a way of pandering to bourgeois audiences before sneaking some metaphysics into their entertainment. He writes, "Only by inserting such [realistic] details can Ibsen cunningly infiltrate the full content of his dramatic concept into the play and most cogently and adequately present his full dramatic 'argument'" (*Third Empire*, 274). But the "dramatic argument" is the event that happens in the theater. And it happens not *in spite* of the style of Ibsen's prose plays, but because of it. Ibsen's realism doesn't compete with or merely provide the ground for mythopoeic content, patterned action, metaphoric meanings. It is absolutely integral to these achievements. Ibsen does not need to be rescued from the dramatic artifices of his day, but from the unexamined aesthetic assumptions of our own.

Yet rescue from realism is very much evident in the tone of these influential critics. Like Solness, who in *The Master Builder* (1892) triumphantly decides to build "castles in the air" (Fjelde, 848, 855) instead of houses for people to live in, these critics sweep Ibsen to an artistic height "above" realism, at once saving him from this debilitating art form and from the related, anchoring weight of social concerns. There's plenty of irony, I believe, in the pinnacle achievements of Solness, Rubek (*When We Dead Awaken* [1899]), and Borkman (*John Gabriel Borkman* [1896])—not only because they bring death, but also because they depend on renunciation (usually of a woman, of a child, of a socially engaged life). Still, the efforts of anti-realist critics—Johnston most of all—seem to depend on an exultant reading of these dubious endings. On the other hand, when Ibsen's protagonists are women, they are whisked into metaphoric abstraction so that they can't be read as triumphant, for to find glory in the final acts of Nora, Hedda, or Ellida Wangel (*The Lady from the Sea* [1888]) is to verge on a feminist reading, and that, these critics contend, is the social concern from which Ibsen requires deliverance most urgently of all.

The history of Ibsen scholarship reads, at times, like an argument against feminist (or proto-feminist) interpretations of Ibsen's plays, or at least of *A Doll House* and *Hedda Gabler*. For nearly 100 years, critics have resented, as Robert Brustein puts it, that "Ibsen has been expropriated by the women's movement" (*Critical Moments*, 132). To stave off such hostage-taking, they insist that we overlook the gender of Ibsen's female characters, that we leap immediately to a supposedly neutral image of the universal human being. Thus such proclamations as: Ibsen "was completely indifferent [to the woman question] except as a metaphor for individual freedom" (Brustein, *Theatre of*

Revolt: 105); *A Doll House* "has nothing to do with the sexes" (Meyer, Vol. 2: 266); Ellida Wangel's free choice to remain with her husband instead of running off with the controlling Stranger at the end of *The Lady from the Sea* represents humanity's tragic need "to remain this side of the third empire of the spirit" (Johnston, *Text and Supertext*: 223); "Hedda Gabler isn't a woman, she's a human being"—a declaration I have often heard in the classroom (from young women as well as young men) and even in the rehearsal hall. So it seems necessary, if absurd, to point out that if Hedda, Nora, and Ellida were not female, there would be no dramatic action. Lona Hessel might be addressing Ibsen scholars when, in *Pillars of Society* (1877), she tells Bernick, "This society of yours is a bachelors' club. You don't see women" (Fjelde, 117).

It makes sense that those who dismiss the obvious critique of women's subjugation in the plays are the same critics who denigrate their dramatic style. For if to some extent Ibsen's plays with female protagonists are feminist—at least at the level of the stories they tell—it's because they are realistic. They refer to a recognizable world in which women's lives are confined, constrained, controlled. While they don't make an agit-prop argument for changing that world, they evoke it critically, revealing its consequences. That is, they play on a feminist field, sexist bourgeois values providing the fateful background of Ibsen's mythic work. Anti-feminist critics imply that feminists confuse this background with the plays' foreground; rather, these critics do away with the circumstantial realm that determines the plays' actions, never asking why Ibsen's female protagonists make such great metaphors for the human condition. Henry James said that Ibsen's characters were "caught in the fact" (Gilman, 68), an observation later critics have cited, reasonably enough, to evoke the existential yearning that pleads through the plays, the cry for what Ibsen called "a revolution of the human spirit" (Brustein, *Critical Moments*: 135). But the characters are first caught in facts on the ground—or, more precisely, facts on the stage. For whatever metaphoric value words, props, or characters might take on, because they are on a realistic stage they first have literal meanings. Flowers may stand for death or nature; first they function in the drama as flowers. (Think of how Hedda derides the bouquet sent by Thea.) Hedda may be a tragic or mythic figure; first she is a woman. And she can have tragic or mythic resonance because she is a woman.

Ibsen and the Ladies

To be sure, the association between Ibsen and women's rights movements is not a paranoid invention of those who insist on its irrelevance. We know from a number of Ibsen's own activities and remarks that he considered the issue important. While living in Rome, for example, he argued in a scandalous tirade that the city's Scandinavia Club accept women as voting members and permit them to serve as librarians. He signed an 1884 petition calling for passage of a Norwegian bill that would establish separate property rights for married women—commenting that "To consult men in such a matter is like asking wolves if they desire better protection for the sheep" (*Letters and Speeches*, 228). His notes to *A Doll House* affirm that "A woman cannot be herself in modern society. It is an exclusively male society, with laws made by men and with prosecutors and judges who assess feminine conduct from a masculine standpoint" (Meyer, Vol. 2: 254). And when an Italian translator/producer wanted to put a conciliatory ending on *A Doll House*, Ibsen scornfully replied, "It was for the sake of the last scene that the whole play was written" (*Letters and Speeches*, 300).

Those who assert that Ibsen was not a full ally of the women's movement typically quote his statement made to the Norwegian Women's Rights League, which honored him in 1898 on the occasion of his seventieth birthday. He said, "Whatever I have written has been without any conscious thought of making propaganda. I have been more the poet and less the social philosopher than people generally seem inclined to believe. . . . My task has been the description of humanity" (*Letters and Speeches*, 337). Bear in mind that Ibsen made this disclaimer a number of years after writing *A Doll House*. In any case, Ibsen's statement is relative; he didn't say that he had been nothing of a social philosopher—just not entirely one. Addressing the woman question wasn't his whole purpose, only part of it.

It's impossible to imagine, in fact, that the first productions of *A Doll House* could have been received *without* reference to the "woman question." As Joan Templeton notes in "The *Dollhouse* Backlash: Criticism, Feminism, and Ibsen," her exhaustive analysis of anti-feminist "defenses" of the play, Nora's door-slam resounded through the West in the 1880s, initiating a spate of articles from America, England, France, Italy, Germany, and Scandinavia, in daily papers and highbrow weeklies, describing *A Doll House*'s theme as "the subjection of women by men" (Templeton, 32). Nora's long, justificatory speech in the last act practically quotes, as Templeton points out, texts that pleaded the case for women's rights, such as those by Mary Wollstonecraft, Margaret Fuller, and Harriet Martineau. In the 1890s, she adds, *A Doll House* was recognized "as the clearest and most substantial expression of the 'woman question' that had yet appeared" (Templeton, 32).

Of course Shaw has been much blamed for this widespread recognition, even though he claimed Ibsen for a wider socialist agenda than feminism (and even though the Fabian Society—and Shaw himself—as Jill Davis has shown [see Works Cited], had rather dubious attitudes about the proper place of women, using fiery new terms to relegate them to the same old roles as mothers and men's helpmates). In England, especially, Ibsen (along with Shaw and Leo Tolstoy) was seized on by the critics of the New Woman movement—as though women couldn't have come up with the demand for equality themselves. A satiric 1894 Punch cartoon, for example, depicts a "Donna Quixote" perched in an armchair, squinting into a book over her homely spectacles, as she hoists a tell-tale latchkey over her head. At her feet lies the head of "Tyrant Man." Behind her an amazon battles the dragon "Decorum" as another waves the banner of the "Divided Skirt." A third tilts at the windmill of "Marriage Laws." Books are strewn around her, among them a volume of Ibsen. (This cartoon is reproduced and discussed in Vivian Gardner's Introduction to *The New Woman and Her Sisters*, pp. 5–6. See Works Cited.)

If this cartoon version of the New Woman was nowhere to be found outside the imaginations of those she threatened, the actual New Woman did, in fact, keep volumes of Ibsen around, specifically the New Woman who worked in the theater, one of the few realms where women could enter public discourse. It's no coincidence that during this period, Ibsen was championed—and more important, produced—by the Free Theater movement that began on the European continent and then caught fire in England, and that these were the theaters from which female actor-managers emerged most powerfully, developing a new style of acting to meet the demands of Ibsen's innovations.

Janet Achurch was a producer of the *Doll House* in which she played Nora in 1889 and the *Hedda Gabler* in which she starred in 1891; Florence Farr produced and performed in *Rosmersholm* (1886) in 1891; Elizabeth Robins staged and acted in *Hedda Gabler* in 1891. As Shaw noted in the "Appendix to *The Quintessence of Ibsenism*," all four women who were Ibsen's strongest supporters, producers, and actors (at least in English)—Achurch, Farr, Robins, and Marion Lea—

> were products of the modern movement for the higher education of women, literate, in touch with advanced thought, and coming by natural predilection on the stage from outside the theatrical class, in contradistinction to the senior generation of inveterately sentimental actresses, schooled in the old fashion if at all, born into their profession, quite out of the political and social movement around them—in short, intellectually naïve to the last degree. (Shaw, 5)

These new women had to create a new acting style—a new actress—to meet the demands of Ibsen's characters, who slammed the door on melodramatic mincing and well-made, often sentimental miracles, who staged themselves with a new and liberating self-consciousness, demanding for women onstage, as well as off, a new way to act.

Women and Well-Madeness

So it's no surprise, either, that for some twenty years, as Ibsen produced his cycle of prose plays, the mainstream press throughout Europe carried debates about him. Each new opening presented another occasion for discussion, denouncement, applause, analysis—not only of theatrical performances and dramatic design, but of ideas. No doubt that then, as now, some of the daily reviewers were dunderheads, often failing to note the most profound and innovative aspects of Ibsen's work. But it doesn't follow that the raging discussions degraded a great dramatist into a *pièce-à-thèse* hack. On the contrary, for all the narrowness and outrage of many contemporary Ibsen critics, their assumption that drama engages and affects the most urgent issues of its times would be a welcome remedy to so much of today's theater writing, which makes a proud point of detaching drama from the world it inhabits. Indeed, the solution to reductive readings of Ibsen is not to drain his plays of their social content, as though it were some enfeebling venom injected by dramatically indifferent parties, but to recognize the inextricable relationship of that content to Ibsen's metaphoric and theatrical invention.

There's a related, more profound way in which Ibsen's realism offers a feminist critique: through its implosive critique of dramatic form. After Nora declared that she must forsake husband and children to become "a human being" (Fjelde, 193), Ibsen was, of course, vehemently denounced. Yet today's critics are divided over why Ibsen's contemporaries were scandalized by his plays. Most suggest that they recoiled from Ibsen's unspeakable subject matter, and ignored, as Meyer puts it, "the technical originality" (Meyer, Vol. 2: 264). On the other hand, Johnston insists that the rejection of Ibsen may have *seemed* like a revulsion toward his dangerous topics, but was really "the condition of vertigo" instilled by a dramatic style that made "the 'reality' purportedly presented (our world), and the artistic standpoint from which that reality might be judged" feel as though they were dissolving beneath the audience's feet (*Ibsen Cycle*, 370). Both, of course, are right: the one is not detachable from the other. All the more so when issues of gender are involved, for Ibsen's innovative dramaturgy reveals the artificiality of the well-made play, and, as a consequence, the artificiality of the era's well-made woman. It questions the reliability of the artistic order and, as a result, the reliability of the social, even epistemological, order.

Indeed, in contemporary reviews of Ibsen's plays, the critique of Ibsen's dramaturgy often takes the form of a critique of Ibsen's representation of women—and vice versa. For example, Gerhard Gran's review of *Hedda Gabler* in *Samtiden, 1891* declared that

> drama, in its present state of technical development, can only present comparatively simple characters. . . . Everything that should make this curious being [Hedda] intelligible to us, her development, her secret thoughts, her half-sensed misgivings, and all that vast region of the human mind that lies between the conscious and the unconscious—all this the dramatist can no more than indicate. For that reason, I think a novel about Hedda Gabler could be extremely interesting, while a play leaves us with a sense of emptiness and betrayal. (Meyer, Vol. 3: 156)

Those who were most disturbed by Ibsen's unseemly ideas railed like their Puritanical predecessors, unconsciously attaching Ibsen's internal critique of theatrical form to his critique of gender roles. Clement Scott (who coined "Ibsenite" as a term of opprobrium) was easily the Philip Stubbes of his day. His accusation that anyone who *attended* an Ibsen play was guilty of gender dysfunction recalls the seventeenth century's most virulent condemnation of theater (in such works as Stubbes's *The Anatomie of Abuses*, first published in 1583) as a site of sexuality run amok. Ibsen's audiences, Scott wrote, were

> The sexless. . . . The unwomanly woman, the unsexed females, the whole army of unprepossessing cranks in petticoats. . . . Educated and muck-ferreting dogs . . . Effeminate men and male women. . . . They, all of them—men and women alike—know that they are doing not only a nasty thing but an illegal thing . . . (Meyer, Vol. 3: 173)

Ibsen's plays could provoke such a response precisely because they make social conventions seem as hoary and artificial as theater conventions. In other words, it wasn't just that Ibsen sympathetically represented female characters in untenable social situations. Pointing to the limits of theatrical form, he commented on the limits of middle-class, patriarchal values. Scott's tirade responds to a deeper and more subversive feminism than that carved on the surface of women's stories, one that conjures a complex critique in the interplay between presentational and representational dramatic styles, between the mechanisms of melodrama and the *tarantellian* promise of a new realist form.

Traditional Ibsen criticism makes much of the way Ibsen catapulted drama beyond the well-made play. Somewhat more recently, mythopoeic interpreters of Ibsen have highlighted his self-conscious use of the more formulaic genre, demonstrating how, as Johnston puts it, "Ibsen is alerting us, not just to inadequacies in our idea of the world, but also to inadequacies in our idea of the theater; that is, of the way the world conventionally is represented in the theater" (*Ibsen Cycle*, 368). Benjamin Bennett goes further in linking Ibsen's social critique to his metatheatricality. Ibsen, he says, employs artificial theatrical devices that are *meant* to be recognized as devices, as an arbitrary and disturbingly familiar theatrical language which reminds us, by its nature as a language, that the theatrical performance is an organized communal event in which we are participating. As real life interferes with the play's ideality and calls attention to our status as individuals, so too does an obvious theatricalness interfere with the play's objectivity and call attention to the communal conventions in which we are all involved (Bennett, 305).

Though both Johnston and Bennett cite *A Doll House* and *Hedda Gabler* particularly to illustrate how Ibsen relies on a melodramatic model, mocking it as he moves beyond it, neither critic recognizes a relationship between Ibsen's obvious theatricality and the obviously theatrical communal convention both plays challenge: femininity. But it is precisely in this confluence of theatrical production and social performance that Ibsen's realism creates a current for the "liberating realm of imagery and reference" that Johnston calls the "supertext" (*Ibsen Cycle*, 362).

A Doll House under (De)Construction

Think again of Torvald's misgivings about Nora's *tarantella*. Her dance is too "naturalistic" because it is unbecoming: that is, it is inappropriate behavior for a respectable wife—and for a character in the new realism, as many critics of the day complained. William Archer sounds a bit like Torvald when he chides that the *tarantella* scene "belongs to an inferior order of dramatic effects" ("Theatre," 22). He approved of Eleanora Duse's decision to replace the manic whirling with more contained action, in which she "dons the crown of roses, seizes the tambourine, makes one sweep round the stage, then drops powerless with emotion and fear in a chair" (Archer, "Lyric Theatre": 7). Even Elizabeth Robins charged that the *tarantella* was too stagey, "Ibsen's one concession to the effect-hunting that he had come to deliver us from" (Styan, 24). Robins and Archer derided the dance most likely because they recognized it as a standard occasion for a star turn, an actor's chance to pull out all the stops on a big emotional number, never mind how tenuously it relates to the plot. But Nora's frenetic dance is not merely an outward manifestation of inner desperation—stagey effect-hunting, indeed. Rather, it announces itself as a remnant of that old staginess, and then goes it one better. Not a concession to the old effect-hunting, Nora's *tarantella* is an *appropriation* of it.

Audaciously, Ibsen calls twice on this effect from an inferior dramatic order—first in the staged rehearsal at the end of Act II, then in Nora's offstage performance, on which Torvald reports near the beginning of Act III. Not only does the dance relate to the plot—in both instances, Nora's dervishing forestalls Torvald's trip to the mailbox—it structures the action. Melodramatically, it serves as a relentless, ticking clock. Nora counts the hours until Torvald will learn her terrible secret: "Five. Seven hours to midnight. Twenty-four hours to the midnight after, and then the *tarantella*'s done. Seven and twenty-four? Thirty-one hours to live" (Fjelde, 175). In marking out the end of her life in the *tarantella*, Nora reverses—or so we think—the traditional image of the dance as a remedy, a means of discharging poison. And in this reversal, the *tarantella* takes on its metaphoric meaning, for it also marks the ferociousness with which she must overstep proprieties if she is, in fact, going to live.

Act II ends with Nora's anticipation of doom. She finishes the *tarantella* rehearsal, pulls herself together, ties up her hair, and goes in to supper to give the performance of her life, chirping, "Here's your [little] lark!" (Fjelde, 175). So we await her return in Act III, events wound up in intricate, well-made fashion. (Of course, Ibsen's six years as a stage manager and director at Norway's Christiania Theatre taught him such mechanics well; he directed some 145 plays there, half of them by or in imitation of the Frenchman Eugène Scribe.) Ibsen delays the unravelling of these events. Act III opens with Kristine Linde and Nils Krogstad's romantic reunion. What's more, this reunion gives the well-made devices another twist: though Krogstad agrees to ask Torvald to return his letter unread, Kristine talks him out of it, subverting the savior function that the old dramatic style assumed.

When Nora does enter, she's dragged in by Torvald, pleading with him from offstage for just another hour—as though teasing the audience by trying to put off the resolution it awaits with such pent-up certainty. Finally she arrives, wearing the *tarantella* costume we've seen displayed, passed among women's hands, stitched—and now, worn. The dress itself has enabled much of the dramatic action, serving as Nora's excuse to keep Torvald out of the room, to invite Kristine over for a confidential chat, and to shoo her away. The costume, too, is the instrument through which Dr. Rank's feelings about Nora become known, in the famous "stocking scene" (which Duse and Eva Le Gallienne cut for its immodesty). But the dress, having gathered so much meaning as an image of liberation, impending disaster, and theatrical gear-grinding, acquires most significance in its removal.

"What are you doing in there?" (Fjelde, 189), Torvald asks, when Nora walks out on his declarations of forgiveness. She replies from offstage: "Getting out of my costume" (Fjelde, 189). While she does so, Torvald prattles on about how safe and snug he'll make her now, promising to be both "conscience and will to you" (Fjelde, 190). She returns, of course, in her regular street clothes, dressed for a stunning exit. More than in this literal sense, the *tarantella* serves as Nora's ennobling and enabling act. It exemplifies how profoundly her life—like the well-made play—has been a series of histrionic effects. This is not a sudden realization, at least not for the audience. Ibsen prepares that shocking door-slam with a web of imagery as wide as Shakespeare's, yet moored by realism to the literal accoutrements of a bourgeois life.

Throughout the play Nora is associated with secrecy, deception, and disguise. The very first word she speaks is "hide" (Fjelde, 125); and in the first moments of the play we watch as she sneaks some macaroons and "steals over and listens at her husband's study door" (Fjelde, 125). She plays hide-and-seek with her children. Torvald fantasizes that she is his "secret darling" (Fjelde, 183). Most important, of course, she holds a terrible secret. (Not only that she borrowed money and forged a signature, but that she worked—unfit activity for a married woman of her class. Note that Torvald's first question to Kristine when Nora says her friend needs a job is, "I suppose you're a widow?" [Fjelde, 142]. Indeed, what Nora liked most about working was that "It was almost like being a man" [Fjelde, 137].)

But in another contortion of the well-made form, Ibsen does not make Nora ashamed of her subterfuge. Her ability to borrow money and pay it back through her own labor and sacrifice was "something [I've got] to be proud and happy for" (Fjelde, 135). The lie that drives the old-style plot, in other words, is not the lie that matters in the end. Ibsen provides the expected melodramatic resolution: Krogstad returns the forged note and Torvald ecstatically rips it up and throws it into the fire. But that reprieve merely makes way for a more shattering liberation. The revelation of Nora's instrumental lie discloses another, at once more political and more existential: her marriage is a sham. Being a twittering little lark of a wife and mother is to have a role, not an identity. This ontological fact cannot be extricated from the social conditions that give rise to it, any more than Ibsen's "supertext" can resonate without the sympathetic vibrations of his self-conscious dramatic style: Ibsen's realism trembles to life, one could say, in the tension between melodrama and metaphor.

Nora's association with the New Woman—and with performance—is hinted at throughout the play because she is repeatedly characterized as an actress. She tells Kristine how much Torvald "[enjoys] my dancing and dressing up and reciting for him" (Fjelde, 137). Sewing trimmings on the *tarantella* dress, Kristine remarks, "So, you'll be in disguise tomorrow" (Fjelde, 156). Later, Rank suggests that at next year's party, Nora could masquerade as "charmed life" (Fjelde, 184) by going just as she is. Foreshadowing the play's ending, Torvald complains that Nora didn't understand when it was time to leave off dancing. "An exit should always be effective," he says, "but that's what I can't get Nora to grasp" (Fjelde, 181). In the theater of his own mind, Torvald casts her as a melodramatic damsel in distress when he imagines her "in some terrible danger, just so I could stake my life and soul and everything, for your sake" (Fjelde, 186). But, of course, this is not a melodrama, so such a miracle cannot take place. Finally, in her last-act speech, when Nora makes her most honest, unmediated statements about herself, Torvald ironically believes she is acting. "Ah, none of your slippery tricks" (Fjelde, 187), he demands; and "No more playacting" (Fjelde, 196), as well as "Oh, quit posing" (Fjelde, 188).

Nineteenth-century critics of the play—as well as more recent writers who insist on a "universal" reading of the protagonist—tend to regard Nora's little squirrel act as her most authentic expression of self, and thus to condemn her actions as the thoughtless iniquities of a naïve, immoral hysteric. This, as Templeton shrewdly suggests, is to see Nora through Torvald's eyes (Templeton, 34). She quotes the Norwegian scholar Else Host, arguing that it is the "childish, expectant, ecstatic, broken-hearted Nora" who makes the play immortal, while the coldly analytical character of the last act is psychologically unconvincing and wholly unsympathetic (Templeton, 29). In a 1925 study, Herman Weigand even insisted that *A Doll House* had to be read as a comedy, because surely Nora would race back home and "revert imperceptibly to her role of song-bird and charmer." After all, he reasoned, Nora is:

> an irresistibly bewitching piece of femininity, an extravagant poet and romancer, utterly lacking in sense of fact, and endowed with a natural gift for play-acting that makes her instinctively dramatize her experiences: how can the settlement fail of a fundamentally comic appeal? (Weigand, 64, 68)

More enlightened readings rely on similar essentialist assumptions. For Johnston, Torvald's affectionate nicknames associate Nora with a "strong 'animal' identity," supporting his interpretation of her as a woman unable "to take the universal ethical realm into consideration at all," and as a representative of the "pre-social, instinctual, feminine, and familial" side of the great Hegelian conflict between feminine and masculine principles (*Ibsen Cycle*, 110-111).

Real Nora, Performing Nora

Such commentary ignores not only the way language reveals Nora's femininity as a role, but the way Nora's behavior changes depending on whether Torvald is—or might be—watching her. In the face of all the acts we know Nora to be capable of—striking a deal with Krogstad, working to pay off her debt, consciously manipulating Torvald by playing the infantilized charmer, resolving not to ask Rank for assistance since he has romantic designs on her, staunchly standing up to Krogstad and admitting that she forged her father's signature when she could have lied, determining to leave the imprisoning "playpen" that her marriage has become—in the face of all this, it's impossible to reduce Nora to Torvald's little squirrel. Yet the myth persists, rather like the cliché that Hamlet is incapable of acting, though we see him setting the Players' show as a trap, throwing off Ophelia, confronting his mother, killing Polonius, arranging for the execution of Rosencrantz and Guildenstern, and so on.

Several times, we see Nora alone, and on these occasions she is no mere little lark. She opens and closes the first two acts, framing their hurtling events with her efforts to situate herself safely outside them. The play begins with her giddy entrance. Stage directions call for her to be "humming happily" (Fjelde,

125). She unloads her Christmas packages and gives the boy delivering the tree an enormous tip, then surreptitiously munches some macaroons before listening for Torvald, like an actor peeping through a curtain to see if the audience has arrived. Her merry disposition may seem, at first, merely to correspond to the imminent holiday. And once we see her interact with Torvald, who greets "my little lark" (Fjelde, 125, 128, 175, 182) and "my squirrel" (Fjelde, 126), this may seem, simply, to characterize her. Soon, though, Ibsen gives us a concrete reason with which we can correct our impression and understand her exuberance in retrospect: Torvald will be starting a new, lucrative job and, Nora exults, "Won't it be lovely to have stacks of money and not a care in the world?" (Fjelde, 131). Still later, Ibsen lets us catch ourselves in the act of seeing her through Torvald's eyes by parceling out the true explanation for Nora's happiness, the conclusion of what she calls "the big thing" (Fjelde, 134): she saved her husband's life by borrowing money, then stealthily worked and scrimped to pay off the debt.

Now it will soon be paid in full. No wonder she feels like a lark. And no wonder she ends the act frightened: Krogstad, like a classic melodramatic villain, has crawled out of the past right on cue and threatened to blackmail her. On top of that, Torvald has proclaimed that the sins of the parents ruin the lives of their children (a theme underscored by Rank's tubercular-cum-venereal condition—and taken up by Ibsen's next play, *Ghosts* [1881]). Though Nora challenges Torvald's suggestion that the mother is the one to blame, she takes his words to heart when he retreats to his study, leaving her once again in private. "Hurt my children—! Poison my home?" she wonders, "pale with terror" (Fjelde, 153). Then she rejects this mechanistic view and gets on with the show. In a telling stage direction, Ibsen instructs, "A moment's pause; then she tosses her head" (Fjelde, 153). And Nora says, "That's not true. Never. Never in all the world" (Fjelde, 153).

Yet, the curtain goes up with Nora alone again, this time pacing restlessly past the Christmas tree, now "stripped of ornament, burned-down candle stubs on its ragged branches" (Fjelde, 154). She frets, anticipating that Krogstad will arrive with that Scribean essential—the incriminating letter. She's drawn out of her anxiety only by the maid's entrance with the box of masquerade clothes, which, Nora says, "I'd love to rip . . . in a million pieces!" (Fjelde, 154). Her predicament is bound up with her performance. As already noted, the last time we see Nora alone, she's counting the hours until the *tarantella* is done. Then she bucks up—indeed, larks up—and makes a grand entrance into supper.

These moments are worth noting in detail because they so sharply contrast with the image of Nora that Torvald maintains, and which pervades the play more generally. Kristine imposes a similar interpretation: despite Nora's clear statements that having a rich admirer to bail her out is a fantasy, Kristine can't imagine Nora's taking care of herself. But the audience holds the privilege of irony, of double-vision, weighing Kristine's and Torvald's reactions against our own heightened perceptions. Nora's no-nonsense moments alone, her clearly manipulative way of stringing along Kristine and seducing money out of Torvald, demonstrate that this is no frail little fledgling but a woman who has learned her part expertly. Indeed, Nora doesn't really panic until her performance fails to persuade: despite her virtuoso pleas, Torvald rejects her suit that Krogstad be reinstated in his job.

In more subtle ways, too, Ibsen associates Nora with the profession of acting. In the "stocking scene," where she flirts with Rank, she unabashedly displays a pair of flesh-colored stockings—exactly the costume item that was scandalizing critics of Europe's popular theater forms. As the historian Tracy Davis notes, pink-colored tights were "the article most heavily invested with indexical signification of skin, eroticism, and sexual stimulation," in pornographic novels, ballet, pantomime, opera bouffe, burlesque, music hall, and acrobatic performances of the period" (*Actresses as Working Women*, 134). "The female leg, naked in tights," she says, "became synonymous with the female performer, with enjoyment, and with the theatre itself" (*Actresses as Working Women*, 135).

Ibsen even goes so far as to intimate the common association of the period between actresses and prostitutes. Describing to Kristine the odd jobs she's taken, Nora lists "needlework, crocheting, embroidery, and such—(*Casually.*) and other things too" (Fjelde, 132). And when Krogstad asks her if she knows of some sure, quick ways of getting money, Nora replies, "None that I'm willing to use." Finally, on hearing what she's done, Torvald accuses his wife of being a "hypocrite, a liar . . . [and] a criminal" (Fjelde, 187)—a series of epithets not far from contemporary railing about actresses. The actress thus served as a heady, even cautionary, image of the New Woman. Ibsen invokes her as a double-emblem of the question blazing inside the theater and beyond: how should—how could—women act?

For nowhere was the critique of gender constraints and theatrical representation more accessible than in the tension between old and new styles of acting. Despite our twenty-first-century assumptions about internal, naturalistic, cinematic acting, the most successful Ibsen performances a century ago came from what Tracy Davis calls the combining of "realistic characteristics with sensational behavior," the striking of "the right balance between truthful embodiment and theatricalized effect in accordance with the audience's taste for modernism and their long experience of presentational acting" ("Acting in Ibsen," 113). As Davis notes, Achurch's Nora was generally more acclaimed than Duse's understated performance. Duse's "dread of becoming melodramatic," Archer explained, resulted in her failure to be "legitimately dramatic" (Davis, "Acting in Ibsen": 116).

Ibsen's stage directions periodically call for actors to smile "almost imperceptibly" (Fjelde, 574, 583, 713, 1053) or for even more subtle actions, like "suppressing an involuntary smile" (Fjelde, 753, 776). Surely these instructions are most telling in what they mean to counteract: the actor's temptation to make points. They contrast with, rather than negate, that possibility, marking the places where high-flown histrionics are not appropriate. The tension between the two styles provides a means of pointing to characters as themselves self-dramatizing—a feature of Ibsen's men as well as his women. Nora certainly does this when she puts on her larkish behavior to cajole Torvald, tease Kristine, or flirt with Rank. And in doing so, she reveals the performance-like nature of femininity. But she is no match for Ibsen's *diva* of self-dramatization, Hedda

Gabler, who stages her predicament most violently by quoting grand theatrical gestures.

Directing Hedda, or Past, Present, and Future

Perhaps Brian Johnston sounds a bit like a true-believer who's seen the face of Jesus in a pizza pie when he suggests that Friedrich Nietzsche's *The Birth of Tragedy* (1872) is concealed within Hedda Gabler (*Ibsen Cycle*, 145), but Hedda's appeal to classical models is undeniable. As Johnston and Elinor Fuchs (see Works Cited) have shown, Ibsen's references to Greek mythology reach beyond Hedda's dreams of vine leaves in Eilert Løvborg's hair to produce an imagistic atmosphere that rings with Attic echoes. More immediately, as Johnston notes, *Hedda Gabler* evokes Scribe as the art of the past. Indeed, in *Hedda Gabler* Ibsen out-Scribes Scribe, forcing immense, mythic subject matter into an intolerable confinement (*Ibsen Cycle*, 144-145). Even more than in *A Doll House*, Ibsen oils the machinery of the well-made play with irony, setting up the form's devices and then deflecting them toward open, inexplicable ends.

To take just one example, the possibility that Løvborg will compete with George Tesman for his academic post—apart from offering Hedda a frisson of spectatorship—introduces a conflict that could drive the plot of this play had Scribe or one of his imitators written it. Ibsen intimates, then steers away from this plot when Løvborg announces, to Tesman's relief and Hedda's dismay, that he will not make his splash until after Tesman's appointment is secured. Ibsen thus arouses his audience's anxiety in a familiar way, only to yank it in new directions. For if the contest between Tesman and Løvborg is not over a job—or over a woman, as Hedda quickly rejects Løvborg's assumptions of intimacy—our attention is focused on something else. Indeed, the dramatic action turns out *not* to center on the conflict between two male rivals at all, though the play's first mention of Løvborg sparks just that possibility when, in the first scene, Aunt Julia Tesman uncharacteristically gloats that Tesman's former competition has fallen miserably and is "lying there now, in the bed he made—poor, misguided creature" (Fjelde, 701). Yet that creaky conflict is denied. And what brings relief in the old drama brings Hedda nothing but boredom.

In this and so many other instances of roused and rerouted expectations, Ibsen trains attention on Hedda's response to the action, offering a point of view through which we might consider the limitations of a plot that once satisfied. It's a complicated ruse, for we see Hedda desire a melodrama for her own amusement and recognize her disappointment as a more fascinating and mysterious subject than the melodrama itself. But Hedda, too, realizes the inadequacies of the narrative she would impose. So she tries to shape events into a grander form, or at least to give the sordid old plot the trappings of classical significance. Yet even those corny vine leaves can't confer heroism on bourgeois banalities. By the time Hedda hands a pistol to Løvborg, she tells him, "I don't believe in vine leaves anymore" (Fjelde, 762). For Hedda can't find diversion, much less salvation, in forms of the past that just won't shape themselves to the petty concerns of the drawing room (though we, of course, can find it in Ibsen's staging of this tension). She yearns for—but can't quite imagine—a form of the future, where she can play protagonist in her own life. Ibsen has put her at the center of a new drama in which she labors vainly to make herself the center of an old action.

Straining toward both past and future to find meaning is an essential action—and process—of *Hedda Gabler*. The play moves relentlessly forward in its embrace of this vigorous, sublime tension, as it attenuates—but never obliterates—the dramatic present. The unfulfilled rivalry between Tesman and Løvborg centers on this cosmic contest—Tesman studies handicrafts in the Brabant during the Middle Ages, Løvborg has given birth to a visionary treatise on the future. Of course, we never do learn the substance of Løvborg's prophecies (in an early draft of the play, Ibsen revealed that his work presaged a true camaraderie between men and women) because Hedda herself expresses no interest in the book's content. Still, Løvborg's grandiose work seems as distant and unreal—as academic—as Tesman's pedantic research. But the present—that uncatchable moment made palpable in the theater—is precisely what everyone but Hedda ignores. While others locate themselves between what's come before and what they hope is yet to transpire, Hedda gets little thrill from memories, and even less from expectations. Indeed, *expecting*, in both senses, is just what Hedda cannot stand to be. She hungers for an unmediated immediate, in short, for a theater of her own devising. Yet when faced with the yawning emptiness of the present, she has nothing to fill it with. That's when "these things come over me, just like that, suddenly. And I can't hold back" (Fjelde, 728). Such rashness, as she says, has consequences, each of them more dire than the last—her marriage to Tesman, their acquisition of the Falk house, her pregnancy, her destruction of Løvborg's manuscript, her suicide.

Ibsen parallels this restlessness with—and restlessness in—the present with his retrospective and anticipatory method. Intensifying and deepening the suspense of the well-made play, Ibsen creates a pull between past and future in our experience of viewing his drama. Expository material is meted out only as it has the capacity to excite our expectations. Information about the past or about offstage events—for example, Aunt Rina's illness, Thea's escape from her lifeless marriage, Løvborg and Hedda's former *tête-à-têtes* (re-enacted in the photo album scene)—does much more than the ordinary work of filling in the dramatic world or rounding out its characters. It creates a state of guided apprehension, our readings of past events changing as new information is provided. In this way, we perceive events and then, in an ongoing process of reconsideration, revise our understanding of them as more and more details accumulate. Thus Ibsen re-creates the very idea of dramatic sequence, allowing events to proceed in overlapping succession, like runners staggered for a relay race. Encouraging us constantly to reassess our conclusions, this innovation calls melodramatic conventions into question and, with them, the gender conventions they inscribed.

Ibsen points this imbricated sequence in two directions. For example, Aunt Rina's sickness makes us expect her death and anticipate that she will be replaced, as Aunt Julia suggests, with someone else who needs care. At first, we think, that will be Hedda's child, but that presumption is deflected toward the nurturing Thea. Rina's death, when it does come—along with the stage full of people dressed in mourning that death brings with it—foreshadows the deaths of both Løvborg and Hedda. (Even the letter announcing Rina's last moments, which the maid brings in after the night of Løvborg's debauch, seems, at first, as though it will bring news about Løvborg.) Similarly, Thea's past stirs questions about Hedda: will she—can she—flee? Thea's line of action, of course, overlaps the others. Her loss of respectability puts her in need of Aunt Julia's ministrations; her collaboration with Løvborg recalls Hedda's intimacy with the latter. And so on. Every gesture, every line of dialogue, every event, takes its place in an action tugged inexorably forward toward a future implied by an everchanging past.

This sense that the action of *Hedda Gabler* is being pulled along is emphasized by what Rolf Fjelde refers to as the play's stichomythic dialogue ("Introduction," 690). If this phrase recalls the Greek echoes in the play, it also describes the way so much of the exposition is elicited by means of interrogation. As Hedda once goaded Løvborg to tell her about his demi-monde adventures, she questions Thea Elvsted about her arrival in town and interrogates Judge Brack about Løvborg's comportment. Aunt Julia examines the maid about Hedda and Tesman. Brack questions Hedda about her marriage. The play thus acquires an interrogative mood, encouraging our process of taking in, retrospectively reviewing, and modifying our responses.

Løvborg, man of the future, exists almost entirely in the past: though he makes two much-ballyhooed appearances, we learn most about him by report. What we actually see him do—chat with Hedda over the album, change his mind about going to Brack's party, lie to Thea about the loss of his manuscript, confess to Hedda and go off with her pistol—is orchestrated by Hedda. Though he'd be the hero in a more traditional drama, here he's a figure in a drama Hedda is stage-managing or even directing. In this respect, she's rather like the duke in Shakespeare's *Measure for Measure* (1604), who reneges on his responsibilities, puts a tyrant in his place, and then manipulates the action he has unleashed, steering it toward a comic ending. Hedda's manipulations don't bring such a felicitous, if phony, outcome; she aims for tragedy. Still, just as critics have labored to understand the duke's motivation, they have psychoanalyzed Hedda, searching for explanations for her impossible actions.

Critics, Actresses, and *Hedda Gabler*

From the sympathetic diagnoses of Lou Andreas Salomé (see Mandel in Works Cited) to the more consciously feminist analyses of Gail Finney, who sees Hedda as "the personification of the hysterization of the female body, or the reduction of the woman to her status as female" (Finney, 151), Hedda's womanhood has supplied a clinical explanation for her actions. (Even non-feminists have drawn such conclusions: Michael Meyer suggests that Hedda "should have been born a boy" (Vol. 3, 154); director Mel Shapiro, who cast Charles Ludlam as Hedda in a 1984 production at Pittsburgh's short-lived American Ibsen Theater, justified this decision by arguing that Hedda was "trapped in the wrong body" [R. Davis, 2-3].) But plausible as some of these interpretations may be (though Shapiro and Meyer might remember that craving male privilege is not the same thing as wanting to be a man), none of them is big enough to contain Hedda. As Hedda herself says, dismissing the very idea of motivation, "Oh—reasons—" (Fjelde, 725). Her suicide is so overdetermined that any explanation, taken alone or in sum, feels insufficient. It's not just the boredom, the baby, Brack's blackmail, Løvborg's botched nobility, Thea's new partnership with Tesman, or Hedda's last-ditch attempt to see something done beautifully. None of these explains the size of her gesture, at once self-destructive and self-aggrandizing. And yet that gunshot rings with inevitability—and meaning.

Critics in Ibsen's day complained precisely of this fact. When it premiered, *Hedda Gabler* received the most venomous notices of any of Ibsen's prose works. One reviewer chided, "We do not understand Hedda Gabler, nor believe in her" (Meyer, Vol. 3: 156-157). Another called her "a horrid miscarriage of the imagination, a monster in female form" (Meyer, Vol. 3: 156-157). A third resented that "Certain traits are perhaps truthfully portrayed, but the psychological combination of these traits is without logic" (Meyer, Vol. 3: 156-157). What's noteworthy about these criticisms isn't simply that the writers made the right observation but the wrong judgment about it; it's that from today's vantage point, we assume they are comparing Hedda to "real women," when in fact they are complaining about a new kind of dramaturgy. At a time when the theater, in Joseph Donohue's words (123), was "crowded to overflowing with images of yielding, often helpless, feminine women" (and with cardboard villains), they rejected Hedda not because she was unlike any actual person—a criterion that was hardly operative (or relevant)—but because she didn't behave like other female characters.

This distinction is important if Hedda's gender is to be understood as something more than the symptom psychoanalytic critics make of it. True, on one level she is a woman trapped in social conditions that leave no room for her individual expression, much as she is a figure trapped in the wrong kind of play, and a human spirit trapped in the mundane degradations of the material world. But our understanding of these suffocations—and of their mutually reflecting nature—comes from recognizing Hedda's divergence from a melodramatic norm. Gay Gibson Cima persuasively argues that, seen in the light of the new performance style wrought by Elizabeth Robins and other female actor-managers, "Hedda simultaneously mocks and enacts the role of woman as ideal victim" (Cima, 48). Balancing the "realistic" with the "melodramatic," Robins's performance as Hedda, says Cima, "attempted to enact and kill off the melodramatic image of the self-sacrificing woman, to show the ludicrousness as well as the seductiveness of her very sacrifice" (Cima, 49).

Without diminishing the contributions of Robins and other actresses to this subtle critique of women's depiction on the turn-of-the-century stage, I think it's fair to credit Ibsen with the play's ability to self-consciously deconstruct. The play's self-referentiality and its constant provision of alternative interpretations make subversive readings of representation possible, rather than, as Cima suggests (57), promoting "the dominant ideology almost as fiercely as melodrama had." (Performance traditions that ignore the metatheatrical pointings of the play, however, may very well promote dominant ideology.) As in

A Doll House, the gender critique is opened up in part by the comparison of the protagonist to an actor.

Like Nora, Hedda refuses to play her traditional role, while those around her take refuge within the "character types" that cozily dictate their behavior. Like Nora in her "stocking scene," Hedda is associated with the icons of actress and theater when Brack guesses that she won't jump off the figurative train of her marriage because someone on the platform will look at her legs. When Tesman finally catches on about his wife's pregnancy, Hedda blurts out, "Oh, I'll die—I'll die of all this." Tesman asks, "Of what?" and she replies—in Fjelde's translation—"of all these—absurdities" (767). But James McFarlane translates this line as "of this farce" (251), reinforcing Hedda's refusal to take her place within a suffocating and decaying dramatic form, a form that by definition denies her honor, heroism, and action. Hedda's final exit is her most self-consciously theatrical gesture of all. Retiring to her inner space, her own little stage behind a curtain, she pokes out her head in a that's-all-folks sort of salute, promising that "from now on I'll be quiet" (Fjelde, 777).

Responding to the play's metatheatrical pulses does not have to lead to a reading that merely spirals back on itself, nor to one that turns the drama into an abstraction, a symphony that has no discursive meaning. On the contrary, feeling the claustrophobia of the proscenium enables us to feel Hedda's claustrophobia of *polis* and personhood. And it should enable feminist critics to reconsider assumptions about the possibilities of realistic drama—or at least of Ibsen's realistic drama. Ibsen, especially, deserves such a circumspect review, for the gender critique implied in his bending and breaking of realistic form may yet be as powerful as the most postmodern "queer" performance. In the later twentieth century, productions of Ibsen began to fasten on to this possibility. For more than two decades, starting in the late seventies, pioneering directors tried to pry Ibsen loose from the encrusted habits and cherished convictions of audiences and producers alike. Offering versions of the plays that broke out of box-set illusionism, they attempted to retrieve Ibsen from the yoked constraints of canonical reverence and an enervated realism.

If Robert Brustein's 1978 production of *The Wild Duck* (1884), for example, went too far in literalizing Brustein's metaphorical reading—the upstage wall of the Yale Repertory Theatre stage was an enormous camera shutter—it did help catapult Ibsen out of the museum. More successfully, Travis Preston's 1984 *Little Eyolf* (1894) at the American Ibsen Theater in Pittsburgh, with its presentational acting, dance-concert side-lighting, abstract set (a boat stood vertically on end, as though planted in the floor, throughout Act III), and open stage, created a chilling tone in which the human experiences of loss, grief, recrimination, and guilt acquired the weight of spiritual disintegration—and renewal. Both encouraged a willingness to regard nineteenth-century realism as a deliberately self-conscious form, one that, as Gordon Craig remarked in 1911, was just another "example of a new artificiality" (Craig, 290).

Bergman and Warner: A Match Made in (Theatrical) Heaven

It's not surprising, though, that the most powerful productions have been those that have grounded their metatheatricality in a heaving, hortatory realism, nor that they have been the plays that most directly take on gender. Ingmar Bergman's *A Doll House* and Deborah Warner's *Hedda Gabler* seemed to begin from an understanding that Ibsen's realism never demanded total immersion in the fictive world of the play: to peer into a recessed box at the end of a darkened theater and grant plausibility to the events that took place there was not to relinquish awareness of artifice; to identify setting and the behavior of characters as comparable to one's everyday environment and actions was not to surrender critical faculties and enter a dreamworld with a life of its own. Realism's aim, J. L. Styan has written, "was to create the illusion of natural space within the unnaturally rigid frame of the proscenium arch" (Styan, 15). Like Ibsen, both productions acknowledged that blaring, gilded, unnaturally rigid frame, which tugs against the very illusion within it, defining an experience of both engagement and detachment. As a result, Ibsen—and these directors—drew attention to the rigid frames that constrain human fulfillment, among them those erected by the entire sex-and-gender system.

Bergman's 1981 *A Doll House* for Stockholm's Royal Dramatic Theatre (seen in New York ten years later at the Brooklyn Academy of Music) streamlined the play and set it on a sparsely furnished, island-like platform. Behind this stage-upon-a-stage, photographs of intricate interiors were projected onto a giant screen. Actors sat outside the platform's perimeter, watching the action until it was time to join it. Pernilla Östergren played a spirited and sensual Nora, leaping onto a tabletop—another stage surface—to dance a wild *tarantella*. Bergman's bold intervention was to split the final scene, setting Nora's farewell in the couple's bedroom, where, we can't fail to assume, they have just had sex. Bergman even implies that Torvald may have forced himself on Nora. The second half of the scene begins with Nora entering the bedroom dressed in traveling clothes, carrying luggage, and rousing her husband to announce her departure. Torvald, naked in bed, modestly pulls the sheets to his chin, an ineffectual shield against his wife's astonishing argument. In a startling, ambiguous image, Bergman has the couple's daughter (he replaces the play's three children with one girl) creep quietly into the bedroom and stand as silent witness to this horrifying—yet somehow promising—primal scene. Nora then makes her final escape from her suffocating home/stage by fleeing into the audience.

The most thrilling Ibsen I've seen was Warner's *Hedda Gabler* at Dublin's Abbey Theater in 1991. Departing from two traditional takes on Hedda—solving the psychological puzzle of her enigmatic personality, or presenting her as simply unimaginable within the terms of her society—Warner and actress Fiona Shaw sculpted a muscular hero who was all too imaginable within her constraining world. Like many before her, Warner introduced Hedda in a silent prologue. (Shaw prowled the stage in the wee hours of the night, checking her nightgown for signs of her period, striking her belly, and weeping with pregnancy.) Hedda was portrayed not as a monster, but neither as a didactic victim of a society that offers her no options but motherhood. The production was played at a breath-taking pitch, with an all-out but controlled eruption of emotion. Tesman hovered near hysteria as he realized that, financially, he was in over his head. Løvborg was virtually operatic in his grief. Most exciting, Thea became a gathering force of strength and action, a potent contrast to Hedda's entrapment.

As for Shaw, she was an elegant wild horse refusing to be broken. She hauled furniture around the stage, flinging chairs here and there as if trying to make her domestic prison—and theatrical jail—somehow inhabitable, as if trying to break through its frame. With each scene, the room became sparser and sparser. The final moments were played on an almost barren stage. When Hedda burned Løvborg's manuscript, rather than deliberately peeling it apart, sheaf by sheaf, she hurled it into the fireplace in a single, desperate gesture. When she gave Løvborg one of her pistols, the act was as shocking as it was inevitable. By the last act, the accumulated tension had reached a level that was absolutely unbearable. I found myself not only waiting for Hedda's gun to go off, but wishing for it, longing, like Hedda, for the release that this final blast would bring. When Judge Brack remarked "People don't *do* such things" (Fjelde, 778), he might as well have been talking about Ibsen. It's no way to end a play—unless, as Warner and Shaw so stirringly demonstrated, it's the only way. And Ibsen was the only one to do it—in *Hedda Gabler* as in *A Doll House*.

Works Cited

Archer, William. "The Theatre." *World* (April 27, 1892): 22.

----------. "Lyric Theatre, Ibsen in Italian." *Daily Graphic* (June 10, 1893): 7.

Bennett, Benjamin. *Modern Drama and German Classicism*. Ithaca, N.Y.: Cornell University Press, 1979.

Brustein, Robert. *The Theatre of Revolt: Studies in Ibsen, Strindberg, Chekhov, Shaw, Brecht, Pirandello, O'Neill, and Genet*. New York: Atlantic-Little Brown, 1962.

----------. "The Fate of Ibsenism." In Brustein's *Critical Moments: Reflections on Theatre and Society, 1973–1979*. New York: Random House, 1980. 124-138.

Cardullo, R. J. *Understanding Drama: A Student Companion*. Delhi: Primus Books, 2022.

Cima, Gay Gibson. *Performing Women: Female Characters, Male Playwrights, and the Modern Stage*. Ithaca, N.Y.: Cornell University Press, 1993.

Craig, Edward Gordon. *On the Art of the Theatre*. 1911. New York: Theatre Arts Books, 1957.

Davis, Jill. "The New Woman and the New Life." In *The New Woman and Her Sisters: Feminism and Theater, 1850–1914*. Ed. Vivian Gardner & Susan Rutherford. Ann Arbor: University of Michigan Press, 1992. 17–36.

Davis, Rick. "Buried Truths to Light: Mel Shapiro on *Hedda Gabler*, Charles Ludlam, and Other Classics." *The Repertory Reader: Newsletter of the American Ibsen Theater*, 1.3 (Spring 1984): 2-3.

Davis, Tracy C. "Acting in Ibsen." *Theatre Notebook*, 39.3 (1985): 113-123.

----------. *Actresses As Working Women: Their Sexual Identity in Victorian Culture*. London: Routledge, 1991.

Donahue, Joseph. "Women in Victorian Theatre, Images, Illusions, Realities." In *Gender in Performance: The Presentation of Difference in the Performing Arts*. Ed. Laurence Senelick. Hanover, N.H.: University Press of New England, 1992. 117–140.

Egan, Michael, ed. *Ibsen: The Critical Heritage*. London: Routledge & Kegan Paul, 1972.

Finney, Gail. *Women in Modern Drama: Freud, Feminism, and European Theater at the Turn of the Century*. Ithaca, N.Y.: Cornell University Press, 1989.

Fjelde, Rolf, trans. *Ibsen: The Complete Major Prose Plays*. New York: Plume/New American Library, 1978.

----------. "Introduction to *Hedda Gabler*." In *Ibsen: The Complete Major Prose Plays*. Trans. Rolf Fjelde. New York: Plume/New American Library, 1978. 690-692.

Fuchs, Elinor. "Mythic Structure in *Hedda Gabler*: The Mask Behind the Face." *Comparative Drama*, 19.3 (Fall, 1985): 209-221.

Gardner, Vivian, & Susan Rutherford, eds. *The New Woman and Her Sisters: Feminism and Theater, 1850–1914*. Ann Arbor: University of Michigan Press, 1992.

Gilman, Richard. *The Making of Modern Drama*. New York: Farrar, Straus, & Giroux, 1974.

Holtan, Orley I. *Mythic Patterns in Ibsen's Last Plays*. Minneapolis: University of Minnesota Press, 1970.

Ibsen, Henrik. *Letters and Speeches*. Ed. Evert Sprinchorn. New York: Hill & Wang, 1964.

----------. *Four Major Plays*. Trans. James W. McFarlane. New York: Oxford University Press, 1981.

Johnston, Brian. *To the Third Empire: Ibsen's Early Drama*. Minneapolis: University of Minnesota Press, 1980.

----------. *Text and Supertext in Ibsen's Drama*. University Park: Pennsylvania State University Press, 1989.

----------. "The Turning Point in *The Lady from the Sea*." In Johnston's *Text and Supertext in Ibsen's Drama*. University Park: Pennsylvania State University Press, 1989. 193-234.

----------. *The Ibsen Cycle: The Design of the Plays from "Pillars of Society" to "When We Dead Awaken"*. Rev. ed. University Park: Pennsylvania State University Press, 1992.

Mandel, Siegfried, ed. & trans. *Ibsen's Heroines*. New York: Proscenium/Limelight, 1989.

Matthews, John F., ed. *Shaw's Dramatic Criticism, 1895-1898*. New York: Hill & Wang, 1959.

Meyer, Michael. *Henrik Ibsen*. Vol. 2: The Farewell to Poetry, 1862–1882. London: Granada Publishing, 1971.

----------. *Henrik Ibsen*. Vol. 3: The Top of a Cold Mountain, 1883–1906. London: Granada Publishing, 1971.

Shaw, George Bernard. "Appendix to *The Quintessence of Ibsenism*" (1891). In *Shaw on Theatre*. Ed. E. J. West. New York: Hill & Wang, 1958. 1-18.

Styan, J. L. *Modern Drama in Theory and Practice*. Vol. 1, Realism and Naturalism. Cambridge, U.K.: Cambridge University Press, 1981.

Templeton, Joan. "The *Doll House* Backlash: Criticism, Feminism, and Ibsen." *PMLA*, 104.1 (Jan. 1989): 28-40.

Weigand, Herman. *The Modern Ibsen: A Reconsideration*. New York: Holt, 1925.

"The Mystery of Shaw's *Candida*"

Candida and Mystery

George Bernard Shaw's *Candida* (1894) was first performed at the Theatre Royal, South Shields, on March 30, 1895; it was revived by the Independent Theatre Company, at Her Majesty's, Aberdeen, on July 30, 1897. *Candida* was first performed in London at the Stage Society, The Strand, on July 1, 1900. However, it was not until late 1903, when Arnold Daly mounted a production in New York, that the play became a success. Daly's production was quickly followed by another one in London: the first public performance in London occurred on April 26, 1904, at the Royal Court. Yet, for all this attention to *Candida*—it was so popular that the phenomenon became known as "Candidamania"—Shaw felt that the play had been misinterpreted by some of its public. As a result, he wrote his short 1904 comedy *How He Lied to Her Husband*—which depicts a farcical version of the same situation—as a kind of reply to *Candida*. Whence did such misinterpretation of the latter play derive? Perhaps in part from Shaw's own subtitling of it as "A Mystery."

Elsie B. Adams was the first to take Shaw's subtitle to mean that *Candida* is "a modern mystery play of the Madonna and Child, which will be performed in the modern equivalent to the medieval cathedral, the theatre where the catholic religion of Creative Evolution lives" (Adams, 437). Indeed, Candida is the name of a first-century Neapolitan Saint recognized by both the Catholic Church and the Church of England. The young poet Eugene Marchbanks himself raises the Candida of the play to the level of the Virgin Mother in his own mind, and both he and her husband, Reverend Morell, are children to her, the one to be educated for passage into the mysterious night—according to Shaw, the "true realm of the poet"—the other to be coddled within the sanctuary of marriage. (Following the Wagner of *Tristan and Isolde* (1865), Shaw described night as the "true realm of the poet" in a 1920 letter concerning the "secret" of *Candida* [Riding, 506; Stanton, 168].)

The truth about Candida, however, as Morell's secretary, Prossy, says in Act I, is that "she's got good hair and a tolerable figure" (*Candida*, 99), and is "very nice, very good-hearted" (*Candida*, 100). Candida's name in secular usage (the English Word "candid" comes from the Latin *candidus*, meaning "white" or "bright") suggests that she is a figure, not of mystery, but of accessibility: she is open in her knowledge and openly knowable. The eighteen-year-old prodigal Marchbanks, in need of an illusion with which to fall in love and embrace as his own, poeticizes her, only to discover at the end of the play that the woman he enshrined as an earthly variant of Titian's Virgin is rather an efficient homemaker and caring wife, the participant in a relationship in which she needs her husband (for her defense, livelihood, and dignity, as he puts it [*Candida*, 157]) as much as he needs her. Realizing that there is no glorification of woman possible in marriage, Marchbanks chooses to live freely outside the stultifying, compromising happiness of its bonds and attain exaltation through devotion to his art and reverence for female beauty.

This is the "secret heart" (*Candida*, 160) that Shaw refers to in the last stage direction, and of which Candida and Morell are both ignorant. She knows that Marchbanks "has learnt to live without happiness" (*Candida*, 159); she does not know that he predicates his ability to create great art on his unhappy existence, on the frustrations and tensions that he will simultaneously transfigure and defuse in his work. Candida cannot perceive this, since she has no real interest in art and how it is made. Indeed, *Candida* is a modern mystery to the extent that it celebrates the birth of a poet's art. Just as the medieval mystery plays focused on the life, death, and resurrection of Christ, Shaw's drama centers on the life and death of the boy Marchbanks and his rebirth as a man, as an artist. The mysteries juxtaposed paganism against Christianity, temporal happiness against eternal peace; *Candida* juxtaposes life against art, joint marital comfort against self-dramatization or self-transmutation. Candida and Morell, unbeknownst to them, thus become Marchbanks's spiritual mother and father, and they are comparable in their ignorance to Joseph, if not to Mary.

For reasons of health as well as for practical theatrical and artistic ones, Shaw had Candida leave her two children behind, ill, when she returns to London in the play: he was an outspoken critic of the exploitation of child actors; always a careful theater man, he was keeping *Candida*'s cast to a manageable size by excluding the children; and, as long as their existence was established, the children were not needed onstage—they would not be useful to this drama as Shaw conceived it. The effect of their exclusion, however, as opposed to Shaw's immediate reasons for it, is to emphasize Candida and her husband's role as *Marchbanks's* parents.

On the surface, moreover, it appears that the dramatist made Morell a pastor partly out of irony: this man of the cloth fathers, not his likeness, not a servant of God, but a man of letters. In fact, to return to Adams's equation of the theater with a modern cathedral, Morell fathers a modern Jesus, an artist-genius who discerns "the distant light of the new age" and "keeps on building up his masterpieces until their pinnacles catch the glint of the unrisen sun" (Preface, *Plays Pleasant*: 9). Morell himself is the one to point out, in the play, that art has something in common with religion: "I well know that it is in the poet that the holy spirit of man—the god within him—is most godlike" (*Candida*, 116). And as the servant of Shaw's new catholic religion, Creative Evolution, Marchbanks will have the responsibility, in Adams's words, "to represent through his art a vision of a world not yet evolved" (Adams, 432).

Art, Shaw, and Religious Drama

By depicting the artist as a Christ figure and presenting his birth in the form of a mystery play, Shaw pays homage to the religious drama of the Middle Ages in addition to arguing for Creative Evolution as the religion of the twentieth century and for artists as prophets. The medieval period, he believed, created the last great art before the Renaissance because it provided "an iconography for a live religion" (Preface, *Back to Methuselah*: lxxix); with the Renaissance came religious skepticism and a resultant decline in the quality of art. Shakespeare, Shaw writes,

> could not become the conscious iconographer of a religion because he had no conscious religion. He had therefore to exercise his extraordinary natural gifts in the very entertaining art of mimicry, giving us the famous "delineation of character" which makes his plays . . . so delightful. Also, he developed that curious and questionable art of building us a refuge from despair by disguising the cruelties of Nature as jokes. . . . He would really not be great at all if it were not that he had religion enough to be aware that his religionless condition was one of despair. (Preface, *Back to Methuselah*: lxxxii-lxxxiii)

"Ever since Shakespeare," Shaw continues, "playwrights have been struggling with the same lack of religion" (Preface, *Back to Methuselah*: lxxxiii). He includes among them the two giants of his own time, Ibsen and Strindberg, who "refused [their audiences] even the Shakespearian-Dickensian consolation of laughter at mischief, accurately called comic relief" (Preface, *Back to Methuselah*: lxxxiv).

Although Elsie B. Adams perceives that *Candida* is a modern mystery play of the Madonna and Child, she neglects to see the other ways in which it either imitates or extends the form of the medieval mystery. She also gives short shrift in her essay to what I shall call the secularly mysterious aspects of Shaw's play, over which many critics have puzzled and which they have taken as the sole evidence for its subtitle. It is my contention that Shaw carefully interweaves secular *and* sacred mystery in *Candida*: that he introduces mysterious elements into the action, thereby raising questions about the plot whose answers come or are underlined, paradoxically, in the fulfillment of drama's sacred mystery.

Marchbanks introduces the first element of mystery into the play: we want to know what this eighteen-year-old disheveled aristocrat is doing in the home of Reverend and Mrs. James Morell. They have children of their own and are busy enough looking after them and Morell's congregation; therefore why would they take a stranger in? In response the question of her father, Burgess, about Marchbanks's identity, Candida says, "Oh, Eugene's ones of James's discoveries. He found him sleeping on the Embankment last June" (*Candida*, 108). For what, then, has Morell discovered Marchbanks? What plans does the pastor have for the young man?

It should be clear from their confrontation before lunch in Act I that Morell wishes to domesticate Marchbanks, to set an example for him, to demonstrate to him that marriage and the family unit are the ideal state in which to live. Morell may not have been conscious of his purpose when he first brought the young man into his house, but he seems to be conscious of it by the time Candida and Eugene return to London. The pastor tells his young charge at one point, "I'm very fond of you, my boy; and I should like you to see for yourself what a happy thing it is to be married as I am" (*Candida*, 113). At another point, Morell declares, "Some day, I hope and trust, you will be a happy man like me. You will be married; and you will be working with all your might and valor to make every spot on earth as happy as your own home" (*Candida*, 116).

Ironically, Marchbanks falls in love with the pastor's own wife; equally ironically, Eugene learns through his relationship with her and her husband that marriage is not for him. That he elects at the end of the play to live the solitary life of an artist instead of ever taking a wife is the final indication that his entire education in the Morell household has tended toward the making of this choice: it was laid before him there (and there is no evidence that he had considered marriage before meeting the Morells), he discerned it, and he made his decision. Now that his education is complete, he may leave. Analogous in some ways to Christ's mission to go to earth and incarnate the sacred mystery that is God, Marchbanks's mission will be to plunge into the night and intimate, through his art, the mystery that is a perfect world. In order to do this he must, like Christ, remain single: marriage must not be allowed to interfere with his idealization of women, love, and beauty, which is in the service of his very idealization of a future world.

The second element of mystery in the play concerns the rivalry between Morell and Marchbanks for Candida's love. The drama would appear to lie, as in conventional romantic comedy, in that rivalry. But there can be little question that Candida's love is not someone's for the taking. As she herself says in Act II,

> Ah, James, how little you understand me, to talk of your confidence in my goodness and purity! I would give them both to poor Eugene as willingly as I would give my shawl to a beggar dying of cold, if there were nothing else to restrain me. Put your trust in my love for you, James, for if that went, I should care very little for your sermons—mere phrases that you cheat yourself and others with every day. (*Candida*, 135)

The play is a mystery, then, to the extent that Marchbanks is never a serious contender for Candida's love, yet manages to precipitate a spiritual crisis in the Morell marriage.

The crisis occurs because, as Candida makes clear, the pastor misunderstands the nature of his wife's love for him, believing that "it was [in the pulpit] that [he] earned my golden moment, and the right, in that moment, to ask her to love me" (*Candida*, 46). Morell thinks that Candida married him for his vocation, and that she is bound to him, in goodness and purity, out of duty and obligation. Thus, when Marchbanks implies toward the end of Act I that Candida merely tolerates the moralist (or Morell-ist) and windbag in her husband, the pastor feels that his marriage is threatened, that he may lose his wife to the young poet. Uncannily, as if in anticipation of this crisis in his marriage, Morell had telegraphed *before* the play to the Guild of St. Matthew to say that he would not be able to speak on the evening of the day Candida comes home. (The telegram from the Guild to which he responds in Act II is their urgent request that he change his mind; his reply here is therefore not his initial breaking of the speaking engagement as a result of his clash with Marchbanks on Act I, as is often thought, but a reiteration of the earlier cancellation.)

Aside from being mysterious in the secular sense, the trouble in the Morell marriage adds up to a religious mystery, as well. The Roman Catholic and Eastern churches recognize marriage as one of seven sacraments (actually called mysteries in the latter church), which are certain acts, ceremonies, or practices distinguished from all others among Christian rites as having been instigated by Christ as the visible means by which divine grace is sought and conferred. The

Church of England, of which Morell is a clergyman, officially accepts only two sacraments, baptism and Holy Communion; nevertheless, it naturally recognizes marriage, as the following declaration by the Anglican bishop in *Getting Married* (1908) indicates: "To me there is only one marriage that is holy: the Church's sacrament of marriage" (*Candida*, 236).

Morell himself gives marriage the quality of a sacrament when in Act I he says to his assistant, the young curate Lexy, "Ah, my boy, get married; get married to a good woman; and then you'll understand. That's a foretaste of what will be best in the Kingdom of Heaven we are trying to establish on earth" (*Candida*, 98). The pastor says virtually the same thing to Marchbanks later in the same act: "[In marriage] you will be one of the makers of the Kingdom of Heaven on earth" (*Candida*, 116). By the end of the play the Morell marriage itself is reborn or reconfirmed, having found its true identity in the charity and humility espoused by Jesus Christ. In Candida and James's final embrace—their sacred union, as it were—the secular mystery of their marital crisis is dispelled once and for all.

Triangles, Realistic and Mysterious

Burgess introduces the third element of mystery into *Candida*: we want to know why he is visiting his daughter and her husband for the first time in three years. He says that he has come out of "family sentiment" (*Candida*, 104): that he wants to make up the quarrel he had with James over the low wages he, Burgess, was paying to his workers. Morell does not believe him and finally declares, "Come now: either take your hat and go; or else sit down and give me a good scoundrelly reason for wanting to be friends with me. That's right. Now out with it" (*Candida*, 106). But Burgess does not give his son-in-law a good scoundrelly reason; instead he avoids the issue by flattering Morell, by saying that he now thinks more highly of clergymen than he once did and has come to tell James so.

Burgess is telling the truth: he now does think more highly of clergymen—but only because they have been gaining influence in the business world. He wants to reconcile with Morell so that the latter will introduce him to some big jobbers. The pastor suspects this, and we learn it when Burgess is invited to hear him speak before the Guild of St. Matthew (James decides to give the talk after all) but declines to do go until Morell says that his father-in-law can meet the "chairman" there. This man is a member of the Works Committee of the County Council and therefore has some influence in the awarding of contracts. Candida's father treats the chairman, Lexy, and Prossy to a champagne supper after Morell's speech, virtually assuring that he will receive favorable treatment from the Works Committee in the future.

Burgess thus leaves his daughter's house having achieved exactly what he came for. The irony is that he has been encouraged in the pursuit of her husband's friendship and its advantages by Morell himself. Burgess has been encouraged, that is, in the open and honest pursuit of his capitalistic deviltry by a Christian Socialist. Morell tells his father-in-law, "So long as you come here honestly as a self-respecting, thorough, convinced scoundrel, justifying your scoundrelism and proud of it, you are welcome. . . . I like a man to be true to himself, even in wickedness" (*Candida*, 105-106). Like Marchbanks and like the Morell marriage, Burgess himself is reborn at the conclusion of *Candida*—not as a repentant Christian, but as a confirmed devil. He is comparable to the devil in the medieval mystery plays, as I intend to demonstrate, but, unlike them, he gets no comeuppance in the end. In the gradual reassertion of his deviltry, in fact, Burgess clears up the mystery of his sudden appearance in the Morell home.

In addition to being a mystery figure in his own right, Burgess forms, together with Lexy and Prossy, the "realistic" triangle in the play to Marchbanks's, Morell's and Candida's "mysterious" triangle. In this role the former three are not so different from the realistic figures in medieval mysteries, the purpose of whom was threefold: (1) precisely to provide an element of realism or "recognition" with which audiences seeking diversion as well as instruction could identify; (2) to put the figures of the actual mystery play in perspective; and (3) to place the devil in the comic-realistic guise of at least one dramatic character.

Alfred Turco, Jr., has described the "mysterious" triangle in *Candida* as follows:

> Morell embodies genial affection and vigorous dedication to a goal, marred by lack of awareness concerning his true position in both home and pulpit. Candida exemplifies material insight and household wisdom divorced from appreciation of such higher matters as her husband's socialism or her suitor's poetry. While Marchbanks is undeniably a weak personality in some respects, the contrasts to Morell's sentimentality and Candida's mundaneness underscore his comparative toughness of mind and force of imagination. (*Shaw's Moral Vision*, 103)

The "realistic" triangle in the play could be described in contrasting terms. Lexy idolizes Morell and, ironically, enables us to take the latter seriously, for all his pontificating, because he, Lexy, is a pale, comic imitator of his mentor. The unmarried Prossy is in love (from a distance) with Morell, and for this reason is able to see her "rival" with piercing eyes: as she says, "[I] can appreciate [Candida's] *real* qualities far better than any man can" (*Candida*, 100; emphasis mine). Burgess obviously does not worship Morell—he wants to use him; and his very earthly and earthly presence in his daughter's home is, in effect, an argument against the idealization of her by both her husband and Marchbanks. Burgess, Lexy, and Prossy form, I hasten to add, a triangle by default. In contrast with the Marchbanks-Morell-Candida triangle, there is no romantic love among its members. Prossy tells us that Lexy thinks her "dowdy and second rate enough" (*Candida*, 99), and Burgess believes that both of them, as employees of his son-in-law, should be kept in their place.

Marchbanks vs. Burgess

The devilish Burgess, as the Christ-like Marchbanks's opposite in the play, deserves discussion in greater detail. Jacob H. Adler, sensing the mystery of Marchbanks's disruption of the Morell household, has written that "Shaw's whole story is very close to much ado about nothing" (*Candida*, 57). He adds that "the presence of a character [Burgess] who feels this way himself is disarming" (*Candida*, 57). Burgess's response to Morell's sermonizing, Marchbanks's "poetic horrors" (which he gets when he realizes that Candida does menial chores along with the servants), and his daughter's independence of mind is to conclude that all three characters are mad, since they grossly overstate their complaints or opinions. He thus functions as a comic devil who cannot take seriously the "mysteries" unfolding before him, or who simply does not understand them. Candida's father is funny precisely because he combines equal amounts of ignorance and arrogance in the same character.

Like the devil figures of medieval mystery plays, who often were composites of the worst sins that the audience could commit, Burgess is a stand-in for any audience of *Candida*, from Shaw's day to our own, as his name indicates. *Les bourgeois* identify with Burgess. (The archaic meaning of "burgess," derived from Middle English, is "an inhabitant of a town or borough with full rights of citizenship.") This is not to say we completely identify with his point of view on the action—we cannot, the most important reason for this being that he is not onstage at the crucial moments in the Marchbanks-Morell-Candida story. What Burgess does is to drain off our own devilish disbelief in the feasibility of Marchbanks's assault on the Morell marriage. As Adler puts it, "Paradoxically enough, the audience can take events [onstage] more seriously, precisely because Burgess does not" (*Candida*, 57). He pulls us back from the action, so that we can observe it for the insights it contains into marriage—between male and female, on the one hand, and between the artist and his muse, on the other.

If Burgess pulls us back from the action, representing the comically objective point of view on it, Marchbanks takes us into the action, personifying subjective submersion in it. Their opposition is reinforced, paradoxically, by their similarities: both are outsiders—Burgess by virtue of having been estranged from his daughter and her family for three years—and both are alone. Marchbanks is estranged from his own family and has been living outdoors; Burgess has been living by himself in the house he once shared with Candida. (He never mentions his wife, who we may assume is dead, or any other family members.) The two men are at opposite ends of the play's social ladder, however, with the young aristocrat at the top and the old Cockney at the bottom. And they pursue mutually exclusive interests: the one, art for humanity's sake; the other, commerce for money's sake. When they meet for the first time, Marchbanks nearly runs away from Burgess, so dissimilar are they in motive, temperament, appearance, and social station.

Marchbanks has been sleeping on the Embankment (a road and river-walk along the north bank of the River Thames in London), and "in [his] garments he has apparently lain in the heather and waded through the waters" (*Candida*, 109). He was originally called Majoribanks, but this was shortened by Shaw to what would be heard in normal pronunciation. "Majoribanks," it's true, would have offered upper-class echoes to Shaw's audiences, since the name was a familiar one in Victorian life, in both society and government; that Eugene was the nephew of an earl would nonetheless have been believable from his name, despite its blurring by Shaw for the sake of production.

Burgess is clearly Marchbanks's opposite in origin, a Cockney elevated by money into a petty bourgeois. He has been sleeping in his own large house, attended by a servant: the petty bourgeois has enclosed himself in comfort and plenty. (Another origin of "burgess" is the old French "burgeis," meaning a castle or fortified town.) Whereas Burgess dismisses as madness what he cannot understand about his daughter and her husband, Marchbanks takes Morell and Candida very seriously and finally penetrates to their core. He is utterly sincere and completely without humor, Burgess, by contrast, is most insincere and likes a good laugh. Ironically, Marchbanks forgets, in his worship of Candida, that she is a Burgess—her father's daughter, and so named before she acquired through marriage the surname of Morell. It would not have occurred to Eugene that the Virgin Mother herself was of lowly birth, but it would have occurred to Shaw.

The Poet, the Pastor, and the Businessman, or Creative Evolution, Christian Socialism, and Free-Market Capitalism

Perhaps as a deliberate Shavian paradox, *Candida* employs the form of a mystery play to present three "faiths": those of marriage, art, and capitalism. It even makes room for an additional faith nearly heretical to true religion: worship of another mortal, as practiced by Lexy and Prossy toward Morell. The play is hardly a vindication of Victorian marriage, as its original audiences believed, but neither is it a total rejection of marriage as an institution in favor of the solitary pursuit of an artistic vision. *Candida* is not an apology for Burgess's capitalism, either, but it is also not a denunciation of his money-grabbing in favor of selfless devotion to a higher cause. Rather, the play's balanced, humanitarian view simultaneously stresses the necessity of the comparative safety and restricted bliss of domestic life for some people, and the requirement of others that they have the unchecked freedom to plumb the depths of holy, artistic night; the need for some to live their lives in the service or imitation of another, for others to dedicate their energies to self-aggrandizement, to making themselves wealthy and powerful.

As Elsie B. Adams has written, "Religion to Shaw does not signify orthodoxy or sectarianism. [His] Creative Evolution encompasses all sincerely held beliefs, including the Christian Socialism of Morell, the revolution doctrine of John Tanner [from *Man and Superman* (1903)], the Catholicism of Saint Joan [from the 1923 play of the same name], even the capitalism of Andrew Undershaft [from *Major Barbara* (1905)]" (Adams, 431-432: note). Shaw himself had the following to say about Creative Evolution:

> What hope is there then of human improvement? According to the Neo-Darwinists, to the Mechanists, no hope whatever, because improvement can come only through some senseless accident that must, on the statistical average of accidents, be presently wiped out by some other equally senseless accident.

> But this dismal creed does not discourage those who believe that the impulse that produces evolution is creative. They have observed the simple fact that the will to do anything can and does, at a certain pitch of intensity set up by conviction of its necessity, create and organize new tissue to do it with. (Preface to *Back to Methuselah*: xvi)
>
> . . .
>
> Creative Evolution is already a religion, and is indeed now unmistakably the religion of the twentieth century, newly arisen from the ashes of pseudo-Christianity, of mere skepticism, and of the soulless affirmations and blind negations of the Mechanists and Neo-Darwinians. (Preface to *Back to Methuselah*: lxxviii)

Shaw believed that the drive of the will was toward ultimate good. Thus any sincere manifestation of it, even if it appeared evil on the surface (as capitalism does to many), would ultimately contribute to the improvement of the human condition. Artists like Marchbanks may be in the vanguard of Creative Evolution, but they are not the only soldiers in its army. Hence, in addition to Marchbanks, the Morell marriage and Burgess are reborn at the end of this mystery play. The poet, the pastor, and the businessman have each learned to live in self-knowledge instead of self-deception—in candidness, if you will, rather than contrivance.

Works Cited

Adams, Elsie B. "Bernard Shaw's Pre-Raphaelite Drama." *PMLA*, 81.5 (1966): 428-438.

Adler, Jacob H. "Ibsen, Shaw, and *Candida*." *Journal of English and Germanic Philology*, 59.1 (Jan. 1960): 50-58.

Adler, Thomas P. "*Candida* as a 'Mystery'." *Shaw: The Annual of Bernard Shaw Studies*, 2 (1982): 13-15.

Bergman, Herbert. "Comedy in *Candida*." *Shavian*, 4.5 (Spring 1972): 161-169.

Berst, Charles A. "The Craft of *Candida*." *College Literature* 1.3 (1974): 157-173.

Doan, William J. "*Candida*: The Eye on Duty." *Shaw: The Annual of Bernard Shaw Studies*, 22 (2002): 131-147.

Finney, Gail. "Motherhood, Power, and Powerlessness: The New Woman as Madonna; Shaw's *Candida*." In Finney's *Women in Modern Drama: Freud,*

Feminism, and European Theater at the Turn of the Century. Ithaca, N.Y.: Cornell University Press, 1989. 185-206.

Holt, Charles Loyd. "*Candida*: The Music of Ideas." *The Shaw Review*, 9.1 (1966): 2-14.

Huneker, James. "The Truth about *Candida*." *Metropolitan Magazine*, 20 (1904): 632-636.

King, Walter N. "The Rhetoric of *Candida*." *Modern Drama*, 2.2 (Sept. 1959): 71-83. Anthologized in Stanton, 243-258.

Lauter, Paul. "*Candida* and *Pygmalion*: Shaw's Subversion of Stereotypes." *The Shaw Review*, 3.3 (1960): 14-19.

Lazenby, Walter. "Love and 'Vitality' in *Candida*." *Modern Drama*, 20.1 (1977): 1-19.

Nethercot, Arthur. "The Truth about *Candida*." *PMLA*, 64.4 (1949): 639-647.

Riding, George A. "The *Candida* Secret." *The Spectator*, 185 (Nov. 17, 1950): 506.

Shaw, George Bernard. *Getting Married* (1908). In Shaw's *The Doctor's Dilemma, Getting Married,* and *The Shewing-up of Blanco Posnet*. London: Constable, 1911.

----------. Preface to *Back to Methuselah*. London: Constable, 1921.

----------. Preface. *Plays Pleasant*. New York: Penguin, 1946. 7-16.

----------. *Candida* (1894). In Shaw's *Plays Pleasant*. New York: Penguin, 1946.

Stanton, Stephen S., ed. *A Casebook on* Candida. New York: Thomas Y. Crowell, 1962.

Storm, William. "Irony and Dialectic: Shaw's *Candida*." Ch. 3 in Storm's *Irony and the Modern Theatre*. New York: Cambridge University Press, 2011. 73-103.

Turco, Jr., Alfred. *Shaw's Moral Vision: The Self and Salvation*. Ithaca, N.Y.: Cornell University Press, 1976.

Woodfield, James. "Shaw's *Candida*: A Comedy." *English Studies in Canada*, 16.4 (Dec. 1990): 433-452.

Yarrison, Betsy C. "Marchbanks as 'Albatros': An Interpretation of *Candida*." *The Shaw Review*, 20.2 (1977): 71-82.

"A World in Transition: A Study of Brecht's *A Man's a Man*"

Changeable Character

In his article "Brecht's Concept of Character," Walter Sokel writes that

> . . . from the beginning Brecht was unable to accept the concept of dramatic character as the ultimate, absolute, and fate-determining quality which it had been for the traditional European drama, "the drama of Renaissance and classicism," as Peter Szondi called it. He had to reject it because that concept is rooted in the religious and metaphysical idea of an indivisible and eternal soul. (Sokel, 177)

Brecht had to reject such a concept because it is also rooted in the idea of an unchangeable world. The drama of Renaissance and classicism accepts the world as it is, and the focus of this drama becomes a man's suffering because of his flaws, because of "human nature." Man may change at the end of the great Western tragedies in the sense that he learns something significant about himself. But his knowledge almost always comes too late, since he gets it in dying or in experiencing some other form of great misfortune. And it is generally not the kind of knowledge from which audience members can profit, though they may have been purged emotionally by watching the protagonist's journey from darkness to light. The likelihood is that they themselves will have to go through a similar experience in order to learn similarly.

Brecht wanted, according to Sokel, to portray "permanent changeability in place of unity and consistency of characters. [His] characters are 'without qualities,' or rather, are equipped with changeable, exchangeable, and mutually contradictory traits" (Sokel, 178). Brecht wanted to portray permanently or fundamentally changeable characters whose change came about less through some internal process, from what is called "tragic recognition," than from some change in their environment or circumstances. He wished to take the focus away from the internal man in an unchanging world and place it on the external man, the one of observable actions rather than hidden motivations, in a world changed by this individual and others. This, Brecht thought, was the only way in which the world, specifically the capitalist- and imperialist-dominated one, could be changed: by showing that man is not tragically isolated from an unchangeable and insensate society, but rather is a product of the societal conditions under which he lives. A change in them for the better, according to Brecht, should lead to a change for the better in so-called immutable human nature, an improvement in the relations of human beings with one another. A change for the worse, or no change at all in already bad conditions, as in *A Man's a Man* (*Mann ist Mann*, 1926), can lead only to further deterioration in the relations among men. Unless, that is, *a man* takes action. What is important for Brecht is that man himself must make the changes in the social system that are going to improve his life. They will not occur miraculously.

A Man's a Man is the first play Brecht wrote in which man is portrayed as changeable. Galy Guy is a poor Irish porter in British India in 1925 who, as a result of his poverty and "soft nature," is turned into a human fighting machine whose nature is so hard that he can destroy 7,000 refugees and declare, "But what's that to me?" (*Man's a Man*, 70). Brecht is at pains to point out that Guy changes, or is led into change, not only because he is good-natured and open to experience, but also because he is a member of an exploitative (colonial) economic system. He may buy a cucumber from Widow Begbick, for example, because he does not want to disappoint her, even though he had originally gone out to buy a fish. But the point is that he is placed in the position of buying the cucumber by the porter's work he does for Begbick in order to earn extra money.

Guy is very poor, he has "nothing to lose," as Uriah says (*Man's a Man*, 29), so throughout the play he places himself in progressively more vulnerable positions where he can earn money or refreshment. He goes with the soldiers to Begbick's canteen at first only in return for a cigar. Then, "as a docker [porter] . . . obliged to look after [his] own interests in any situation" (*Man's a Man*, 17), he bargains for five boxes of cigars and eight bottles of beer as payment for answering the absent Jeraiah Jip's name at roll call. Finally, Guy grabs at a share in a business deal that involves an elephant, for to own such a great beast of burden is, as any porter knows, a gold mine. Once he gets the elephant, however, Widow Begbick talks him into selling it to her; he is only too happy to do so, since it is obviously not a real elephant and can be of no use to him.

This is the turning point of the play: Guy has been set up by Uriah, Jesse, and Polly. They have exploited his poverty, for they knew that he would take the fake elephant for a real one as long as there was a buyer for it. Now he is to be shot "for sealing an army elephant and selling it, which is theft; [and] for selling an elephant that wasn't an elephant, which is fraud" (*Man's a Man*, 47). The soldiers make Guy think that he is actually going to die, and even fire into the air at the execution after he has fainted out of fright, just so he can hear that he is "dead." They want him to give up the identity of Galy Guy and assume that of Jeraiah Jip, the fourth member of their detachment whom they lost while looting a pagoda, because without a replacement they will be discovered as thieves.

Wise Man, No Tragedy

Walter Benjamin himself called Galy Guy a wise man:

> He introduces himself as a docker "who doesn't drink, smokes very little, and hasn't any passions to speak of." He is not tempted by the offer of sex with the widow whose basket he has carried. "To be frank, I'd really like to buy some fish." Yet he is introduced as a man "who can't say no." And this too is wise, for he lets the contradictions of existence enter into the only place where they can, in the last analysis, be resolved: the life of a man. Only the "consenting" man has any chance of changing the world. (Benjamin, 8-9)

Unlike Sergeant Fairchild, Galy Guy lets the contradictions of existence enter into his life. Sergeant Fairchild is a strict disciplinarian, a man of order, who cannot tolerate the enormous sensuality within himself. Because he cannot, and because he gives in to it and goes to see Widow Begbick in his black suit and bowler hat, as she asks, he eventually shoots off his "manhood." He will be troubled by sensuality and women no more, but he will also have lost his instinct for battle. In the final scene, for instance, he ineffectually tries to stop Guy from knocking out the fortress of Sir el-Djowr. Guy hears Fairchild fire the shot that destroys his manhood on the troop-train bound for battle on the northern border, and it is this event more than any other that persuades him to assume Jeraiah Jip's identity—that of a murderous soldier—and like it, or else he might find himself dead or maimed.

Unlike a classical tragic hero, Guy will not kill himself or allow himself to be killed in order to avoid killing others as Jip. In this sense he is Benjamin's thinking or wise man as dramatic hero. He is in an untenable situation not entirely of his own making, when one considers his economic situation; he does not want to kill, and he does not want to be killed. He is in a tragic situation, but does not take tragic action. He does not destroy himself: he destroys others. Brecht exaggerates here to make his point. I think we should place less emphasis on Guy's destruction of the fort and the refugees than on the fact that he does not destroy himself. The knowledge that Guy gets in the course of the play—that "a name is uncertain, you can't build on a name" (*Man's a Man*, 63); that "one man is no man. Someone must call out to him" (*Man's a Man*, 56)—he finds himself applying to a terrible cause: the slaughter of 7,000 refugees. His knowledge is thereby defamiliarized and made to stand out all the more for us: for "knowledge is something we usually think of as being applied in a constructive way; here it is applied in a destructive manner.

What is important is the knowledge that Galy Guy gets. That he gets it, and then finds he has to murder poor people like himself because of it, is more a comment on the society that produced him and the conditions under which he must live than it is on him as an individual. This was indeed the view that Brecht came to have toward the end of his life. In his essay "On Looking Through My First Plays" (1954), he wrote:

> [In *A Man's a Man*] I had a socially negative hero who was by no means unsympathetically treated. the play's theme is the false, bad collectivity (the "gang") and its powers of attraction. . . . [Galy Guy's] growth into crime can certainly be shown, if only the performance is sufficiently alienating. (245)

In 1926 Brecht was more interested in stressing, in essentially the same work (*A Man's a Man*, like most of his plays, underwent several revisions), the positive attributes of the "collective," the positiveness of a man's sacrificing his identity for the good of the mass or the whole. "This Galy Guy," he writes in the preface to *A Man's a Man*,

> is by no means a weakling: on the contrary he is the strongest of all. That is to say he becomes the strongest once he has ceased to be a private person; he only becomes strong in the mass. And if the play finishes up with him conquering an entire fortress this is only because in doing so

> he is apparently carrying out the unqualified wish of a great mass of people who want to get through the narrow pass that the fortress guards. No doubt you will go on to say that it's a pity that a man should be tricked like this and simply forced to surrender his precious ego, all he possesses (as it were); but it isn't. It's a jolly business. For this Galy guy comes to no harm; he wins. And a man who adopts such an attitude is bound to win. (Willett, *Brecht on Theatre*: 19)

Understandably, at the time of the play's initial writing and production, Brecht saw the power to effect social change in the strength of the masses. What he overlooked in his zeal, incredibly, was that his Galy Guy joins a murderous mass intent on anything but social change to benefit the poor. However significant it is that Guy is portrayed as a changeable human being, his change *in the text* is still distinctly negative. Brecht grappled with this "problem play" throughout his career and only in 1954, it seems, realized that "[Galy Guy's] growth into crime can certainly be shown, if only the performance is sufficiently alienating" ("On Looking Through My First Plays," 245). A production of *A Man's a Man* must therefore stress Guy's changeability, but it must also stress the causes of his change and its immediate results.

Had Guy committed suicide rather than killed others, he would have been deemed "noble" from the point of view of Aristotelian tragedy. He may not be noble for what he does in Brecht's play, but he is wise: he has learned, and he is still *alive* and open to experience, so he may apply his knowledge eventually to changing the world. The tragic hero, by contrast, often takes his knowledge to the grave. The Brechtian wise or undramatic hero—who, precisely because he has so much knowledge, uses it in a way that is not immediately clear or does not have immediate consequences—remains alive at the end of the play, ready to admit yet another contradiction into his existence. (Benjamin writes that "the undramatic nature of the highest form of man—the sage—was clearly recognized by Plato a very long time ago" [17].)

The wise or undramatic hero is not unlike the Spanish *picaro*, who gains knowledge about the ways of the world—typically, the world of the city, to which he journeys from the country—and uses it in order to survive. The *picaro* adapts himself to a corrupt world that cannot be constructively changed, however; he sees it as such and resolves not to try obstinately to change it for the good of everyone, but to triumph over that same world for his own gain. Like the classical tragic hero, the *picaro* remains essentially isolated from society; like Galy Guy, he is untragic. Unlike the latter, though, he gives no hope for a new and better future.

Picaresque Hero

Surely Brecht was drawing on the picaresque tradition in creating Galy Guy—he drew on it in *The Threepenny Opera* (1928), which was written at about the same time as a *Man's a Man*, and he was to tap it again later in *Mother Courage and Her Children* (1941). Brecht's era was a time of profound social upheaval, like the second half of the sixteenth century. Harry Sieber has suggested how the earlier age gave birth to the term *picaro*, or at least to a new meaning for it:

> The Habsburg kings were committed to empire-building and waged war on a scale that the world had never seen before. Vast armies of Spanish pike-men (*picas secas* and/or *piqueros secos*, from the verb *picar*) had to be provisioned, garrisoned, transported, and occasionally paid to defend Spain's far-flung territories. Geoffrey Parker has recently assessed the difficulties the Spanish military faced in the late sixteenth century: "The increasing resort to criminals as a source of recruits can only have accentuated the innate unruliness of the troops, especially when the men were lodged in overcrowded private houses away from the supervision of their officers" [*The Army of Flanders and the Spanish Road, 1567-1659* (Cambridge, U.K.: Cambridge University Press, 1972), 180]. The efficiency of the Spanish military decreased in the second half of the century . . . deserting soldiers joined the ranks of other countries, but many attempted to return home, begging and stealing on the way. It is possible that some of the deserters carried their previous military title of *piquero* with them into "civilian" life. (Sieber, 6)

In the first half of the twentieth century—Brecht's precise era, as he lived from 1898 to 1956—war was waged (twice, from 1914-18 and 1939-45) on a scale never seen before, and there was a worldwide depression (1929-39). Human life became more expendable than it had ever been, and this is reflected in part by Galy Guy's exchange of one identity for another, as well as by his decision to kill others rather than be killed. Like the piqueros—the criminals recruited into the British army—he is recruited into the British army. Unlike them, he does not desert and turn to a life of stealing and vagrancy; forced to remain a soldier, Guy remains a wise man.

Changeable Structure

If Brecht rejects through the character of Galy Guy the idea of man as unchangeable or character as fixed, character-as-destiny, then he is careful to reject throughout *A Man's a Man* the idea of virtually anything as unchangeable. He creates an atmosphere of flux to support his idea of man and the world's being in flux. The very structure of the play stresses the idea of changeability. To wit: *A Man's a Man* consists of eleven scenes in seven different locations, not two or three acts in a single setting. The seven locales in India are Kilkoa (Galy Guy's flat); a street outside the Pagoda of the Yellow God; a highway between Kilkoa and the army camp; Widow Begbick's canteen; the interior of the pagoda; a train; and the battlefield before the mountain fortress of Sir el-Djowr. Significantly, the one locale that is repeated four times, Widow Begbick's canteen, is itself in a state of flux. Uriah promises Begbick that he and his men will pack it up for transport to the front if she tells Guy that she would like to buy his elephant.

As if to emphasize the slow taking apart of the canteen, Brecht takes apart Scene 9 itself, dividing it into five smaller scenes. By Scene 9, Number 4a, the canteen has been packed inside a wagon that will travel to the front, and by Scene 9, Number 5, "Galy Guy" has been shot and buried and the new Jeraiah Jip is ready to be transported to the front to fight. Widow Begbick's canteen behind the lines has been dismantled to become a new one near the battle, and the peaceful porter Galy Guy has been dismantled to become the fighting machine Jeraiah Jip. Just as a canteen has no independent existence of its own—unless men frequent it, one might as well not speak of it as existing—Guy has no independent existence of his own. The smallest unit of social existence, according to Brecht in his *Short Organum for the Theatre* (1949), is two persons, not one (Willett, *Brecht on Theatre*: 197). Accordingly, Galy Guy is dependent upon others for his economic survival: that is why he carries Begbick's basket of cucumbers, answers roll call for Jip, and accepts the gift of the elephant. He agrees to transform himself into Jeraiah Jip because he is made to believe that, as Galy Guy, he will cease to have a social existence: not only will he no longer be able to work as a porter, he will also be shot. He wishes to survive—the correct, "unheroic" instinct, Brecht would say—so he assumes the identity under which he can survive. He becomes a soldier, killing the enemy in return for his food and clothing: killing others, paradoxically, in return for the confirmation of his own existence. Begbick's canteen needs the army if it is to survive, and so, finally, does Galy Guy.

As the canteen is being dismantled in Scene 9, the elephant "Billy Humph" is being constructed, itself to be partially dismantled by the end of Scene 9, Number 2. A real elephant in the wild may lead a more or less autonomous existence, but Billy Humpf is obviously a fake elephant: he is Polly-and-Jesse covered by canvas, and he becomes dependent on Galy Guy for the confirmation of his existence. Guy confirms it, as I have pointed out, only when he discovers that there is a buyer for the elephant. Even as a canteen could not exist but for the men who support it, so too can a product or service be said not to exist unless someone is willing to buy it. Once Guy is trapped into service and a fake elephant is no longer needed, Billy Humpf runs away—to turn back into Polly and Jesse, who are needed again as soldiers.

Changeable Characters

Not only do the set and objects on it transform themselves in the course of the play, but characters other than Galy Guy do also. Jeraiah Jip, in fact, undergoes his transformation before Guy. In Scene 7 Wang transforms Jip into a god to whom supplicants offer money. Uriah, Jesse, and Polly have stolen Wang's alms box, but instead of handing the captured Jip over to the police, Wang decides to make a god out of him. He will get his stolen money back (and more)by doing this, whereas had he handed Jip over to the police, he would have got only justice. But justice is of no use to Wang for his survival; Jip as the god of his pagoda is of use. Wang needs Jip, and Jip needs him: for in return for serving as a god—in essence, for sitting around and doing nothing—Jip will be fed beefsteak and beer. as a soldier risking his life in combat on the northern border, he would have been fed rice rations and water. Jip could run away from Wang's pagoda, but does not do so: he likes his steak and beer.

Once Jip finally does leave Wang's employ and attempt to join Uriah, Jesse, and Polly at the front, he is rebuffed. Jesse says to him, "You couldn't possibly be our Jip. Our Jip would never have betrayed us and abandoned us. Nothing would have delayed our Jip. So you can't be our Jip" (*Man's a Man*, 67). Ironically, Jesse is right, even though Jip is standing right in front of him: the Jip that would never have betrayed and abandoned his comrades does not exist. There never was any such Jip, for the concept of unified and consistent character is false. Jip is the Jip who was willing to transform himself into a fake god in order to stay out of battle and live well for a time. He is the Jip who did what he felt was necessary in order to survive, despite his feelings for his friends. he is closer to Galy Guy than to the Jip his comrades thought they knew.

Like the Galy Guy who did not return to his wife, Jeraiah Jip did not return to his friends; like the Guy who transformed himself into a human fighting machine in return for extra rice and whisky rations, Jip transformed himself into a god for beefsteak and beer. It is no accident that in Scene 11 Guy gives Jip the papers of Galy Guy so that he, Jip, will have some form of identification to present to the authorities, and that the latter thanks him by saying, "You're the best of the lot. You've got a heart at least" (*Man's a Man*, 68). In a sense, Jeraiah Jip *is* Galy Guy; he is another Galy Guy, or Guy's alter ego. If for no other reason than their being the only characters in the play whose first and last names begin with the same letter, this should be clear.

Unlike Jeraiah Jip, the Widow Leokadja Begbick may not change in the course of *A Man's a Man*, but it is clear from her poetic interruptions to the text that she has changed at some time in the past. This is the reason Brecht chooses her as his choral figure, to deliver up to the audience the wisdom of one who has undergone a change and has survived because of it. She has not followed the troops with a canteen her whole life; once she lived in the same place for seven years and was married to a man who supported her. After her husband died unexpectedly, she had to learn to support herself and live alone. Brecht specifically calls her the Widow Leokadja Begbick because the widow is not the same person that the wife Leokadja Begbick was; the different title points up the different identity she now has.

Everything Begbick does in the play confirms her instinct for survival. We first see her selling Galy Guy a cucumber he does not want at a "discount," with the money he saves becoming his payment for carrying her basket. Then she sells Wang beer that will keep Jip happy in the pagoda—the same beer she sells to his comrades, who need him or another fourth man if they are to survive roll call and the upcoming battle. Begbick agrees to buy the fake elephant from Galy Guy and thereby force him into becoming Jeraiah Jip, in return for help moving her canteen to the front. And on the train taking the soldiers to the northern border, she agrees to lie down with Guy so that he will feel better and stop asking questions, in return for seven weeks of a soldier's pay. In short, Widow Begbick profits off war, like her more famous descendant Mother Courage.

We may be tempted to judge Begbick harshly for her actions, even as we may be tempted to judge Galy Guy, but Brecht's point is that in a different world these people would not have to act in this way. For them to act differently in the world in which they live—for Guy not to transform himself into Jip, for Begbick not to buy the "elephant"—would be suicidal, "tragic." It would confirm the inalterability of the world and their surrender to it; the focus would thus be placed on them and their suffering. Brecht, by having them adapt to the world, places the focus on that world and what it drives people to do in order to survive. That the world changes Begbick and Guy is significant, for it shows that man is indeed changeable; and if man is changeable, then the world is too, for it is, finally, only other men. Brecht portrays the "negative" changes of Guy and Begbick, not because he wants us to think that these characters are bad, obviously, but because the spectator must see what an evil and exploitative world can do to a human being before he or she can resolve to change it. In the same way that the world changed Guy and Begbick, Brecht would like his play to change us. He would like us to be able to encounter a wise man like Galy Guy, absorb his knowledge, emulate his openness to experience—and change the world.

Poetic Interruption, Prosaic Contradiction

I have spoken of the very structure of *A Man's a Man* as changing, of its location as shifting from scene to scene. Galy Guy's environment changes substantially—from home to army camp—and *he* changes as a result. The location for several scenes, Widow Begbick's canteen, is also in the process of change, of being dismantled to be carried to the front, where it will be reassembled. Begbick herself has changed, and, befitting that, her words undergo change of a kind throughout the play. She who has changed and survived speaks of the merits or inevitability of change in her poetic interruptions to the text, which are a transformation from the prose the characters speak to each other in the drama:

> No matter how often you look at the river, lazily
> Flowing along, never will you see the same water.
> Never will what flows down, never a drop of it
> Turn back to its source. (*Man's a Man*, 21)
>
> Oh, cling not to the wave
> Breaking against your foot. As long as your
> Foot stands in the water
> New waves on it will break. (*Man's a Man*, 36)

It is as if Brecht is saying at moments like these that, if his drama can go against the realistic convention of time and stop itself, changing into poetry or song, into a condensation or illustration of what has occurred in the dramatic action, then man can go against the psychological convention of thinking of himself as a fixed and unified entity and begin to think of himself as changeable and open to experience. He can, in *his* new form, learn from his past and use it to adjust to the present, even as Widow Begbick does in her poems and songs—along with the play itself. The play seems to catch up with itself during Begbick's "interruptions," to draw the necessary conclusions from its action before moving on. So much so, that after Scene 8 there is even an Interlude in which Begbick speaks for Brecht himself in the perfect marriage of form and idea:

> A man's a man, says Mr. Bertolt Brecht
> And that is hardly more than you'd expect.
> But Mr. Bertolt Brecht goes on to show
> That you can change a man from top to toe. (*Man's a Man*, 35)

She who has changed speaks about change in a form that itself represents change, that exists outside the action of the play *per se*, and in this way could be said to represent change in its purest state.

Significantly, Galy Guy speaks in verse only three times: in Scene 4, when he debates whether he should go back home to his wife or stay with the soldiers (*Man's a Man*, 20); in Scene 9, when he decides to help bury "Galy Guy" and to assume the identity of Jeraiah Jip (*Man's a Man*, 56-57); and in Scene 11, when, as Jip, he takes on the leadership of the machine-gun detachment (*Man's a Man*, 70). Guy speaks in verse, in other words, only at critical moments in the process of his change: when he decides to stay in the army camp and thereby lays the groundwork for his change; when he resolves to change into Jeraiah Jip; and when he transforms himself from the commanded into commander Jip, when, that is, his change into Jip is at its most complete. Guy's shift from prose to verse thus underlines his change from one man into another.

Even Guy's prose, or how others respond to it, underlines his change into Jip, his allowing a contradiction of existence (one must kill in order not to be killed) to enter into his life, the only place, according to Walter Benjamin, where it can be resolved. In Scene 3 Guy says to Widow Begbick, "I'm a man of great imagination; I've had enough of a fish, for instance, before I even lay eyes on it" (*Man's a Man*, 10). He proceeds to describe comically how other, richer people do not have it as easy as he does, because they have to go to the trouble of buying the fish, taking it home, then cooking, eating, and digesting it; they have no imagination, alas. Begbick turns Guy's words around for her own benefit. She makes his description of his privation sound like a description of his selfishness, and then *she* becomes selfish by talking him into buying a bargain cucumber instead of a fish:

> I see, you're thinking only of yourself. (*Pause.*) Hm. If you think only of yourself, I suggest that you take your fish money and buy this cucumber, which I'll let you have as a favor. The cucumber is worth more, but you can keep the difference for carrying my basket. (*Man's a Man*, 10)

In Scene 4 the same kind of "contradiction" occurs. Uriah, Jesse, and Polly lure Galy Guy to Widow Begbick's canteen, but, once there, Guy says, "I have to hurry home. I've bought a cucumber for dinner, so you see, I can't do exactly as I should like" (*Man's a Man*, 14). Jesse replies, "Thank you. Frankly, it's just what I expected of you. You can't do as you'd like. You'd like to go home but you can't" (*Man's a Man*, 14-15). Jesse makes Guy's declaration of his obligations to his wife sound like a declaration of his powerlessness, his submission to the will of the soldiers. He turns Guy's words around for his own and his friends' benefit: they, of course, need Guy to substitute for Jeraiah Jip at roll call. Galy Guy submits to the soldiers' will here, just as he bought Widow Begbick's cucumber. He accepts the contradiction of his words, the changing of them into something he did not mean, even as he will eventually accept the contradiction of his existence, his change into something he was not before: Jip, the human fighting machine.

Changeable Genre, Grotesque Figure

If the structure, language, characters, and scenery of *A Man's a Man* all stress the idea of changeability, surely the generic form of the play must also stress this idea. Brecht calls *A Man's a Man* a comedy, but then he calls the protagonist "Galy Guy" in the list of characters, and this man is not "Galy Guy" at the end: he is Jeraiah Jip. To be sure, *A Man's a Man* is not a tragedy and Guy does not take tragic action; however, he does gain wisdom that has the potential to alter the fabric of his society, and in this sense the play is not formally comic. Galy Guy's wisdom is so momentous that, unlike truly comic characters, he has changed by the end of the play not simply in his perceptions of the world, but from one character into another. He is Walter Benjamin's wise or undramatic hero: untragic because he chooses not to die with the great insight he has gained about the world and his place in it; uncomic because, although he survives, he does so as a different man—not just as a man with a different outlook.

A Man's a Man is neither a tragedy nor a comedy, then. It has altered the nature of both to become something else, a form that combines to a new end the best feature of each: profound wisdom, on the one hand, and abiding life, on the other; wrenching change and sure survival. Brecht calls the play a comedy, but it changes into something else right before our eyes. For if a man can change fundamentally and can change the world, then the dramatic form that represents him must necessarily change as well: it cannot be exclusively comic, nor can it be solely tragic. It must combine select elements from both, because these forms are tied to an unchanging world in which—so the mythology goes—man either dies in deep, painfully acquired knowledge or lives happily ever after in ignorance and compromise.

It would be a mistake, though, to call *A Man's a Man* a tragicomedy, for the premise of tragicomedy is that man *suffers* in ignorance. It combines, if you will, the worst features of tragedy and comedy. Samuel Beckett was probably our greatest modern writer of tragicomedy in the twentieth century, and there can be little doubt that he and Brecht are far apart in their views of human existence. Rather, *A Man's a Man* has more affinities with the grotesque than with the tragicomic. (Marianne Kesting's "Die Groteske vom Verlust der Identität" ["The Grotesqueness of Identity-Loss"] is the only study I know of that brings up the grotesque in relation to *A Man's a Man*; but Kesting's article [see Works Cited] is primarily a discussion of the differences between the first published version and subsequent editions, not an examination of the grotesque element in the play.)

"The grotesque," writes Bert O. States, "is the phenomenon we characteristically get when the serious and the comic attitudes seem about equally mixed and, as a result, appear to be mocking each other" (States, 75).

States sees the grotesque as a mode with an "essentially detached view of humanity as an object of manipulation for the idle ironist who has nothing better to do than to make 'masterpieces' of moral confusion" (States, 83). He regards the grotesque's primary tendency as "to strip from tragedy its spiritual equilibrium, yet leave it with its sense of inevitability and defeat" (States, 78).

A good example of a "grotesque tragedy," according to States's definition, is John Webster's *The Duchess of Malfi* (1614). Webster seems to use the grotesque in this drama to detach himself from humanity and express his fundamental ambivalence toward human existence: he would live, yet he finds life evil, loathsome, and hopeless. Brecht differs from Webster in that he uses the grotesque in *A Man's a Man* to distance, not himself, but the *audience* from the characters. What is important in the play is not that one be inundated by the evil of existence, but that one see evil as the result of specific sociopolitical conditions in society—see that it is not inherent in humanity, as Webster would perhaps have us believe. One must be distanced from the characters in order to understand their origins and how they have become what they are.

Therefore, by the time we witness Galy Guy stuffing rice into his mouth and singlehandedly knocking out the fortress of Sir el-Djowr with five cannon shots—the last of several superb grotesque images in *A Man's a Man*—we should be aware that Guy is not merely "evil," but in fact has learned to kill in order to survive. Unlike the grotesque characters of Webster, he must not die: he must live, to unlearn his murderousness. We are not given the opportunity in the play to identify with a fixed and unified, three-dimensional Galy Guy, one who could never change from the murderer that he becomes. Instead, we concentrate on Guy the two-dimensional character construct, the comic grotesque, who in the end contains knowledge of human relations that can be applied to the creation of a better world. Galy Guy, Brecht has shown us, is eminently changeable, so there is no reason to believe that he will remain a murderous soldier: the very nature of the drama, as well as his own character, contradicts this idea.

Critics and Epics

Few critics deny *A Man's a Man*'s importance in Brecht's career as a transitional work, but most find the play flawed in a way that I do not. Only Eric Bentley notes that, generally speaking, *A Man's a Man* marks a switch from the tragedy of the previous plays to comedy, and that this comedy is ideally suited to the aims of epic theater, even if Brecht curiously never took it up again with thoroughness except in *Mr. Puntila and His Man Matti*. (Bentley, *Brecht Commentaries*: 76-77.)

The following critics see *A Man's a Man* as a transitional work, from the anarchic nihilism of the earlier plays to the social awareness and didacticism of the later ones; from the depiction of more or less active heroes to the portrayal of a passive one; from relatively straight dramas to a new theater in which Brecht addresses the audience directly in his own name, and in which titles separate scenes and lyrical portions are sharply divided from the main plot: Ewen, 136, 142; Esslin, 259; Ronald Speirs, *Brecht's Early Plays* (London: Macmillan, 1982), 118; and Lyons, 45. Negative critical opinion of *A Man's a Man* as indeterminate, confused, even silly and crude, may be found in: Gray, 45; Hill, 54; Ewen, 136; Needle and Thomson, 35; and Lyons, 67.

A Man's a Man may be one of Brecht's more successful plays, however—even though it comes early in his career—if only because we do not demand the individuality, the private psychology, from its comic grotesques that we seem to demand from the characters in the subsequent, "straighter" plays like *The Good Person of Setzuan* (1940) and *The Caucasian Chalk Circle* (1945), where we do not get it. Brecht finished writing *A Man's a Man* in 1926 as a "comedy," but termed it a "parable" in 1931 (Willett, *Theatre of Bertolt Brecht*: 27). It is a parable, too, of course: a play from which a moral—Brecht would say social—lesson can be drawn. But one cannot help thinking that his calling the play a parable in 1931 somehow influenced him to write *The Good Person of Setzuan* and *The Caucasian Chalk Circle* almost exclusively as sober parables. These two plays would have been substantially improved, I believe, had Brecht suffused them with the comic vitality of *A Man's a Man* instead of limiting their comedy to a specific character or certain scenes.

The comic characters of *A Man's a Man*, and of the equally undervalued later play *Mr. Puntila and His Man Matti* (1948), are in fact closer to the ideal of Brecht's epic theater than the majority of characters in the two parable plays *The Good Person of Setzuan* and *The Caucasian Chalk Circle*. That ideal places the focus not on the psychology of the individual, but on the sociology of existence: man as he molds and is molded by the society of other men. Brecht to the contrary, the plays thought to be his greatest, *Mother Courage and Her Children* and *Life of Galileo* (1939), succeed less on their epic qualities than on the complexity and realistic appeal of their main characters. This is not to demean them; it is to grant *A Man's a Man* the place it deserves in the Brecht canon, and that it has been hitherto denied.

Works Cited

Benjamin, Walter. *Understanding Brecht*. 1966. Trans. Anna Bostock. London: New Left Books, 1973.

Bentley, Eric. *The Brecht Commentaries, 1943-1986*. 1981. New York: Grove Press, 1987.

Brecht, Bertolt. *Gesammelte Werke* [*Collected Works*]. 20 vols. Ed. Elisabeth Hauptmann. Frankfurt am Main: Suhrkamp Verlag, 1967.

----------. *A Man's a Man*. In Brecht's *Collected Plays*. Vol. 2 of 9 vols. (1970-2004). Trans. Gerhard Nellhaus. Ed. Ralph Manheim & John Willett. London: Methuen, 1977. 1-70.

----------. "On Looking Through My First Plays" (1954). From "*A Man's a Man*: Notes," in *Collected Plays*. Vol. 2 of 9 vols. (1970-2004). Trans. Gerhard Nellhaus. Ed. Ralph Manheim & John Willett. London: Methuen, 1977. 245.

----------. *Bertolt Brecht on Art and Politics*. Ed. Thomas Kuhn & Steve Giles. London: Methuen, 2003.

Esslin, Martin. *Brecht, A Choice of Evils: A Critical Study of the Man, His Work, and His Opinions*. 4th rev. ed. New York: Methuen, 1984.

Ewen, Frederic. *Bertolt Brecht: His Life, His Art, and His Times*. New York: Citadel, 1967.

Gray, Ronald. *Brecht*. London: Oliver & Boyd, 1961.

Hill, Claude. *Bertolt Brecht*. Boston: Twayne, 1975.

Kesting, Marianne. "Die Groteske vom Verlust der Identität" ("The Grotesqueness of Identity-Loss"). In *Das deutsche Lustspiel 2*. Ed. Hans Steffen. Göttingen: Vandenhoeck & Ruprecht, 1969. 180-199.

Lyons, Charles R. *Bertolt Brecht: The Despair and the Polemic*. Carbondale: Southern Illinois University Press, 1968.

Needle, Jan, & Peter Thomson. *Brecht*. Oxford, U.K.: Basil Blackwell, 1981.

Sieber, Harry. *The Picaresque*. London: Methuen, 1977.

Sokel, Walter. "Brecht's Concept of Character." *Comparative Drama*, 5.3 (Fall 1971): 177-192.

Speirs, Ronald. *Bertolt Brecht*. New York: St. Martin's Press, 1987.

States, Bert O. *Irony and Drama: A Poetics*. Ithaca, N.Y.: Cornell University Press, 1971.

Willett, John, trans. & ed. *Brecht on Theatre: The Development of an Aesthetic*. New York: Hill & Wang, 1964.

Willett, John. *The Theatre of Bertolt Brecht: A Study from Eight Aspects*. 1968. London: Methuen, 1977.

11. *Hedda*, dir. Trevor Nunn, 1975

12. *Hedda Gabler*, dir. Alex Segal, 1962

13. Arnold Daly, *Candida*, 1903

14. Peter Lorre, *A Man's a Man*, 1931

15. Brecht's *Antigone*, Living Theatre, 1967

16. Brecht's *Turandot*, University of Washington, 1969

17. *The Caucasian Chalk Circle*, Berlin, 1954

18. *The Doctor's Dilemma*, New York, 1927

POSTLUDE

"Why Should My Name Be Remembered?" (1936), by Bertolt Brecht

1
Once I thought: in distant times
When the buildings in which I lived have collapsed
And the ships in which I traveled have rotted
My name will still be remembered
With others.

2
Because I praised the useful, which
In my day was considered base
Because I battled against all religions
Because I fought oppression or
For another reason.

3
Because I was for people and
Entrusted everything to them, thereby honoring them
Because I wrote verses and enriched the language
Because I taught practical behavior or
For some other reason.

4
Therefore I thought my name would still be
Remembered: on a stone
My name would stand; from old books
It would get printed in new books.

5
But today
I accept that it will be forgotten.
Why
Should the baker be sent for if there is enough bread?
Why
Should the snow that has melted be rejoiced over
If new snowfalls are impending?
Why
Should there be a past if
There is a future?

6
Why
Should my name be remembered?

(Translated by Robert Conard in *Bertolt Brecht: Poems 1913-1956*. New York: Methuen, 1976. 382.)

"The Difficult B.B., The Complex E.T.: Rethinking the Theory and Practice of Brechtian Theater"

Overture

Any account of the life and work of Bertolt Brecht would have to be "multiplex" (to use a word from our age's electronic-cum-scientific jargon), because he was complex (the old-fashioned word). Luckily, the idea of "pluralism" is still fashionable right now, hence we can feel less anxious than we did, say, thirty years ago about approaching Brecht from many points of view, rather than just one or a few. The trouble is, this stylish idea of pluralism has also given rise to a widespread urge to re-write everything, as if the commanding assumption were that true knowledge comes only from granting equal validity to every possible point of view. So, whereas we may now be spared the kind of single-category presentations of Brecht's work that appeared in the 1950s and 1960s ("Brecht the Marxist," "Brecht the Theorist," "Brecht the Poet," and so on), we nevertheless must confront new estimations that endeavor to present his work as meaning whatever someone wants it to mean ("Brecht for All Seasons," "Brecht the Chameleon," "A Feminist Reading of Brecht," and so on). The complexity of this artist is not adequately honored, however, by the breezy "Whatever" approach, which more than ever seems to be an excuse for not thinking.

The pluralistic stance and the re-writing mission probably came into vogue when they did because they offered apparent remedies for new philosophical difficulties, especially in the realm of political discourse if not personal conduct itself. Those difficulties have been with us now for roughly forty-five years (since the assassination of John F. Kennedy and the beginning of the Vietnam debacle), during which we have been living in an era that intellectual historians have agreed to call "post-modern." This expression means many things. Generally, though, it means that the "modern" era, which began around 1890 and was chiefly characterized by a repudiation of the influences of earlier tradition, has been replaced by an era that is characterized by the acceptance of all earlier influences—not as "true" in any particular way, but rather as "value-free" data. And it is in the fields of literary criticism and theory that this generalized inclination to accept rather than combat previous influences takes on a more specific philosophical intention.

Two schools of post-modernist criticism, for example—"deconstructionism" and "new historicism"—are linked by the conviction that almost everything we accept as valid or "known" has been falsified in some way by the values defining those cultures which have transmitted our knowledge. This conviction also belongs to another system of post-modernist thinking called "post-structuralism," the general idea of which is that we should cease believing that objects (natural, artistic, or political) are knowable through a grasping of their inherent "structured-ness," because the very means we use to define "structures" are themselves unconsciously "structured" and consequently deceptive as sources of knowledge. We should, therefore, take apart—"deconstruct" (or its obverse, "rehistoricize")—all the constructed modes by which we have ostensibly come to know everything, in order to start again building a trustworthy basis for knowing anything surely.

In this spirit Shakespeare himself began being subjected to critical re-writing in the 1980s (a re-writing, I might add, that continues apace). One collection of essays from 1988 was called *The Shakespeare Myth*, and Gary Taylor published a book in 1989 titled *Reinventing Shakespeare*. The assumption behind both books is that the Shakespeare we think we know was always some kind of cultural fabrication—a "myth" or "invention"—passed down through four hundred years of editing, criticizing, theatrical (as well as filmic) production, and teaching. Once we understand this, the argument goes, we might see him more accurately: as a poet reasonably respected in his own time, but not necessarily as the "universal genius" now encrusted with four centuries of "Bardolatry." For another example, feminist critics (of Shakespeare or anyone else) declare that most modern literary views rest upon layer after layer of received thinking which is implicitly defined by a male point of view, and that this is causing flawed or erroneous critical judgments because we cannot "see" otherwise. The remedy is to re-write literary history from a point of view that "deconstructs" such unquestioned premises, especially the "phallocentric" premise of assumed male dominion.

With regard to Brecht, this critical climate is responsible for some strange occurrences. He has not become as large a cultural myth as Shakespeare, but he certainly has a legendary aura about him and has had since the 1960s. At the same time, the German language of his works has kept him essentially inaccessible to readers of English, a situation that has not been remedied by translators. (The "Translation Problem" is a huge Brecht topic, largely because Brecht's dialogue has the quality of dialect even though it is completely understandable to someone who knows High German.) Nonetheless, largely due to the bloated scholarship industry, Brecht has managed, in the fifty years since his death, to become a "difficult" case in any language.

So much so that more recent critics have not yet wholly succeeded in deconstructing the political or Marxist (though some insist on "Communist") dramatist of older critical definition. But neither has any more recent critic opened people's eyes fully to the *aesthetic* nature of Brecht's works, particularly in the context of the other artworks of his time. Yet this is something that the "new historicism," by its own avowed premises, should be trying to do. One book did appear in 1989—at what could be called the onset of the age of the critical re-writing of canonical authors—called *Postmodern Brecht: A Re-Presentation* (by Elizabeth Wright), which in its early chapters promised an exciting re-evaluation of earlier convictions about Brecht's work, but which relapsed toward its end into a largely ideological assessment of him in post-structuralist terms. (It is thus as if an old idea, namely, that writers are philosophers or playwrights thinkers, had not been successfully "deconstructed" by this author.)

One of the most unfortunate things that have happened in this new critical climate, however, is the development of a critical estimation of Brecht which is essentially personal. It might be labeled (with a post-1960s unabashedness) "Brecht the Asshole." To wit: in certain accounts published over the last twenty years or so, there have come to light some previously unknown facts about Brecht's private life that certain critics have seized upon and made the basis of a "deconstructed" human being. It is therefore now possible to conclude that he was an even more objectionable fellow than we had suspected. Not only did he consider himself gifted enough to deserve certain personal privileges, but he also treated like servants the several female intimates who were his artistic collaborators, while cheating other, male collaborators (especially Kurt Weill).

These illuminations augment the suppositions and rumors that surrounded Brecht's reputation in the years immediately following his death. He was arrogantly outspoken, we heard, and he wasn't above insulting actors and directors whom he considered stupid. People pointed out that he always seemed to have a three-day growth of beard, that he often smelled unwashed, that his wearing of working-class clothing was both ostentatious and phony; and, of course, they also objected to his habit of incessantly smoking all those cheap, smelly cigars. We were told, as well, that Brecht "converted" to Marxism in his mid-twenties and later greatly admired Stalin—yet he kept elitist company with many of Europe's leading artists and intellectuals. And, it was said, he was a hypocritical (or at least inconsistent) Marxist in making sure to keep Swiss bank accounts, so that he could have easy access to his money for purchase of material goods like big cars and leather jackets. Brecht felt no compunction, moreover, about lying to the government officials of several countries in order to obtain the things he wanted: visas for the countries of his exile, continued freedom in America, citizenship in Austria, a theater in East Berlin.

The English poet W. H. Auden even went so far as to say that Brecht was one of the few people who deserved the death sentence, adding: "In fact, I can imagine doing it to him myself." Auden's antipathy was later illuminated by James Fenton, in a review of a book on Brecht:

> Brecht was quintessentially a noncombatant and I suspect that this was what noncombatant Auden disliked in him. . . . From the moment of his espousal of communism, Brecht stood on the sidelines, cheering on a party he most emphatically did not wish to join, recommending that others submit to a discipline which he himself refused. (Fenton, "Aimez-vous Brecht?" [see Works Cited])

An American academic joined the fray when, writing about Brecht the director, he asked the following insinuating rhetorical question: "Did his production method actually require the steady availability of several people (usually women), each willing to respond to his express needs virtually at any time of the day or night?" (John Fuegi, in an essay contributed to the 1986 collection *The Play and Its Critic: Essays for Eric Bentley*, and later incorporated in Fuegi's controversial book *Brecht and Company: Sex, Politics, and the Making of Modern Drama* [1994]). The tone in this comment and other personal ones about Brecht is harshly moralistic. Whereas in an earlier era such a paradoxically unsavory artist might have been an attractive character, today it is considered wrong to be the kind of person Brecht was.

However, even without this contemporary shift towards judging talented people by their "personal politics" (another neo-moralistic expression), Brecht's reputation by itself furnishes plenty of instances of contradiction, division, and finally uncertainty. In America, for instance, he is probably better known as a Communist playwright than as the author of forty plays, three volumes of poetry, four collections of prose fiction, and eight books of essays on theater, film, literature, art, politics, and society. Among theater artists themselves there is wide disagreement about the basis of his genius: is his theory of Epic Theater more, or less, important than his introduction to theater practice of elements like the half-curtain and the mixing (in a serious play) of singing and action? Will Brecht be remembered, finally, more for his work as a director than for his work as a dramatist? As the dramatist, or "librettist," of *The Threepenny Opera* (1928), he is prized by Broadway theater devotees and lovers of showbiz; yet many of these same people would be repelled by the idea that he wanted to rewrite the screenplay for the movie version of *Threepenny* to make it much more clearly anti-capitalist. (Brecht eventually sued the film company for not accepting his screenplay, lost the suit, published his version under the title *The Carbuncle*, then in 1931 re-cast his anti-capitalistic treatment of the story in *The Threepenny Novel.*

For its part, *The Measures Taken* (1930)—which is about Communist Party workers reporting their execution of a comrade—cannot be swallowed whole by some Western admirers of Brecht, but it was also rejected by orthodox Communist critics. Furthermore, probably only a few people aside from academic Brechtians know that he set the *Communist Manifesto* (1848) in hexameters, that he worked on adaptations of Synge's *The Playboy of the Western World* (1907) and Beckett's *Waiting for Godot* (1953), or that he wrote a long prose work called *Me-ti/Book of Changes* (1934-40), based on the Chinese writings of Mo Di and on the *I-ching*. Even his chief literary critics cannot agree on whether he is more important as a poet or as a playwright, despite their accord that two or three of his plays are among the best of the twentieth century. And, while no one disputes that the theater company Brecht founded with his wife Helene Weigel, the Berliner Ensemble, was the most influential and significant national theater company of the twentieth century, many people cannot accept its having been located in the capital of the Communist German Democratic Republic.

There are thus many things about Brecht and his artistic achievement that are either unaccepted, unknown, misunderstood, or disputed by a majority of people, including those who already possess firm ideas about his character, his worth, and his politics. *Forty plays, really? More than Shakespeare! But they couldn't all be as good.* (Who other than a Brecht scholar can name five of those forty plays?) *Well, of course he was a Communist: didn't he testify before HUAC, the House Un-American Activities Committee?* (What is the difference between a Communist and a Marxist, anyway? Between a political artist and an artist who nonetheless has his own set of political views?) *All right, so Brecht wrote a theory of theater, but it doesn't apply to his plays: they have their own artistic life. Besides, creativity and theorizing don't go together; you can't create if you think too much.* (Where did this idea come from? Is it true? Is it true of Brecht?) *Brecht was a*

German, and the Germans are all heavy thinkers; that's why nobody reads them anymore. (Name a German that nobody reads anymore.) *Brecht is the inventor of Epic Theater and the "Alienation Effect." This is theater that alienates the audience.* (Is it a good idea to "alienate" the audience?)

All of these notions about Brecht have been heard in the best and in the worst circles. Yet despite them, as well as because of them, he has achieved the status of "classic" artist, in the process becoming an academic staple: university professors lecture on him because he must be "covered," even if they do not appreciate him or his artistic accomplishments. (It is surprising how many academic Brecht "specialists" don't even like him!) At the same time, his innovations in dramatic form and theatrical style have become clichés: indeed, he has already been rejected by many theater people who hastened to copy those innovations without understanding them. Brecht's Berliner Ensemble itself degenerated into a bureaucratically loaded state theater, with lots of untalented people and a tightly controlled state aesthetic. Given his recent dismissals by both the academic and the commercial theater worlds, then, Brecht is in danger of becoming a legend without ever having been thoroughly known. But it remains true that knowing him thoroughly is very difficult—and altogether necessary.

First Movement: What, Where, When; or Life, Art, and Politics

Eugen Friedrich Berthold Brecht (1898-1956) lived his first twenty-five years in Augsburg, a middle-class city of some 150,000 inhabitants located forty miles west of Munich, and perched somewhat eccentrically between the southern German cultures of Swabia and Bavaria. Founded in 53 B.C. by the Roman emperor Augustus (its Latin name was Augusta Vindelicorum), Augsburg enjoyed a long history as a mercantile center, starting out as a key city in the Roman trade routes to the "barbaric" territories of Germania. By the early sixteenth century, it had become known as well for its political and religious liberalism.

When, for example, Martin Luther was summoned to Augsburg by Cardinal Cajetan to answer the Inquisition's charges of heresy, the nuns of St. Anna helped him to escape through a secret door in the city's Roman wall. (This door is still known as the Luther-Gate.) The Religious Peace of Augsburg, one of several "treaties" between warring Catholic and Protestant princes, was signed there in 1555, and shortly thereafter Augsburg established the first combined Protestant-Catholic church in Europe, the Church of St. Ulrich. The city is also the site of the first social living settlement in modern history, the Fuggerei—still supported by the Fugger family, one of the richest in feudal Europe and creditor to more than one pope. Moreover, some of Germany's foremost Renaissance artists are Augsburg's native sons, among them Elias Holl and Hans Holbein the Elder, and its main downtown street, Maximilianstrasse, is still called "Renaissance-Strasse" for its row of house façades in the architectural style of the period.

Today Augsburg's rich historical character is hard to discern, submerged as it is beneath the clutter of consumerism and the bustle of affluence. By the age of twenty-five, Bertolt (which he changed from Berthold because the suffix "-hold" in German means "lovely") Brecht himself had come to resent the city for its bourgeois smugness and provinciality, even though he had earlier drawn personal and poetic inspiration from the combination of its medieval humanism and its individualistic character. He had begun to move away as early as 1918, when he graduated from the Realgymnasium and transferred to Munich for the ostensible purpose of studying medicine. (World War I was still in progress, but medical students were deferred from service.) Brecht never really studied medicine, however. Instead, he spent a lot of time talking and drinking with other students, attending a theater history seminar and other lectures as he chose, composing a lot of poetry, and writing some plays. All the while, he continued to maintain his attic room in his parents' house in Augsburg, where he also did a lot of schmoozing and hanging out, wrote a lot of poetry, and (according to his *Diaries, 1920-1922*) had his share of sexually-charged romantic encounters.

During these years in Augsburg and Munich, Brecht produced his first four full-length plays: the quasi-expressionistic trio of *Baal, Drums in the Night,* and *In the Jungle of Cities*, together with *Life of Edward the Second of England* (after Marlowe). *Baal* was begun in 1918, revised twice, and first produced in Leipzig in December 1923, after both *Drums* and *Jungle of Cities* had had their premières in September 1922 and May 1923, respectively. In 1924, Brecht directed *Edward II* himself at the Kammerspiele in Munich, in collaboration with its co-author, Lion Feuchtwanger (a novelist who knew English literature), and the artistic director of the Kammerspiele, Bernhard Reich. During these same years, Brecht also worked in the company of the famous Munich cabaret artist Karl Valentin. By 1919, he had fathered a son, Frank, with his Augsburg girlfriend Paula ("Bie") Banholzer. And in 1922 he married the actress Marianne Zoff in Munich, where she bore a daughter, Hanne, early in 1923. (Brecht's son died on the Russian front in World War II; his daughter became the respected German stage-and-screen actress Hanne Hiob.)

By now Brecht had broken upon the German literary scene. Herbert Ihering, one of Berlin's two leading drama critics, quickly recognized his genius and proclaimed that he had "overnight altered the physiognomy of German literature" with a new kind of drama "which had its own laws and dramaturgy" apart from those of realistic and naturalistic drama. (The other prominent critic was Alfred Kerr, who would later accuse Brecht of plagiarizing song lyrics for *The Threepenny Opera*.) Ihering's praise was one of the reasons Brecht was awarded the Kleist Prize in 1922 for *Drums in the Night*. After another year in Munich, he was ready to make a permanent move to the German capital and Europe's most exciting artistic center.

In Berlin, Brecht made good on his promise as a brilliant young playwright and dramaturg. He joined the dramaturgy staff, first of Max Reinhardt at the Deutsches Theater, then of Erwin Piscator's experimental "Political Theater," where he worked on adaptations of Shakespeare (*Hamlet* [1603] and *Macbeth* [1605]), Dumas's *La Dame aux Camélias* [1852], and the Czech novel *The Good Soldier Schweik* [1921-23, Jaroslav Hašek]. He also began in these years (1924-1927) to work on the plays *A Man's a Man, The Little Mahagonny* (a *Songspiel*, or play consisting solely of songs), and *The Rise and Fall of the City*

Mahagonny—after which he began the remarkable group of experimental works called *Lehrstücke* (teaching or learning plays). These comprise nine plays, all begun between 1928 and 1931: six short "musical *Lehrstücke*" (*The Flight of the Lindberghs, The Baden-Baden Learning Play on Consent, He Who Says Yes/He Who Says No, The Measures Taken,* and *The Exception and the Rule*) and three full-length works, *St. Joan of the Stockyards, The Mother,* and *Roundheads and Peakheads.*

It was during the twenties, as well—1924, to be exact—that Brecht met Elisabeth Hauptmann, who would become his life-long, faithful collaborator. Also in 1924, his son Stefan was born to Helene Weigel, whom he had met the year before and who was to become the most famous "Brechtian" actress of the twentieth century. They would marry in 1929 and produce another child, Barbara, in 1930. Today, when people speak of the "Brecht estate," they refer both to Stefan, an American citizen, who owns the translation and production rights to his father's work in the West, and to Barbara, who was a citizen of the German Democratic Republic, co-directed the Berliner Ensemble there, and now controls those same rights in Eastern Europe.

Brecht lived and worked in Berlin until 1933, when Hitler's already obvious totalitarianism drove him into exile (along with many other German artists). His greatest success of the period was undoubtedly *The Threepenny Opera,* with the famous music by Kurt Weill, which had its première on August 31, 1928, in Berlin's Theater am Schiffbauerdamm. It was also during these years that Brecht started formulating his theory of "Epic Theater," mostly in essays and notes to productions of his plays, while publishing early versions of the plays in a series of soft-cover editions bearing the title *Versuche* (attempts or experiments). Connected with his essays and production notes, he began reading Karl Marx in 1925 or 1926, and thereafter couched much of his theoretical discussion of the theater in terms drawn not only from Marx, but from Lenin and Engels as well.

In 1932, a year before leaving Germany, he met Margarete Steffin, another influential collaborator (and mistress), who would help him write much of his full-length drama of the European exile years and would inspire most of his mid-life love poetry, but who would die of tuberculosis in Moscow in 1941. Brecht's European exile lasted from February 28, 1933 (the day after the Reichstag fire), until May of 1941, when he boarded the Trans-Siberian Express in Moscow bound for Vladivostok, whence he would travel by ship to the United States. In his first few months of exile, he stayed briefly in Prague, Vienna, Zürich, Lugano, and Paris (where, with Kurt Weill, he wrote the ballet *The Seven Deadly Sins of the Bourgeoisie* [1933]). Thereafter he, Helene Weigel, the two children, and Margarete Steffin lived in two neighboring houses in Skovsbostrand, near the Danish town of Svendborg. Ruth Berlau, a Danish actress, had helped to arrange these quarters.

In Denmark for six years, from 1933 to 1939, Brecht worked on plays such as *Roundheads and Peakheads, Fear and Misery in the Third Reich,* and *The Rifles of Señora Carrar*, numerous poems, a wealth of essays on theater, literature, and culture, and a book to be called the *Tui-Novel,* about the behavior of intellectuals during this fascist period of history. In addition, he indulged in endless conversation with artists and thinkers similarly exiled from Germany, like Walter Benjamin, Karl Korsch, Hanns Eisler, and Stefan Zweig—to name just a few who turned up in Scandinavia. And Brecht traveled to Moscow, Paris, London, and New York for writers' congresses as well as to see productions of his plays. (In New York it was the Civic Repertory's 1935 production of *The Mother*, which he loathed.) In Moscow, he met many old friends (such as Bernhard Reich, Erwin Piscator, and the actress Carola Neher [wife of the stage designer Caspar Neher], who had been the quintessential Polly Peachum in the Berlin production of *The Threepenny Opera*), and he was also extraordinarily affected by the performances there of the Chinese actor Mei Lanfang, about whom he wrote in a 1937 essay titled "Alienation Effects in Chinese Acting."

During these years, as well, Brecht conducted his written debate with Georg Lukács and other Soviet theorists on the topic of "socialist realism," much of which appeared in the Moscow journal *Das Wort* (*The Word*, of which Brecht was co-editor). He further proposed the formation of an organization for the collection and dissemination of information about experimental theater work, to be called the Diderot Society. Several important essays were also written during this period, among them "The Street Scene" (1938), "On Experimental Theater" (1939), and those essays in conversational form that would later be called *The Messingkauf Dialogues* (1939-42). Brecht's collection known as *Svendborg Poems* itself was published in 1939, and exemplary short stories like "Socrates Wounded" and "The Trophies of Lucullus" were completed around the same time.

The landmark dramas of this period were *Life of Galileo* and *The Good Person of Setzuan*. The first version of *Galileo* was finished in three weeks in November 1938, overhauled in December after Brecht had received news of the splitting of the atom, and then sent out to theaters all over free Europe. The idea for *Setzuan* had been in Brecht's mind since 1930 under the working title *The Commodity of Love*, but he did not take it up again until early 1939. Meanwhile, Denmark was becoming unsafe for German exiles, so Brecht arranged through friends for a move to Sweden.

The Brecht entourage lived there, on the island of Lidingo near Stockholm, for just a year, from May 1939 to April 1940, when Nazi troops marched into Denmark and Norway. From that year came two linked one-acts, *Dansen* and *What's the Price of Iron?*, further work on *The Good Person of Setzuan* (which had faltered for a while), and, by November of 1939, a completed *Mother Courage and Her Children*. A week of furious work immediately thereafter produced the radio play *The Trial of Lucullus* (1940). Ruth Berlau now joined the Brecht "group" as another indispensable mistress and collaborator, and they all moved to a safer Scandinavian locale: Helsinki, Finland. Living for just over a year in several dwellings in or near Helsinki, Brecht worked again on *Setzuan* and on a prose work called *Conversations in Exile* (a.k.a. *Refugee Conversations*, 1941), while also completing *Mr. Puntila and His Man Matti* in three weeks during 1940 (August 27 to September 19) and *The Resistible Rise of Arturo Ui* in one month of 1941 (March 10 to April 12). Later in that same month of April 1941, the world première of *Mother Courage and Her Children* took place in Zürich.

On May 15, 1941, Brecht left Helsinki with his family and his artistic collaborators Margarete Steffin and Ruth Berlau. The long-awaited American visas for all six had finally been granted, but because Hitler's troops now occupied the northern Arctic port of Petsamo—from which Brecht and company had intended to sail from Europe—they had to travel via Russia. But Steffin, severely weakened by the living conditions as well as the weather in Finland, had to be admitted to a hospital in Moscow, and Brecht was advised by his Soviet writer friends not to delay his trip, since the Nazis were expected to march on the Soviet capital any day. So, leaving Margarete Steffin in his friends' care, Brecht, Berlau, and family embarked on the trip to Vladivostok via the Trans-Siberian Railway, only to receive the news in mid-journey of Steffin's death. Then, on June 13, 1941, they boarded the Swedish ship *Annie Johnson* bound for San Pedro harbor in Los Angeles, California.

Arriving there in July 1941, Brecht subsequently lived in American exile until October 1947. He left the United States on the afternoon of Halloween—the day following his appearance before the House Un-American Activities Committee. His six years in America had been more arduous, if in a very different way, than his eight years of European exile, for here he was definitively cut off from his native-language theater. So from his residence in Santa Monica, he set about trying to earn a living by writing film scripts for Hollywood, at the same as he busied himself with promoting Broadway productions of his plays. But Brecht experienced only repeated frustration in the face of America's "entertainment industry," for he discovered that nothing was valued in the United States unless it was marketable.

Even the landscape appeared to him as something transmitted according to the laws of the market: "It all looks as if it's behind panes of glass, and I find myself involuntarily looking at every chain of hills or lemon tree for a little price tag," he wrote in his *Arbeitsjournal* (*Work Diary*, 1944; my translation, as are all others except where noted). Earlier European theater associates like Kurt Weill and Elisabeth Bergner had themselves been drawn into the prevailing climate of American "show business"—Weill, especially, with his Broadway successes—so much so that Brecht could not persuade either of them to work with him on any of his pending or completed scripts. He desperately wanted a Broadway production in order to establish himself in this new country, but he also wanted it on his own terms, which were antithetical to the commercial principles governing the aesthetics of playwriting and theatrical production in the United States.

For most of 1942, then, Brecht earned his living through screenwriting—in particular, as one of two screenplay writers for the movie *Hangmen Also Die*, directed by another European acquaintance, Fritz Lang. It was the only film script for which he was paid while in America, but his name was not included in the screen credits. At the same time, he was collaborating again with his old friend Lion Feuchtwanger on yet another Joan of Arc play, eventually to be titled *The Visions of Simone Machard* (1943). The seeds of *Schweik in the Second World War* (a.k.a. *The Good Soldier Schweik*) were also sown, or in any event replanted, in this, Brecht's first full year in the United States. And early in 1943, *The Good Person of Setzuan* had its world première in Zürich.

For the rest of that year, Brecht traveled between Santa Monica and New York; worked on film projects with actor friends like Peter Lorre in mind; planned, with Kurt Weill, both an unrealized Broadway production of *Setzuan* and a collaboration on *Schweik* (with Lorre as the prospective Schweik); had a quite public falling out with Thomas Mann over the issue of "proper conduct" on the part of leftist German émigré writers; set to work with the poets H. R. Hays and W. H. Auden on an adaptation (in English) of Webster's *The Duchess of Malfi* (1614); and signed a contract for an adaptation of *The Chalk Circle* (based on the 1927 play by Klabund [Alfred Henschke] and on Brecht's own 1940 story "The Augsburg Chalk Circle"), to be written for the émigrée actress Luise Rainer. In these same months—particularly toward the end of 1943—Eric Bentley undertook a translation, with Elisabeth Hauptmann's help, of *Fear and Misery in the Third Reich*, which would be produced two years later under the title *The Private Life of the Master Race*; *Life of Galileo* had its world première in Zürich in September; and, in November, Brecht's son Frank was killed in Russia.

The year 1944 was taken up mostly by work on what was now known as *The Caucasian Chalk Circle* (with various translation problems connected with the adaptation, as a result of which first Christopher Isherwood, then W. H. Auden, withdrew from the project), and by a re-working of *Life of Galileo* in collaboration with Charles Laughton, whose close acquaintance Brecht had made early in the year. With his erstwhile musical collaborators Hanns Eisler and Paul Dessau, Brecht also had long discussions on the use of music in the Epic Theater. In 1944, as well, Ruth Berlau gave birth to Brecht's third son, but he died within a few days. Later in that year, Brecht and Berlau began systematically experimenting with photographing dramatic performances for archival preservation, a practice that came to fruition later in the Berliner Ensemble *Modellbücher* (*Model-Books*), where one can see moment-by-moment groupings, blocking, and postures which show "attitudinal" definition—what is meant by "gestical" in Brecht's theory of theater (more on this later).

The following year, 1945, saw the production of *The Private Life of the Master Race* in New York, the completion of the "Laughton Version" of *Galileo* (conceptually altered yet again to reflect the dropping of the atom bomb in August) and of the English-language *Duchess of Malfi* (with Berlau and Auden as collaborators in the end), and work on a few uncompleted screenplays. In late 1946, *Malfi* was produced in Boston and New York; at about the same time, Eric Bentley's *The Playwright as Thinker* appeared, the first book in English to champion Brecht's kind of theater intelligently. In December Brecht was already writing his boyhood friend and the designer of *Baal*, Caspar Neher, that he planned to travel to Zürich the following June, and that he had received an offer from East Berlin to use the Theater am Schiffbauerdamm.

Then in March of 1947, Brecht and Weigel both received an "exit/re-enter permit" for the country of Switzerland. On July 31 of the same year, Charles Laughton played Galileo in the première of the American version of this work at the Coronet Theater in Beverly Hills, California, as directed by Joseph Losey. Three months later, on October 30, 1947, Brecht testified before the House Un-American Activities Committee. (His testimony is recorded on Folkways records

[1961], with commentary by Eric Bentley.) Meanwhile, for safety's sake, friends were microfilming his works in New York. He flew to Zürich the next day.

Brecht attempted at his hearing to deliver a statement, but he was not permitted to do so. The last two paragraphs of it (the statement in its entirety is included in Bentley's notes to the Folkways recording) read as follows:

> Being called before the Un-American Activities Committee, however, I feel free for the first time to say a few words about American matters: looking back at my experiences as a playwright and a poet in the Europe of the last two decades, I wish to say that the great American people would lose much and risk much if they allowed anybody to restrict the free competition of ideas in cultural fields, or to interfere with art, which must be free in order to be art. We are living in a dangerous world. Our state of civilization is such that mankind already is capable of becoming enormously wealthy but, as a whole, is still poverty-ridden. Great wars have been suffered, greater ones are imminent, we are told.
>
> One of them might well wipe out mankind as a whole. We might be the last generation of the specimen man on this earth. The ideas about how to make use of the new capabilities of production have not been developed much since the days when the horse had to do what man could not do. Do you not think that, in such a predicament, every new idea should be examined carefully and freely? Art can present such ideas clearly and even ennoble them.

It should be remembered that the purpose of this committee, which had begun its work as early as 1937, was to root out of the American entertainment industry all Communists or fellow-travelers. As a result, by the late 1940s and early 1950s, many artistic careers had been ruined by witnesses before HUAC who named Communist (or purportedly Communist) colleagues in Hollywood and on Broadway.

Brecht did not see the short New York run of Laughton's *Galileo* in December 1947. He also did not take his son back to Europe with him, for Stefan had become an American citizen. Brecht himself remained officially in Zürich from 1947 until the spring of 1949. In the last five weeks of 1947, as "busy work," he adapted Friedrich Hölderlin's 1803 translation of Sophocles' *Antigone* (441 B.C.) in collaboration with Caspar Neher (who was engaged at Zürich's Schauspielhaus); it was intended for production at nearby Chur, and Brecht said its main purpose was to give Helene Weigel a long overdue opportunity for a major role in German. The première took place on February 15, 1948. Ruth Berlau, recently arrived from New York, had photographed the entire performance three days earlier, and now she and Brecht assembled the *Antigone-Modellbuch.* Plans were also set in motion for a Zürich production of *Antigone,* at the same time as *Mr. Puntila and His Man Matti* was being readied for its Schauspielhaus première on June 5, 1948. Negotiations were additionally begun so that Brecht could work with Neher in Salzburg, whence the latter had moved in the meantime. For neither Brecht nor Neher was heartened by Swiss acting or theater practice, each of which seemed to have deteriorated from pre-war standards.

In August of 1948, Brecht finished his major theoretical work, *A Short Organum for the Theater*. In September he secured permission from Swiss authorities to travel to Berlin, where the new East German government had invited him to stage *Mother Courage and Her Children*. Having had his German citizenship revoked legally by Hitler in 1935, he was not allowed to travel through the American sector of West Germany, so he and Weigel journeyed to Berlin by way of Salzburg (where he negotiated further with Salzburg Festival officials about the possibility of his working there) and Prague. In October Brecht began rehearsals for *Mother Courage* at the Deutsches Theater, using many young East German actors.

The most famous theatrical première of the European postwar years then took place on January 11, 1949, in ruined East Berlin. Helene Weigel portrayed Mother Courage; Teo Otto designed; and Brecht co-directed with Erich Engel, the original director of *The Threepenny Opera*. Thus did the world see for the first time an authentically "Brechtian" production. And from this production was born the Berliner Ensemble, the most impressive national theater (it's worth repeating) in modern history. Helene Weigel was officially its artistic director, Brecht its chief stage director. This theater's first official production under the name Berliner Ensemble was of *Mr. Puntila and His Man Matti*, on November 8, 1949, as directed by Brecht and Engel and designed by Neher, with music by Paul Dessau. There followed quickly a production of Maxim Gorky's *Wassa Schelesnowa* (1910/1936), on December 23rd. Meanwhile, Brecht continued to negotiate with people in Salzburg for a position there, all the while still waiting to be granted an official Austrian passport, so that he might have free access to German-language theater in its entirety.

The new year—April 15, 1950, to be precise—saw the first of several productions by the Berliner Ensemble of Brecht's adaptations of world drama: *The Court Tutor* (1774), by the German dramatist J. M. R. Lenz. This would be followed in the next four years by re-worked versions of Gerhart Hauptmann's *The Beaver Coat* (1893) and *The Red Rooster* (1901), Gorky's *The Mother* (1906; first adapted by Brecht in 1931), Goethe's *Urfaust* (1772-75), Shakespeare's *Coriolanus* (1605-08), Anna Seghers' 1930s radio play *The Trial of Joan of Arc at Rouen, 1431*, Molière's *Don Juan* (1665; which opened the Berliner Ensemble's new permanent house, the refurbished Theater am Schiffbauerdamm, in March 1954), and Farquhar's *The Recruiting Officer* (1706; under the title *Drums and Trumpets*). The Berliner Ensemble also produced Brecht's *The Rifles of Señora Carrar* (1937) and *The Caucasian Chalk Circle* (1945) under his direction. By the mid-1950s, *The Days of the Commune* (1956), conceived by Brecht in Zürich, was in rehearsal, as were *The Good Person of Setzuan* (1940) and a number of other adaptations in which Brecht had at least a partial hand, including Synge's *The Playboy of the Western World* (1907) and Beckett's *Waiting for Godot* (1953).

Brecht had spent more and more time during late 1954 and all of 1955 at his house in Buckow, near East Berlin, where he was writing a collection of poems called the *Buckower Elegies* and his last play, *Turandot, or The Congress of Whitewashers*. The Berliner Ensemble made several tours at this time (once to

Warsaw, twice to Paris), and Brecht traveled frequently to other European cities, either to consult with producers of his plays or to attend various cultural events. He was also involved during these years in repeated efforts to make a film of *Mother Courage*, and he was constantly engaged in production discussions with his several young assistant directors, chief among them Manfred Werkwerth, Benno Besson, Egon Monk, Peter Palitzsch, and Carl Weber. Then in May 1955, Brecht traveled to Moscow to receive the Stalin Peace Prize. His last major directing effort was still another revised version of *Life of Galileo*, which he began in December of 1955. Rehearsals were well underway when he died of a massive heart attack on August 14, 1956. He is buried in the Dorotheen-Friedhof, next to his city residence at 125 Chausseestrasse, Berlin, in the former GDR. His tombstone is a large gray rock bearing no epitaph.

A late poem of Brecht's reads:

I require no gravestone, but
If you require one for me
I would wish that it might have written on it:
He made suggestions. We
Took them up.
Through such an inscription would
We all be honored. (*Collected Poems*)

Second Movement: The Experimental Playwright, the Theater Theorist, and the Artist-as-Critic

Everyone who knows the name Bertolt Brecht also knows that he enjoys the reputation of being the twentieth century's most influential dramatist and theater practitioner. At the same time, he is widely known as a troublesome person (see the Overture of this essay) and a politically problematic artist (having never quite shaken the twin stigmata of "Marxist ideologue" and admirer of Stalin). It didn't help matters, either, that the Berliner Ensemble and the East Berlin cultural ministers had by the 1970s effectively defined him as "an important figure" in the historical development of socialist theater in the GDR; or that a younger generation of German writers, most prominently Peter Handke and Heiner Müller, laid claim to having supplanted him and thus fixed his place in theater history (as opposed to the living theater of the present).

But the most pervasively troublesome thing about Brecht the artist is his theory of Epic Theater. Agreement is hard to find, among critics and theater people alike, concerning the worth of his theory or his "true" reasons for having propounded a theory in the first place. "Is Brecht's theory correct?" "Isn't it too intellectual?" "Doesn't it assume a Marxist 'faith'?" "Does it even apply to his own plays?" These are the basic questions, underlain in part by an ancient skepticism about ever resolving the dichotomy between theory and practice in the arts. They have been answered variously, and with equal conviction, by explicators on both sides of the erstwhile Political-Ideology Curtain, as well as by progressive theorists of theater and drama—some of whom are sure we have "gone beyond Brecht."

At the risk of oversimplifying, let it be said that in the present American climate of thinking (or not thinking) about the theater, Brecht's theory is either embraced erroneously as calling for a revolutionary political theater (i.e., theater that advocates the abolition of capitalism or systems of government that are based on capitalism), or it is discarded as irrelevant to the practical work of creating theater. Thus we most often see Brecht productions that are stridently "Marxist" in an agit-prop mode, on the one hand, or which are independently "artistic" adaptations—the products of their directors' sovereign imaginations—on the other. There are historical causes for this situation. Whereas the British theater received a large injection of Brechtian drama and theory in the mid-1950s (due chiefly to the Berliner Ensemble's 1956 visit to London), the American theater missed out on any such mainlining influence. It became heady instead (especially after the dull, Eisenhower-dominated 1950s) with a mixed or eclectic, American-style avant-garde: experimental theater inspired by Artaud and Grotowski, a "turn-on-drop-out" politics, a religion of "peace and love," and a pop-psychological social ethic featuring self-help, ego-training, and a "value-free" morality.

It may be that we have left behind most of the extreme convictions of those combined Theaters of Self-Exploration, Therapy, and Force-Fed Political Consciousness—all of them versions of Peter Brook's "Holy" and "Immediate" theaters (see his 1968 book *The Empty Space*)—even if we have not achieved any kind of dominant theater that all would acknowledge as inspiring, or even good. We still have an experimental, avant-garde theater, it's true, but it is not nearly as noisy as it was in the 1960s and 1970s. We still have, of course, the commercial theater of entertainment, although it does not exactly flourish. And we have, in both these realms, that thing commonly known as "Director's Theater."

The feverish and self-consuming experiments of the 1960s and 1970s, for their part, had two pervasive effects. First, they reinforced the Romantic assumption, long cultivated among ordinary theater-goers, that ART is subjectively esoteric and ARTISTS are both specially endowed visionaries and self-indulgent weirdoes who live "beyond good and evil." Second, these experiments drove an almost moralistic wedge between the idea of *doing* theater and the idea of critically *analyzing* it. This deed was perpetrated chiefly by the insistence that words, particularly the words that made up the playwright's text, were inimical to the theater's true aim: *to celebrate, preferably in ritualistic form, the inarticulate urges residing deep in the collective human psyche.* But this assumption of a subjectivist autonomy for art and artists only recapitulated another longstanding assumption among many critics of theater and drama—namely, that the work of art exists beyond any theoretical definitions, even those articulated by its author. Indeed, this notion has long propelled a good portion of post-structuralist theory and criticism of art. And it has always informed the aims of "Director's Theater," which insists that the text is raw material for the theatrical production and that the director who fashions this production is therefore as much the play's "author" as the playwright himself.

Brecht's theory and practice, taken together, complicate this situation. On the one hand, it is well known that Brecht altered his own scripts readily, both as a director of those scripts and as a tireless textual reviser. Not only that, but he also freely adapted the plays of other authors to suit his own needs. On the other hand, he insisted on precision of interpretation, both by actors and by directors (not to mention readers, philosophers, and politicians), and he always stood ready to illuminate his own plays, whether in published notes or ephemeral conversations. Moreover, even though Brecht subscribed to the "changeability" of the world and human nature, he believed in such things as "correctness" and "knowability." He would therefore not have shared the chief premise of post-structuralist epistemological questioning—namely, that human beings are necessarily unable to discern truth because they already are victims of "received untruth." On the contrary, Brecht's favorite slogan was "truth is concrete." And although he postulated a reality that was in constant flux because of self-contradictoriness—in fact, he reveled in dialectics—he was a materialist. For him reality would never lose its materialist character in favor of a spiritual one, never become transcendent. For this reason "truth," which arose from reality rather than being imposed abstractly upon it, would always be ascertainable, useful, and particular, as opposed to absolute, eternal, and general or universal.

If we of the twentieth and twenty-first centuries are ourselves accustomed to saying that "truth is relative," it is because we have learned to look at reality in a more provisional way than our forebears did. We have learned, for instance, that to know "the real" requires an understanding of how contextual and contingent everything is. With this understanding, we may then conclude that something need not eternally be the way we know it to be here and now, under these circumstances. At the same time, however, to know something thoroughly in its contextuality and contingency is to know it *concretely*. And this means that "truth" can indeed be had, as well as enjoyed. The phrase "truth is relative" is usually employed to persuade someone that there is no such thing as "truth." By contrast, the phrase "truth is concrete" reminds us that, however shifting, temporary, or conditional it may be, the "truth" is something we can get and use.

For Brecht, then, the proper philosophical attitude for inhabitants of the twentieth century and beyond, heirs to the "scientific age" of Bacon, Galileo, and Newton with their inductive metaphysics and concrete epistemology, was the "critical attitude." This consists in seeing reality as containing contradictions and therefore as capable of changing—or being changed. It is an attitude that is premised upon the possibility of seeing objectively and complexly. It assumes that human beings are capable of detecting the sources of mental confusion or delusion, understanding the causes of human stupidity or ignorance, and grasping the means for rectifying or improving the human condition. In other words, more than the emotional experiences or the unconscious reservoirs, Brecht prized the sapient powers of *homo sapiens*.

The trouble with Brecht's theater theory, therefore, is that it rests firmly on the principle of criticism. And once we have understood this, it is possible to appreciate exactly how his theater is "didactic." *Theoretically*, Brecht's kind of theater aims to teach its twentieth and twenty-first century audiences a new *aesthetic* attitude: the critical attitude. His most radical pronouncement on this subject may well be this one from the late 1930s:

> The critical attitude is the only productive one, the only one worthy of human beings. It signifies cooperation, going forward, living. True aesthetic pleasure is impossible without a critical attitude. (*Gesammelte Werke* [*Collected Works*, 1967], Vol. 19: 393)

In Brecht's view, this critical attitude already defined modern man's engagement with the natural environment. He observed that "criticizing the course of a river means improving, correcting it. Criticizing society means revolution. This is criticism carried out, practical criticism" (*GW* 15, 378). Such an attitude is also deeply enjoyable in itself, Brecht averred, because it betokens a "moment of productivity." He continued: "And if, in our ordinary linguistic usage, we apply the word 'arts' to those enterprises that improve people's lives, why should Art proper remain aloof from such arts?" (*GW* 15, 378). Brecht considered it unthinkable to perpetuate a theater that did not address itself to this productive human disposition. So he articulated a theory of theater that did so; and he wrote plays which he called "experiments" in that theory. His aim was not merely to address, but also to incorporate into a new theater, that "critical attitude" by which modern man takes pleasure in contemplating the world with a view towards changing it.

This is what people misunderstand when they decide that Brecht's *plays* advocate social or political change. Those who repeat this erroneous commonplace are missing the main point of his *theory*. Brecht does not say that his plays for an Epic theater teach a Marxist recipe for altering the world. Rather, he says that the pleasurable attitude of criticism, which we all practice in our daily lives, should become part of our *theater* experience as well. Furthermore, he says that the theater of our time must represent the present-day world in such a way that, no matter how familiar it seems, it can simultaneously be held at a distance, perceived to be full of contradictions, and therefore be understood as alterable. Only thus can the work of both audience members and theater practitioners be described as *critical*.

As for the aesthetic side of the critical attitude, Brecht wrote the following in his *Arbeitsjournal* in 1944: "To explain the political usefulness of non-Aristotelian dramatic art is child's play; the difficulties begin in the aesthetic sphere. A wholly new aesthetic experience in the theater must be established." He went on to speak of the usual aesthetic experience as something antiquatedly metaphysical, something linked to transcendental ideas such as Fate, the gods, or "Human Nature," supposedly immutable forces which govern human fortune. These are the notions that belong to what he called "Aristotelian" theater; and they are ideas we may still find informing many a textbook on drama and theater. Brecht considered uncritical the notion that aesthetic experience was something immutable, something predicated on operations of the human mind like "willing suspension of disbelief" and "empathy." These, he declared, diminish the spectator's consciousness of reality for the ostensible purpose of transporting him emotionally out of himself and into the fictitious "world" of play. But why should we continue to assume that this is the definitive way in which human beings take pleasure from dramatic art?

To be sure, it is an *easy* way. It means merely surrendering one's productive self to the manipulation of others, becoming a *victim* of the work of art rather than a collaborator in its use or in trying to make it useful. To illustrate this unacceptable situation, Brecht drew an analogy from social life: speaking of the masses, he said that as long as they remain *objects* of political manipulation, they "can only regard what happens to them as their destiny; they learn as little from catastrophe as the laboratory specimen learns about biology" (Program Note, Berliner Ensemble production of *Mother Courage and Her Children*, 1949). But, said Brecht, we live in an age of conscious productivity. And in this age,

> when science has been able to change nature to such an extent as to make the world seem well-nigh habitable, . . . it is no longer possible to describe man as a victim, as the object of a fixed but unknown environment. It is scarcely possible to conceive of the laws of motion if one looks at them from the point of view of the tennis ball. (*Brecht on Theatre*, 275)

If we translate this analogy into the terms of theater experience, it goes like this: "It is no longer possible to assume that humans are victims or objects of a fixed, enigmatic aesthetic environment; it is hardly possible to conceive of the laws of human relations if one looks at their theatrical representation from the point of view of characters who are buffeted by unknown forces." Thus, for Brecht, to allow oneself to be carried away by the "fates" of invented *dramatis personae*, according to rules considered mysteriously unchanging, was a most un-modern aesthetic activity and an unworthy human one. It therefore had to be supplanted.

Accordingly, Brecht argued, the new theater should create (and live from) pleasure in the fashioning of human relations. (He did *not* argue that the new theater would create new human relations.) This pleasure includes the rational pleasure of understanding *how* human relations are fashioned. "Fashioned" is the key word here. It is (*pace* the deconstructionists) what the playwright does: he shapes, forms, designs—"fashions." In everyday life, human beings "fashion" their social and personal relations, which are ever-changing; in the theater, human beings (artists) "fashion" from life imitations of social and personal relations. And it is this *process* of forming and making that Brecht wanted to become the focus of the theater-goer's aesthetic experience: the shaping process of the theater itself, no less than the human relations which are the object of that shaping. So he wrote plays that made this complex "fashioning" process their content, and which therefore demanded a new *theatrical* style, both to suit the new content and to achieve the aim of making its perception *pleasurable*. Both his new dramatic form and his new theatrical style are described in his theory.

Yet Brecht was an instinctive artist who knew that theory alone would not change the theater. The theater itself would have to "re-educate" its audience. But even the term "the theater itself" requires critical addressing. When we say it, we implicitly acknowledge that it is "eternally" the same. Nonsense, said Brecht: the theater has changed constantly throughout its history. The trouble was, the theater of his early life—the continental and German institution of the 1920s—was an implacable monster that devoured everything which came its way. As he ruefully conceded in his 1931 notes to *The Threepenny Opera* (*Brecht on Theatre*, 43-47), "it 'theater-tizes' everything" (*Es 'theatert' alles 'ein'*). The only hope for altering this powerful institution was to continue writing experimental plays—that is, plays which aimed to change the existing theater—for a discerning *reading* audience, who would become "experts" and therefore demand changes in the existing theater practices. And so it would be these new plays that would "teach" the way to a new theater.

The audience, however, could not be expected to establish an innovative theatrical style. This would have to be accomplished by the theater's own artists: actors, directors, designers, and composers. Consequently, we read in Brecht's theory numerous essays devoted to the means by which theater *artists* should fashion a new theater. But these means were basically aesthetic ones, as Brecht succinctly put it in the first paragraph of a 1940 essay called "Short Description of a New Technique of Acting which Produces an Alienation Effect":

> What follows represents an attempt to describe a technique of acting which was applied in certain theaters with a view to taking the incidents portrayed and distancing them for the spectator. The aim of this technique, known as the alienation effect [*Verfremdungseffekt*], was to make the spectator adopt an attitude of inquiry and criticism in his approach to the incident. *The means were artistic.* (*Brecht on Theatre*, 136)

A later group of writings, called "New Technique of Acting 2," written between 1949 and 1955, bears an even more significant epigraph: "There are two arts that need developing: the art of acting and the art of spectating" (*GW* 16, 710; this line itself was written to advertise the Berliner Ensemble's 1952 publication *Theaterarbeit* (*Theater Work*), a valuable dramaturgical document on the company's first six productions). These essays, about a hundred pages in length and mostly untranslated, are a mine of illumination. Here, for instance, Brecht writes a short list of "General tendencies that the actor should combat." At the top is "Striving for the middle of the stage." There follow some paradoxically paired warnings, such as "Constantly looking at the person being spoken to" and "Not looking at the person being spoken to"; and "Not investigating the intentions of the playwright" yet "Subordinating one's own experiences and observations to the presumed intentions of the playwright." (These are translated from *Theaterarbeit* in *Brecht on Theatre*, 239-246.) In such examples, we can see Brecht's characteristically dialectical thinking.

There are also dozens of "oughts" for the new, "Epic" actor. For instance: young actors ought to practice observation and imitation in their playing, the one by means of the other; moreover, they ought to imitate and observe not only real people and their behavior, but also other experienced actors and their performing behavior. Young actors in addition ought to learn "to recite lines as if from memory." (This is no easy trick.) As professionals, they ought to avoid the common temptations of the profession, such as holding themselves aloof from other people, or its opposite, imposing themselves on other people. And the actor ought to study constantly what manifests itself as "law" in the conduct of human beings towards one another. Says Brecht: "Society is his command giver; he studies *it*." Social feeling is indispensable, but it should not replace *knowledge* of social conditions or the constant study of them. The actor must thus develop a "perfect pitch" for the sound of truth. In the process, the actor should not cut himself off from any joy or any suffering: "He needs these feelings for his work, since above all he must aspire to remain a human being" (*GW* 16, 742-744).

Brecht constantly stresses the Epic actor's need to develop his aesthetic invention by unself-indulgent practice and by critical observation of both social and artistic behavior. Finally, after all the training and hard work, the actor must strive to master the most crucial technique of stage performing: *effortlessness*. (Brecht's word is *Leichtigkeit*, which connotes both ease and lightness.) To achieve this, says Brecht, he must know the stage like a blind man, savor the text as if it were a part of him, and orchestrate his movements so that their very rhythm and plasticity will make them enjoyable. For, Brecht continues, "if the actor does not make it effortless for himself, he will not make it effortless for the audience, either" (*GW* 16, 746).

Regarding the actor's working methods and approach to the text, Brecht offers much concrete instruction throughout his theoretical writings. For instance, in his *Short Organum for the Theater* (translated in *Brecht on Theatre*, 179-205, 276-281), we may read that "the Epic actor masters his character by first mastering the play's plot [*Fabel*]" (200). He does this by "walking all around the entire episode, letting himself be amazed by the contradictions in its various attitudes, knowing that he in turn will have to make them amaze the audience" (*Brecht on Theatre*, 200). Furthermore, he must show his own stance towards the character and the character's circumstances, which he does by "presenting" the character more than by crawling inside the character's skin. Presenting the character, says Brecht in the *Short Organum*, does not necessarily mean "that if he is playing passionate parts he must himself remain cold; it is only that his feelings must not *at bottom* be those of the character, either" (*Brecht on Theatre*, 193). Empathy, or self-identification with the character, must be reserved for rehearsals—there to be used "as one of a number of methods of observation" (*Brecht on Theatre*, 195)—but avoided in performance.

Although Brecht admits that empathy has led to subtle delineations of personality in the contemporary theater (he did not reject Stanislavsky altogether, as is commonly believed), he states in the *Short Organum* that it has nonetheless been applied in an indiscriminate way:

> It is the crudest form of empathy when the actor simply asks: what should I be like if this or that were to happen to me? What would it look like if I were to say this and do that? Instead he should ask, have I ever heard somebody saying this and doing that? So as to piece together all sorts of elements with which to construct a new character such as would allow the story to have taken place—and a good deal else. (*Brecht on Theatre*, 195-196)

Brecht concludes this paragraph with a most provocative statement: "The unity of the character is in fact shown by the way in which its individual qualities contradict each other." Underlying these theoretical ideas is Brecht's prizing of earlier, non-naturalistic styles of acting: those of the classical Chinese, the street balladeer and carnival puppeteer, the marketplace pitchman or mountebank, and the improvised, *commedia*-like styles as preserved in vaudeville, burlesque, cabaret, and silent film comedies by actors like Charlie Chaplin.

Underlying Brecht's theoretical ideas are also the terms he invented or used in a special way—some of which have caused certain difficulties in interpretation. A simple definition of the dramatic-cum-theatrical technique he termed *Verfremdung* (which I shall henceforth call "alienizing," but which could also be called "defamiliarizing") is this: "to render unfamiliar that which is simultaneously familiar." The root of this half-coinage (partly derived from *Entfremdung*, which means estrangement or alienation in the strictly psychological sense) is *fremd*, meaning "alien" or "strange." The idea is to make something we regard as familiar seem strange, so that we will not be lulled by its familiarity into thinking it immutable. The trick to comprehending an "alienizing effect" in Brecht's dramaturgy is to remember that the object rendered "alien" must at the same time be recognizably familiar.

It may be of assistance here to recall that the first psychoanalysts were termed "alienists"—that is, specialists in the technique of making patients able to see themselves as "other," which implied an ability to "distance" the self from self. Presumably, the cure for mental disorder would be more likely be effected if the patient could see himself "as if from the outside," that is, "objectively." But, as we all know, this is something that usually requires the agency of someone else. Therefore, in the theater, it must be the artists, beginning with the playwright, who are the agents of *Verfremdung*. A Brecht text contains "alienizing effects" in its dramaturgy; and theater artists must translate them into the theater's terms, using the new style of theater being developed—or continued—by them.

We come now to another troublesome term, "Gestus." Brecht defined this Latinate coinage in several places as including the meanings of "gist" (a word that can be intellectually complex enough) and "gesture," in the sense of both a physical movement, like nodding, and a more elaborate spiritual motion, as in the phrase a "noble gesture" or a "token gesture." He says that

> by Gestus, we understand a whole aggregate of single gestures of the most varied kind, in combination with utterances, forming the basis of a single remarkable incident among human beings and referring to the totality of attitudes of all those involved in the incident (the condemnation of a person by others, a consultation, a fight, etc.); or, an aggregate of gestures and utterances which, by appearing in a single person, sets certain events in motion (the delaying attitude in *Hamlet*, the professings in *Life of Galileo*, etc.); or, even just the basic attitude of a person (like contentment or waiting). A Gestus marks the relations of human beings with each other. (*GW* 16, 753)

Thus abstractly defined, "Gestus" is difficult to grasp. The concept gains clarity, however, if we know one description of an exercise for an Epic actor. It occurs among the group of writings from 1935-1941 called "New Technique of the Art of Acting," under the sub-heading "Producing the A-Effect." The description's own title is "Alienizing Gestus," and it reads as follows:

> A simple method by which the actor can alienize Gestus consists in separating it from mimicry [*Mimik*]. He need only put on a mask, and follow his playing in a mirror. In this way he will easily arrive at a selection of gestures that are rich in themselves. Precisely the fact that the gestures are selected will produce the Alienizing-Effect. The actor should then carry over into his playing something of the attitude he assumed before the mirror. (*GW* 15, 369-370)

The thinking in this deceptively brief paragraph is astonishing. Not only does the actor, by playing in a mask before a mirror, see himself as "strange" (because he is masked), but he also sees himself as an experimenter in the "selection of gestures." That is, he sees his definition as "actor" itself alienized. It is as if he were thereby enabled to say, "So that's what an actor does! He simultaneously wears a figurative disguise and makes deliberate choices about how to move his body." Thus the exercise reinforces the fundamental point that the actor is someone who is both *other* than the mask and *other* than the figure known through a particular selection of gestures. The distinction between "Gestus" and mime or mimicry, then, rests on the performer's abiding consciousness of the separation between himself and the masked, gesturing figure. That consciousness remains constant during the exercise because the actor watches himself in the mirror.

But then Brecht wants the actor to take that consciousness with him into performance. There, too, it must remain constant: the Epic actor must maintain, as if he were still before the mirror, that observation of himself making deliberate choices about how his character will be seen. He can do this only by holding an analogously "mirrored" distance between himself and his "imaged-forth" creation. In short, he must bring into, and maintain in, his actual performance a *critical attitude*. And now we can understand the specific meaning of such an attitude: it is "dialectical seeing." It defines Brecht's notion of *Verfremdung* as the presentation and seeing of objects for *what they are* and simultaneously for *other than they are*. This notion embraces the "object" of actor as well as performance, of performer as well as production.

The Epic Theater, therefore, requires thinking actors who are capable of enjoying contradictions, but who also understand that their art consists essentially in making critical choices about their stage behavior. They must additionally understand, however, that the same critical disposition which they bring to their art has to be brought to the dramatic text, for it is the substantive source of their performances. These "fashioners of gestical behavior" consequently need to develop their skill in the critical reading of plays. With Brecht's drama this means something different from the Stanislavskian training of actors, where character, plot, and action are translated into terms like "through-line," "objective," and "super-objective," and where it is usually assumed that actors already know how to discover these elements in a text. For Brecht, "critical reading" means that the actor must comprehend the play in its total "gestical" action, which in this dramatist's work consists basically of contradictions.

The actor must then discover how the play "imitates" the contradictions of human behavior in the modern world. Moreover, he must read with an eye to representing the play's contradiction-filled action *as such* to an audience, so that they too might be able to *see* the drama's action as being "gestically" imitative of life's contradictoriness. And the audience will not be able to see a Brecht play's representations of present-day reality in a critical way—the way he wanted them to—unless the actors themselves "interpret" the play critically. It follows that the new theater will not be able to induce the critical disposition in audience members, as their own wholly new aesthetic experience, unless actors develop the same disposition and make it the chief ingredient of their artistic work.

The Brechtian actor-artist, for this reason, must be quite the opposite of that self-absorbed, psychologizing person whom the students in most acting programs strive to become, and about whom the public loves to read in their show-biz, celebrity magazines. Instead of someone who goes to work, Method-like, "from the inside out," who must "get in touch with himself" and "find out who he is" before he can "embody" a character "truthfully," the Brecht actor is someone who starts working from critical observation of human social behavior and brings that same disposition to his study of the text (which is not the same thing as working imaginatively or transformatively, like an Olivier or any other classically trained actor, "from the outside in"). Rather than seeing the play's action from a psychological point of view, inside his character, the Brecht actor endeavors to see the whole action, including his character, from a critical distance. He might express his attitude as follows:

> This play will teach me a way of regarding human behavior in aggregate, something I may think I understand already, but which I must acknowledge as always changing. The play will teach me essentially how to see social life critically. I must then transform this instruction, by means of an artistic work that I share with other artists, into a clearly understandable but also uniquely enjoyable theater presentation. The purpose of this theatrical event is likewise to afford my audience the experience of seeing human life, or social being, critically. The members of that audience are not used to such an experience in the theater of our time, so my performance must be equally entertaining and intelligible. That is, I must not disappoint either the playwright's or the audience's rightful expectation of pleasure, as well as instruction, from theater art; I can assure this pleasure by showing my own in creating it. Finally, I must not forget that my art should increase my own capacity for living productively in society.

The counterpart, in Brecht's theater, of this critically inquiring actor is the director who puts both the text and the audience above the idea that his own "concept" enjoys preeminence. To be sure, when he is directing plays from another time, he must "select a [conceptual] mode of reading" that will interest his own time, said Brecht in an essay from the same group of writings on a "New Technique of the Art of Acting" (*GW* 16, 756-757). But his main business is "to bring a story before the audience," using those essential elements that the theater places at his disposal: "the text, a stage, and actors." What is the most important aspect of the story? "Its significance: that is, its social points." How should the director determine the story's significance? "By studying the text, the peculiarity of its author, and the time of its origination." And what is the chief operation by which the director brings the story before his audience? "The *arrangement*: that is, the blocking of the characters, the defining of their stance towards one another, of their changing positions, of their entrances and exits. The *arrangement* must tell the story intelligibly" (*GW* 16, 756-757).

In Brecht's view, there were "heaps of wrong *arrangements*," ones that failed to tell the story intelligibly because they were more interested in doing other things such as "positioning certain actors, the stars, in advantageous places (so that all eyes focus on them), at the expense of the story; conjuring up for the audience certain moods that explain the incidents superficially or falsely; serving generalized tensions and excitement that don't belong to the story; and so on." The prevalent kinds of "wrong arrangements," in this case all from the "art theater," were these: naturalism's imitation of "wholly accidental positionings of characters 'as they occur in life'"; expressionism's merely self-expressive characters; symbolism's figuring-forth of presumably hidden meanings; and formalism's striving for "picturesque groupings" that don't further the story (*GW* 16, 756-757).

In another essay from "New Technique of the Art of Acting," Brecht wrote that "playwrights and actors have the common task of presenting the play's events in an entertaining and profitable way. However, concerning the social function that a performance should have, actors and playwrights can have different ideas." For this reason, Brecht "hated directors who forced the actors 'to embody their ideas,' and likewise abhorred hearing that actors ought simply 'to serve the poet's word'" (*GW* 16, 763). Moreover, in practical terms, the director must recognize that everything in the text is "dramatic action": songs, lighting changes and intensity, specified physical actions, scene titles, written directions for grouping, tone, and tempo, et cetera. He must consequently study the text carefully in order to find out its every "Gestus" and rhythm; nothing guessed at or half-understood should reach the stage. As Brecht was fond of telling collaborators, "When certain directors or actors cannot get out of a play or a scene what is in it, they stuff something into it that doesn't belong" (*GW* 16, 761). Again, it is the basic attitude towards the text and towards the theater's relationship to the audience that distinguishes a Brechtian director from many directors in our contemporary theater. He must be willing to learn from the text and to afford his audience—as well as his actors—a similar learning experience. In other words, he must exercise the "critical attitude."

Neither the current commercial theater nor the so-called "Director's Theater" much resembles Brecht's aesthetic model. Few of us would disagree that our American Broadway and Broadway-aspiring theater (which for some time now has included major regional and university theaters) remain much the way Brecht described them in the mid-1940s, when he was living in Santa Monica, trying to sell scripts to Hollywood and plays to New York. American actors had no opportunity for artistic renown, he said, "only for credit and success." They formed huge communities of "stars"; they spent most of their time "promoting the autograph and fan-mail industry; and every so often, on the advice of their hairdressers and publicists, they modified their stereotyped personalities, but chiefly for their real-life vocation: going to parties" (*Arbeitsjournal*, August 9, 1944). Actors and audiences alike in the United States were kept in thrall—actors to inferior plays (and movies) and an anxiety about their careers, audiences to their cherished illusion that the theater (or film) was reflecting real-life incidents. In truth, said Brecht, the conventional American theater, like its cinematic counterpart out in California, aimed at "achieving more or less primitive shock effects or hazily defined sentimental moods that were to be consumed as substitutes for the missing spiritual experiences of a crippled and cataleptic audience" (*Brecht on Theatre*, 160).

Our commercial theater continues to regard its audiences as consumers, blatantly pandering to a mean level of taste and intelligence in order to stay in business. And it is even outdone in this process by prime-time television "drama." But lest we think that "Director's Theater," with its appearance of artistry, is the satisfactory antidote, consider how it works. With the director and his "concept" (or sometimes the designer and her "concept") furnishing the ruling aesthetic motive, the collaborative artistry of theater is destroyed. The director becomes the chief inventor of the performance's "meaning." The rest of the theater's workers retreat into their specialized domains, thereby disclaiming any responsibility for the production's overall quality. And worst of all, the actors—usually of their own volition—abdicate interpretive responsibility. The play's potential significance for an audience is therefore not developed through the use of contributions, during the rehearsal process, from all the theater's artists; rather, that significance is assumed from the start to be the subjective, foregone conclusion of the director. In this scheme of things, theater work itself loses its mutually inspiring pleasure. Indeed, the play we see in the end may not even be—*need* not be, according to the logic of "Director's Theater"—the original author's.

Coda

At this point, one might reasonably raise a number of objections to, or at least reservations about, Brecht's ideas, at least as they are being represented here. One is: what about plays not written by Brecht? Is there something wrong with them if they don't show the world to be full of contradictions and thus capable of change, or if their characters move us emotionally? Another concern might be: isn't this insistence on the "critical attitude" just too prepossessing, the worst kind of theoretical browbeating? In answer to the first concern, Brecht said the following in a 1949 interview:

> An Epic way of acting isn't equally valid for every classical work. It seems to be the most easily applicable, i.e., to hold the most promise of results, in works like Shakespeare's and in the earliest works of our own classic writers (including *Faust*). It depends on their attitude toward their social function: the representation of reality with a view to influencing it. (*Brecht on Theatre*, 225)

As we know, Brecht adapted several works from the canon of world drama. In light of this fact, perhaps we should ask ourselves whether some of the best plays by the major writers of Western drama, for one, are not already "Brechtian," in the sense that their dramatic actions invited their original audiences to engage them critically. Works like Molière's *The Misanthrope* (1666) and *Tartuffe* (1664), Shakespeare's "problem comedies" (such as *Troilus and Cressida* [1609] and *All's Well That Ends Well* [1601-05]), most of Shaw's plays (as Brecht himself points out in the essay "Three Cheers for Shaw," translated in *Brecht on Theatre*, 10-13), even Ibsen's *The Wild Duck* (1884), *An Enemy of the People* (1882), and *A Doll House* (1879), among many others from varying periods and styles, are alike in refusing to fit easily into our textbook definitions of dramatic genre—and thus in making the question of their genre, and that genre's relationship to reality, one that audiences and readers alike are urged to confront.

In fact, it could be argued that Shaw, Ibsen, Molière, Shakespeare, and let's not leave out Euripides, all wrote "problem plays"—because what these works do, in the final analysis, is pose the problem of their artistically fashioned actions directly to the audience. They seem precisely, that is, to adopt a Brechtian attitude toward the social function of their art: "the representation of reality with a view to influencing it." In other words, these are plays that do not merely "release" the audience into some disposition of cathartic transcendence, or simply reaffirm a feeling of universal harmony; rather, they challenge their societies to question the assumptions and values which underpin the represented dramatic actions, challenge them even to criticize (in the sense of "rethink") the very artistic conventions by which their interest has been aroused, their feelings excited, their expectation of resolution encouraged. Most of these plays, then, can reasonably be interpreted as entertaining and complex provocations to thought. And this is "Brechtian."

As for the second objection above, the best reply will come only from a thoughtful consideration of the concept known as "criticism." Brecht's arguments that the critical attitude can be an aesthetic attitude, and that criticism is the most suitable disposition for us "children of the scientific age," are far too persuasive to be set aside merely because we happen to live in a time which is skeptical about the pleasure of *thinking* in the theater, or which is automatically distrustful of any artist who says he wants to make us think. The fact is, thinking *is* pleasurable. We attest to this in most of our daily endeavors. So why should this pleasure be excluded from our theater-going? For the most part, it is the established theater that excludes thought, by insulting its audiences with puerile fantasies and technical effects designed to provide them with temporary relief from life's cares or concerns. And because this theater has only the specious credit that belongs to entertainment, its customers cannot invest anything in it except the expectation of superficial pleasure. Put another way, they cannot learn a truly artistic pleasure from an institution that merely invites them to escape from thinking—and thus from significance.

In a 1926 essay Brecht invented a little theatrical scenario to illustrate how in his day, too, the theater no longer had any "credit." By this he specifically meant that a figure entering the stage would not be given credit for having any reasons *of his own* for saying or doing something; instead, the audience would immediately question what *the author* was up to in the character's place. In other words, they would insist that the character's behavior be "validated"—that is, verified by their own, as well as the dramatist's, knowledge of "how things are"—before they would give it their objective attention. Brecht's illustrative scenario goes as follows:

> Two men are onstage. The fat one offers the thin one an orange. The thin man refuses the gift derisively. We hear him say he does not care for the orange, so there! Now, the audience could say, "If I were the thin man, I would accept the orange." Or: "I would refuse it, too." Or they could ask, "Why doesn't the thin man take the orange?" But in fact the audience only says, "First of all, nobody offers anyone an orange without a reason; second, nobody refuses an orange without a reason." As the author of this scene, I would allow these points with pleasure, if I could assume that the audience's interest would be increased by the very enigma of such assertions. But the audience has already lost interest completely, for they are now concerned only with the question, "Isn't this utterly improbable? Why are they showing us this incident?" Now the scene continues. The fat man offers the thin man the orange a second time (at this gesture the audience could say, "He has no character," but instead they say, "That's even more improbable"), and the thin man not only refuses it a second time but actually draws a revolver and shoots the fat man dead. (The audience does not now say something like "That's nasty of the thin man," or "This thin fellow has *that* in him"; rather, they say, "That's the climax," and they leave the theater.)
>
> The author's friends had told him so: they had suggested he make it clear that there was already something going on between the two characters. Oh, but had he wanted to listen to them? Had he wanted to read his Gustav Freytag [*Technique of the Drama*, 1863]? As the play bill was being presented, he continued telling himself with sheer bewilderment that, in his opinion, life *was* like that. (*GW* 15, 87-89)

Eighteen years after writing this, in the last paragraph of his 1944 "private lesson" for his American friend Mordecai Gorelik, Brecht stated that

> The modern theater must not be judged by its success in satisfying the audience's habits, but by its success in transforming them. It needs to be questioned not about its degree of conformity to "the eternal laws of the theater," but about its ability to master the rules governing the great social processes of our age; not about whether it manages to interest the spectator in buying a ticket—i.e., in the theater itself—but about whether it manages to interest him in the world. (*Brecht on Theatre*, 161)

To be interested in the world is to be critical. And Brecht was dedicated to transforming the theater into something that would entertain us precisely by offering us "a world-to-be-criticized," rather than something which would divert us by making us forget the world. His Epic Theory proposes a theater that appeals to the human being who, by exercising his critical intelligence, would be "self-productive," in the theater no less than in the world. Does this kind of theater exist now? Should it?

Works Cited

Brecht, Bertolt. *Bertolt Brecht Before the Committee on Un-American Activities: An Historic Encounter*. Ed. Eric Bentley. New York: Folkways Records, FD 5531, 1961.

----------. *Brecht on Theatre: The Development of an Aesthetic*. Ed. & trans. John Willett. London: Methuen, 1964.

----------. *Bertolt Brecht: Diaries, 1920-1922*. Ed. Herta Ramthun. Trans. John Willett. London: Eyre Methuen, 1979.

----------. *Arbeitsjournal*. In *Bertolt Brecht Werke: Journale 2*. Vol. 27. Berlin: Aufbau-Verlag, 1995.

----------. *Gesammelte Werke* [*Collected Works*]. 20 vols. Ed. Elisabeth Hauptmann. Frankfurt am Main: Suhrkamp Verlag, 1967.

----------. *Collected Poems*. Trans. & ed. Tom Kuhn & David Constantine. London: Liveright, 2018.

Fenton, James. "Aimez-vous Brecht?" *New York Review of Books*, 31.4 (Mar. 15, 1984): 25-27.

Fuegi, John. *Brecht and Company: Sex, Politics, and the Making of the Modern Drama*. New York: Grove Press, 1994.

Wright, Elizabeth. *Postmodern Brecht: A Re-Presentation*. London: Routledge, 1989.

"Play Doctor, Doctor Death: Shaw, Ibsen, and Modern Tragedy"

Tragic Criteria

The Doctor's Dilemma was not a great popular or critical success when it was originally produced in 1906, but the play is one of Shaw's most perplexing, intriguing works and deserves a more prominent place in the Shavian canon. Indeed, in his controversial book on Shaw, Colin Wilson goes so far as to declare that *The Doctor's Dilemma* "is the culmination of Shaw's career as a playwright" (Wilson, 198). The absurdity of this opinion aside (among the play's successors, after all, were *Pygmalion* [1913], *Heartbreak House* [1919], and *Saint Joan* [1923]), Wilson's praise for the play is veiled criticism of the philosophical preoccupation that he felt seriously diminished the strength of Shaw's later dramatic writing. Wilson reads *The Doctor's Dilemma* as a return to the nineteenth-century, well-made-play structure that Shaw had effectively adapted earlier; he does not consider the play a serious attempt to write a tragedy, or even as an attempt to write a play of importance. Instead, Wilson praises *The Doctor's Dilemma* as the last hurrah of the "playful" Shaw before the playwright became hopelessly mired in the politics, and drama, of "creative evolution." I want to argue here, by contrast, that *The Doctor's Dilemma* is much more interesting than Wilson contends. It is not simply an oddity or a throwback to nineteenth-century dramatic forms, but a serious attempt by Shaw to confront the traditional criteria for greatness in a play without compromising his own modern aesthetic determination of what a play should be.

One of those traditional criteria for greatness is that a dramatic work should aspire to tragedy, which *The Doctor's Dilemma* does do. Indeed, it was his only major play that Shaw specifically labeled a tragedy. To date, however, critics have not yet fully considered the complex relationship between the formal, classically tragic aspects of *The Doctor's Dilemma* and the play as an example of the new drama that Shaw espoused. And it is precisely this complex relationship between "old" and "new" that renders *The Doctor's Dilemma* problematic and has so often caused the play—its plot, its dramatic structure, Shaw's artistic intent—to be misunderstood.

Shaw came to write *The Doctor's Dilemma* in response to a challenge from his friend and colleague William Archer. Shaw had criticized Ibsen's use of death in his plays in a column written to honor the Norwegian dramatist a few days after his death (*The Clarion*, June 1, 1906). Here is part of Archer's response to Shaw's comments in his own column in *The Tribune*: "Shaw eschews those profounder revelations of character which come only in crises of tragic circumstance . . . it is not the glory but the limitation of Mr. Shaw's theatre that it is peopled by immortals" (*The Tribune*, July 14, 1906). A few weeks later, Shaw answered in the third person through the letters-column, announcing that "Mr. Shaw" was writing a new play that "is the outcome of the article in which Mr. William Archer penned a remarkable dithyramb to Death, and denied that Mr. Shaw could claim the highest rank as a dramatist until he had faced the King of Terrors on the stage" (Henderson, 1911: 390). There can be little doubt that Archer had struck a nerve in his "offensive" defense of Ibsen's tragic drama, and

Shaw could not duck the challenge to his abilities as a complete and serious artist. From its inception, therefore, *The Doctor's Dilemma* was linked directly to Shaw's intellectual relationship with the work of Ibsen.

The Quintessence of Ibsenism

Because of the direct relationship of *The Doctor's Dilemma* to Ibsen's drama, Shaw's *Quintessence of Ibsenism* is particularly relevant in this context, for it provides the most extensive commentary on the nature of drama that Shaw wrote outside of his plays themselves. Moreover, three crucial points emerge from *The Quintessence of Ibsenism* that should bear directly on any analysis of *The Doctor's Dilemma*: the first is Shaw's insistence that the dominant tragic theme in Ibsen is the futility of man's efforts to live up to the ideals he constructs for himself; the second, that tragedy should be focused on living characters; and the third point is that serious drama must be didactic. Connected to these three points is Shaw's plea for technical innovations in the new theater that he himself is espousing.

Bernard Dukore, for one, has attempted to apply the dramatic principles articulated by Shaw in *The Quintessence of Ibsenism* to Shaw's own dramatic works. Dukore focuses on Shaw's analysis of "the technical novelty in Ibsen's plays," the subject that comprises the penultimate chapter in *The Quintessence of Ibsenism*. Shaw characterizes Ibsen's technical novelty, or the structural change in modern drama, as a change from exposition-situation-unraveling to one of exposition-situation-discussion. The emphasis of any dramatic work thereby shifts away from action and towards discussion, which functions as an alternative to violent resolution and can take place anywhere in the play, not just toward the end. Dukore applies this model, as follows, to *The Doctor's Dilemma*: Act I provides exposition; Acts II, III, and IV intensify the situation; Act IV concludes the action; and in Act V that action is discussed (Dukore, 64). The problem with this analysis is that it implies the action of the play concludes in Act IV, and that Act V consists simply of a discussion of that action. While it is true that Shaw wanted to shift the focus of drama away from "situation" and towards discussion of the action, the epilogue of *The Doctor's Dilemma*, as I shall demonstrate below, serves at one and the same time as the culmination of the action proper and a discussion of the ancillary action from Act IV.

Act IV can be seen as the conclusion of the action only if Louis Dubedat is accepted as the tragic hero of the play and his death as the culmination of the tragic action. In a letter written by Shaw at the outset of his work on *The Doctor's Dilemma*, however, he asserts that the hero of this piece was to be a doctor (*Collected Letters*, Vol. II: 639). Shaw kills off Dubedat in *The Doctor's Dilemma* in order to fulfill his pledge to Archer that he was capable of putting a death on the stage, but it is clear just from what Shaw wrote in *The Quintessence of Ibsenism* that the true tragic figure was the character who is forced to live on and not the one who dies: "If people's souls are tied up by law and public opinion it is much more tragic to leave them to wither in these bonds than to end their misery and relieve the salutary compunction of the audience by outbreaks of violence" (*Quintessence*, 200). It is strange that Dukore, who was drawing on *The*

Quintessence of Ibsenism for his analysis, did not realize that Dubedat's death makes Ridgeon the protagonist, and it is therefore only in Act V, when Ridgeon finds out his murder of Dubedat was pointless, that the action of the play is completed. Central to Dukore's misinterpretation of Act V as pure discussion is his assumption that the central premise or motivation of the action is Ridgeon's "dilemma," i.e., whether to cure Dubedat or Dr. Blenkinsop.

Social-Problem Play?

Like Dukore's analysis, most critical approaches to *The Doctor's Dilemma* have chosen to focus on this work as a "problem play" involving a central moral dilemma. While critics have disagreed about the exact nature of this central dilemma, most agree that they are dealing with a problem play and sidestep the issue of the drama as an example of Shavian tragedy. J. Percy Smith does attempt to deal with the play as a tragedy yet ends up discussing it as a problem play instead. He boldly asserts that the "story of this play is simple enough" (Smith, 193), but then offers a synopsis of the plot that is simply mistaken. He states that the central dilemma stems from a scarcity of the necessary serum—a likely medical, as opposed to moral, scenario—but the text gives clear and ample evidence that there is no such scarcity at all.

To wit: at the opening of the play Sir Ralph has already administered the serum to little Prince Henry, and it is the serum itself—albeit incorrectly administered—and not the lack of it that eventually kills Dubedat. It is Ridgeon's knowledge of the correct timing for injecting the serum, a knowledge that he could presumably share, which is critical for the cure. That a number of critics have seized on a scarcity of serum, not the use of it, as the cause of the play's central dilemma may have something to do with their own reluctance to indict the medical profession. Indeed, as Stanley Weintraub reports, the fact that doctors themselves "did not take seriously [Shaw's] implicit and explicit injunctions to examine and heal [themselves] must have irritated Shaw all his life" (Weintraub, 1992: 84).

In fact, it becomes clear as the play progresses that Ridgeon's own account of his dilemma is constantly changing. In Act I, he tells Jennifer Dubedat in all earnestness that he cannot possibly take on another patient without actually sacrificing one of his current patients, but by the end of Act II he has decided that he can squeeze in one more patient without too much trouble. And although he informs Sir Patrick in the play's opening scene that the test for the proper opsonin level is a simple matter, by the end of Act III it is apparently impossible for him to communicate this piece of information to B. B. (Sir Ralph Bloomfield Bonington).

J. L. Wisenthal, for his part, is typical of many critics who read the "problem" of *The Doctor's Dilemma* as the struggle between the artist and the scientist, with the artist ultimately triumphant and his way of life vindicated (Wisenthal, 1974). This reading relies on the acceptance of Blenkinsop as a genuine scientist, but in fact he is an undistinguished general practitioner and an "honest decent man" (*Doctor's Dilemma*, Act II: 56); he himself says in Act I, "I've forgotten all my science" (*Doctor's Dilemma*, 26). The point is not that Blenkinsop is a scientist, but that, unlike Dubedat, he is a morally sound, worthy human being. Wisenthal's reading also relies on an acceptance of Dubedat as someone who himself is a true artist, or, in Wisenthal's words, "a character who embodies perfection of the work—a dedicated professional" (Wisenthal, 1974: 109). The text, however, does not offer convincing evidence that Dubedat values art above all else—except perhaps in his death, where, as he dies, he attempts to craft an inflated image of himself not borne out by the facts of his life: "I believe in Michael Angelo [sic], Velasquez [sic], and Rembrandt; in the might of design, the mystery of color, the redemption of all things by Beauty everlasting, and the message of Art that has made these hands blessed" (*Doctor's Dilemma*, Act IV: 100).

Act III of *The Doctor's Dilemma* itself offers counter-evidence to the view that Dubedat serves his art above all other considerations. This act begins with both Dubedats in the art-making process: Louis is making a painting of Jennifer. They have been discussing his habit of borrowing money and Jennifer has extracted a promise from him that he will not continue to do so. But Dubedat is lying when he promises her that he will not borrow money any more. Dubedat chooses to couch his lie to Jennifer in the words of a romantic artist: "Ah, my love how right you are! how much it means to me to have you by me to guard me against living too much in the skies" (*Doctor's Dilemma*, Act III: 61). The fact that he is lying in this instance is made clear to the audience upon the entrance of Ridgeon and the ensuing conversation between the doctor and Dubedat.

Almost immediately after Dubedat speaks the self-idealizing lines quoted above, early in Act III, Jennifer reminds Louis of the drawings that he owes to a customer. Dubedat responds, "Oh, they don't matter, I've got nearly all the money from him in advance" (*Doctor's Dilemma*, Act III: 62). Shaw chooses to put this exchange at the beginning of Act III because this is the act in which Dubedat will claim to be an immoral moralist. That is, Shaw wants it to be clear that Dubedat thinks only of money, even when his art is in question; he has no commitment as an artist to the drawings themselves, even though he has already begun them and been almost fully paid in advance. Indeed, Shaw specifically indicates that the pictures have been started in order to underscore the expedient, mercantile attitude Dubedat has towards his calling. (Just as Dubedat's possession of any artistic merit beyond that of a "clever brute" is thus subtly undermined by Shaw, so too is the validity of the "science" in the play undercut. To wit: Ridgeon may appear to be a more competent doctor than Walpole, Blenkinsop, and the obviously incompetent B. B., but Shaw was not about to concede that Ridgeon's opsonin treatment was any less ridiculous in its way than the removal of something Walpole calls the nuciform sac.)

Alfred Turco demonstrates that the critical obsession with the surface moral dilemma of *The Doctor's Dilemma*—whether to cure the artist or the scientist—is based on a misreading of the play. Turco points out that Ridgeon himself is lying from the moment he meets Mrs. Dubedat, and that this initial white lie—told in an attempt to avoid having to see the woman for very long—sets off a series of lies which, in effect, bury the doctor. There is no dilemma according to Turco because, as Ridgeon explains to Sir Patrick at the outset of the play, the test for the proper timing of the administration of the serum is a simple matter:

> RIDGEON. Send a drop of the patient's blood to the laboratory at St. Anne's; and in fifteen minutes I'll give you his opsonin index in figures. If the figure is one, inoculate and cure: if it's under point eight, inoculate and kill. (*Doctor's Dilemma*, Act I: 14)

Black Comedy?

Turco concludes that *The Doctor's Dilemma* is a black comedy about the humbug, quackery, opportunism, and unscrupulousness of the medical profession—a comedy, moreover, that blends the sentimental trappings of a well-made, nineteenth-century problem play with such superficial technical elements of classical tragedy as *hamartia*, reversal, and catastrophe. According to Turco, "Ridgeon's *hamartia,* or false step, is a trivial lie within the repertoire of any receptionist; his reversal occurs during a scene in which he succeeds in killing his rival; and the catastrophe is his gradual discovery that he has committed a purely disinterested murder" (Turco, 1970: 25). Turco's reading of *The Doctor's Dilemma* is important because it highlights the absurdity of interpreting the play as the straightforward discussion of one doctor's moral dilemma, and because it also outlines the tragic structure of the drama. By dismissing the tragic structure of *The Doctor's Dilemma* as a form of parody, however, Turco slights the impact of the tragedy as well as that of the play's moral dilemma.

There are two major concerns with Turco's analysis of the resolution. The first of these is his self-confessed inability to account for Sir Patrick, who is normally seen as the voice of reason in the play, and for Sir Patrick's refusal to take action against what he knows to be Ridgeon's murder plans. The other concern is with Turco's emphasis on the lie itself as the false step that makes untenable a reading of *The Doctor's Dilemma* as a straightforward or conventional problem play. Both of these concerns can be removed by expanding on Turco's model of the superficial technical elements of tragedy. Indeed, I would suggest that *The Doctor's Dilemma* is meant to be read as a *modern* tragedy. And, as I shall discuss further, the superficial technical elements of tragedy that Shaw uses for comedic effect also serve as a superstructure for a uniquely Shavian vision of tragedy.

Let us begin with the "problem" of Sir Patrick. Sir Patrick's reluctance to intervene more strenuously to prevent the killing of Dubedat from taking place has troubled many critics of *The Doctor's Dilemma.* "Paddy" is privy to all the relevant information of the play's action. He knows that Ridgeon's dilemma is false, because Ridgeon has already explained to him at the beginning of Act I that his discovery is no more than a simple test at the hospital that takes fifteen minutes to indicate the patient's opsonin level. In Act II, Ridgeon callously (and conceitedly) indicates to Sir Patrick that he has romantic designs on Mrs. Dubedat; Sir Patrick even understands at this point that Ridgeon intends to murder Dubedat. Ridgeon had told him in Act I, "If I wanted to kill a man I should kill him that way" (*Doctor's Dilemma,* 14), referring to the very course of action that he is considering taking against Dubedat at the end of Act II. But Paddy does nothing to dissuade him and goes as far as to help convince him of Dubedat's lack of worth in comparison with Blenkinsop.

As a result, Sir Patrick has been viewed as a knowing accomplice to the murder, an advisor to Ridgeon in his plot to kill the artist (Bertolini, 79). If the character of Sir Patrick is seen in terms of the superficial technical attributes of tragic structure, however, it becomes clear that he fulfills the essential role of choral figure, or leader of the chorus of doctors—medical colleagues and advisors all—to Ridgeon. Viewed in this way, Sir Patrick's frank advice and "arid common sense," as Shaw describes it in the stage directions (*Doctor's Dilemma*, 10), are in keeping with his role. His hearkening back to "ancient history" in the person of his father and to the thirty cures for consumption that he's seen in his long life are also consistent with his character as the play's chorus. Sir Patrick provides advice drawn on knowledge of the past and reminds Ridgeon of the lessons of the past, but like a true Greek chorus he never actively attempts to influence the action of the protagonist. His implication in the crime through his inaction is also consistent with the ancient chorus in such plays as Euripides' *Medea* (431 B.C.), in which the chorus of women exacerbates Medea's homicidal anger at the same time as they seem to be offering her well-considered, if somewhat removed, advice. In his role as a choral figure, Sir Patrick thereby further underlines the overarching tragic structure of *The Doctor's Dilemma*.

Turco focuses correctly, I think, on the entrance of Jennifer Dubedat as the inciting incident of the tragedy, although he does not refer to it as such in his schema of the play. The "white lie" (Ridgeon's telling one of his assistants to call him away quickly from his consultation with Mrs. Dubedat by pretending that he is urgently needed at the hospital) is simply the first complication engendered from that inciting incident. This lie, and subsequent lies told by Ridgeon, are false steps and indications of a character flaw, to be sure, but such lying is not this character's *hamartia*. That *hamartia* is revealed earlier in Act I when Ridgeon confides to Sir Patrick that he has been feeling unwell: "Sometimes I think it's my heart: sometimes I suspect my spine. . . . And there are other symptoms. Scraps of tunes come into my head that seem to me very pretty, though they're quite commonplace" (*Doctor's Dilemma*, 15). Sir Patrick recognizes the symptoms as mild depression combined with adolescent "foolishness" making a mid-life appearance, and warns Ridgeon not to make a thoroughgoing fool of himself, presumably by becoming infatuated with a woman.

Back to Tragedy

This scene reveals the protagonist's *hamartia* as understood by the prevailing model of tragedy that Shaw was attempting to manipulate. The tragic flaw is the mid-life crisis that Ridgeon has brought onstage with him; the tragic false step occurs when Ridgeon refuses to accept, or understand, Sir Patrick's diagnosis. When Sir Patrick advises him that he is not going to die but that he may do something foolish and should be careful, Ridgeon responds with a non-sequitur, "I see you don't believe in my discovery. Well, sometimes I don't believe in it myself. Thank you all the same" (*Doctor's Dilemma*, Act I: 16). Ridgeon may be blind to his *hamartia* at this point, but if we recognize it as the potential for adolescent infatuation, then the "dilemma" of the title is no longer strictly a fictive construct on Ridgeon's part, as Turco suggests. The moral dilemma is false, but a tactical dilemma remains, and it is simply that of a respectable man who has a sexual desire for another man's wife. Ridgeon uses the false moral dilemma, which keeps altering as the play progresses, to mask the true tactical dilemma of how to get the girl without compromising the principles of a "moral" man.

Ridgeon, it must be emphasized, is at the height of his success as a professional man when the play starts—he is knighted on the day the drama begins—and Shaw uses his knighthood to emphasize that he is a tragic hero of noble stature. What also emphasizes his tragic stature is Ridgeon's elevated profession and his unusual first name. He was named after Bishop John William Colenso, who in 1867 was excommunicated from the Anglican church for his heretical religious writings (published between 1855 and 1861), and whose case caused quite a stir in England for many years. Ridgeon's profession, of course, is that of medical doctor, not priest or pastor. Moreover, his character is based on that of Shaw's friend Dr. Almwroth Wright (1861-1947), who played a prominent role, through experiments at St. Mary's Hospital, in advancing vaccination in Britain (Weintraub, 1992: 83). Ridgeon is thus a scientist, and, as the new dramatists of realism and naturalism well knew, science had become the rival god of the twentieth century and doctors its vicars—or heretics. Perhaps Shaw knew, or spoke about, this more than most, as his exhaustive 1917 compilation *Doctors' Delusions: Crude Criminology and Sham Education* attests, as does his preface to *The Doctor's Dilemma*, in which he made it plain that he regarded traditional medical treatment (including vaccination) as dangerous quackery which should be replaced with sound public sanitation, good personal hygiene, and diets devoid of meat.

As evidence of science's godlike status, consider the following. Jennifer comes to beg assistance, or "divine" intervention, at the "shrine" of Dr. Ridgeon, from which he must descend in order to see patients in his consulting-room. Like rival or sectarian Greek gods, Ridgeon and his medical associates squabble about their respective specialties or "territories" and brag about the honors bestowed upon, or obeisance paid toward, them; like the Greek gods also, Ridgeon is not above getting directly involved in the affairs of humans—his patients—on the basis of his own mortal desires. Finally, again like the Greek gods, especially the lesser ones, Ridgeon is not so omniscient as he would like to think. He has his own blindness in his love for Jennifer, and she, a mere human, has her own insight into Ridgeon and the ultimate fallibility of the medical profession. Ironically, Jennifer even has a spiritual side: by the end of the play, she may have lost her faith in doctors as a result of Ridgeon's handling of her husband's case, but she still believes in her husband for all his flaws (which she acknowledges) and despite the fact that he is dead. She may have remarried, but even this she has done on Dubedat's advice: for "Louis disliked widows, and [believed] that people who have married happily once always marry again" (*Doctor's Dilemma*, Act V: 115).

Ridgeon's benightedness is of less interest in this context, however, than the fact that he has been knighted. To wit: when Ridgeon meets Mrs. Dubedat, he is struck by her name, Jennifer, repeating it and its Anglicized equivalent, Guinevere. This seemingly trivial detail is underscored by Shaw at the beginning of Act II when Dubedat calls Jennifer Jinny-Gwinny. The Arthurian legend of a love triangle involving a knight, a king, and a beautiful Guinevere is thus reproduced in *The Doctor's Dilemma*—with an obvious reversal. The new knight, Ridgeon, is the middle-aged bachelor, and the "King of Men," as Jennifer refers to Dubedat in her book on his life, is the young married man. *The Doctor's Dilemma*, of course, is not intended as an extended gloss on this Arthurian legend, but the reference to it serves to enrich the action, superimposing elements of romance over the play's tragic structure.

Genre Confusion

In theory if not in practice, each genre of *The Doctor's Dilemma* that I have examined—problem play, romance, and tragedy—can be considered "closed" or complete unto itself, and as such these genres were incompatible with Shaw's philosophy of the universe. That philosophy saw art, as well as life, as an evolving organism, or, as Shaw quotes Hogarth in the play *In Good King Charles's Golden Days* (1939), "the line of beauty is a curve"—not a straight line from one finite point to another. As we know from his 1930 speech in praise of Albert Einstein, Shaw believed in a curvilinear universe; indeed, this was the idea at the heart of his *Weltanschauung*, or comprehensive view of the world and human existence. He used generic models in *The Doctor's Dilemma* to destabilize each other precisely so that curvilinearity—indeed, non-linearity—would be maintained and closure could not be implied in any satisfying way. In other words, Shaw purposely disturbed the expected resolution of the dramatic forms he used by playing one off the other in a warp and woof of contradiction.

This instability of genre is initiated by Shaw from the outset of the play, because he calls the play a tragedy in four acts and an epilogue. The implication is that the tragedy, as such, is encompassed in the four acts, and that the last act, or epilogue, is simply a summing up distinct from the tragic action *per se*. This conclusion is supported by the fact that the death scene in Act IV seems to be the climax of the play. The chorus of doctors even enacts its own dithyramb to death in which B. B. has a mock catharsis, exclaiming: "How well he died! I feel a better man, really" (*Doctor's Dilemma*, 103).

But Shaw's purpose for phrasing the title in the way he did—*The Doctor's Dilemma: A Tragedy in Four Acts and an Epilogue*—was not to imply that the climax comes in the fourth act. As noted, Shaw set out to put a death in his play specifically in response to Archer's challenge. At the same time, he seized the opportunity to make a statement about tragedy as a dramatic phenomenon and the place of tragedy in modern drama—or in a modern, democratic, prosaic world where the Greek concept of Fate had been taken over by science in the form of heredity and environment, or biology, psychology, and sociology. That is, Shaw wrote a five-act tragedy as a self-conscious quotation of the classical, or neoclassical, requirements of tragic form. But he chose to make the title theatrically self-conscious, or metatheatrical, by explicitly calling the play a four-act tragedy. The title could thus be construed as a typically whimsical touch by Shaw, a kind of intellectual joke in which he is thumbing his nose at tradition at the same time as he is following the traditional pattern for tragedy. Shaw seemed to believe, however, that the tragic is still possible even if pure tragedy is not; and that he could achieve the tragic out of comedy by bringing it forth as a frightening moment, an abyss that opens suddenly.

The meaning of *The Doctor's Dilemma* is inexorably tied, then, not only to the "play" of its forms but also to the wordplay of its title. Indeed, the metatheatrical device of the complete title introduces a motif that continues throughout *The Doctor's Dilemma*, for the play is full of theatrical references and allusions to art in general. A number of these appear in the guise of comic characterization, such as the Macbeth-Hamlet conflation by Sir Ralph at the end of Act IV, or the reference to Browning's play *A Soul's Tragedy* (1846) by Sir Patrick in Act I. The statement by Dubedat in Act III that he is a follower of Bernard Shaw, moreover, has the effect of shocking the audience out of the illusion of reality that has been fabricated onstage. The entire death scene, for its part, is also self-consciously theatrical, as Shaw has Ridgeon draw attention to the histrionics of the moment with his line to Sir Patrick, "Would you deprive the dying actor of his audience?" (*Doctor's Dilemma*, Act IV: 99).

The artistic design of *The Doctor's Dilemma* becomes clearer when such metatheatrical elements are seen as complements to the play's self-consciously tragic superstructure. The tragic elements already enumerated—*hamartia,* reversal, catastrophe, and chorus—themselves can be understood as subtler aspects of the metatheatrical motif in the drama. In this way, the play becomes a kind of palimpsest on which one set of aesthetic or dramatic criteria almost disappears as another set can be discerned on the surface. *The Doctor's Dilemma* has a false moral dilemma, for example, and a true tactical dilemma. It also has a false resolution in Act IV with the death of the artist, in a Dumas-*fils* caricature, and a true, more realistic resolution in Act V. Even the *agon* between the traditional morality of the doctors and the morality of the iconoclast Dubedat is a false agon.

Satire Transcended

Shaw laid out his strategy for toying with the audience's sense of drama and morality in *The Quintessence of Ibsenism*: "Never mislead an audience, was an old rule. But the new school will trick the spectator into forming a meanly false judgment, and then convict him of it in the next act, often to his grievous mortification" (219). *The Doctor's Dilemma*, for its part, continually begs questions of judgment. Characters in the play are morally judged by the doctors, and *all* the characters—including the doctors—are judged by the audience for their moral values in the same way that Dubedat's pictures are judged for their aesthetic ones. It is no accident that Ridgeon himself identifies scraps of tunes that seem pretty but are quite commonplace among his "symptoms" in Act I. Ridgeon's own apparent lack of credibility here as a judge of artistic value is thus linked to his looming infatuation with Mrs. Dubedat and the lack of judgment implied by it.

No character in *The Doctor's Dilemma* has any credibility by the end of the play, and no character or philosophy of life emerges as being any more morally righteous than another. This is one of the reasons that the epilogue is the most frequently criticized part of the play, for it brings home with a vengeance the play's ethical-cum-artistic strategy. In his review of the original production, William Archer praised the play as a masterful comedy but urged Shaw to drop the last act altogether (*The Tribune*, Dec. 29, 1906). If *The Doctor's Dilemma* is understood as a satirical parody of tragedy, the last act or epilogue is indeed superfluous. The final act can be seen in an entirely new light, however, once the multi-layered and metatheatrical structure of the play is understood. The superficial technical elements of tragedy that Shaw introduces and plays with over the first four acts are swept aside in Act V; the chorus itself removed, the entire action of the play is reduced to its barest elements. Once the fourth act ends and with it Shaw's comic satire, the epilogue or fifth act can then be seen as the combined discussion-action-catastrophe of Shaw's modern tragedy.

Ultimately, it is Ridgeon's inability to judge Mrs. Dubedat's character that brings about his catastrophe. He has deluded himself into believing that he killed Louis Dubedat in order to preserve Jennifer's image, or fantasy, of her husband. The catastrophe occurs when Ridgeon realizes that he has misinterpreted Mrs. Dubedat's fantasy, for it is in actuality a full picture that has included her husband's shortcomings all along. Nonetheless, Jennifer's judgment is no less warped than that of any of the other characters. Shaw himself wrote the following to Cathleen Nesbitt (who was playing Mrs. Dubedat in a 1923 London production) in disparagement of Jennifer:

> Jennifer is a sort of woman whom, I, personally, cannot stand, enormously conceited, morally patronizing to everyone, setting herself always in some noble, devoted, beautiful attitude, never looking facts in the face or telling herself or anyone else the truth about them for a moment, and making even her husband's death a splendid opportunity for taking the centre of the stage. (Weintraub, 1996: 91)

Mrs. Dubedat is the "womanly" woman to whom Shaw refers in *The Quintessence of Ibsenism*—the sort of woman who has led a bohemian life only by chance and may well have been equally devoted to the moral shortcomings of her husband had he been a banker or a munitions manufacturer.

With the revelation of Jennifer's real nature, Ridgeon's own self-deception is uncovered and he is forced to confront the fact that he has constructed a series of false moral dilemmas throughout the play in order to conceal the true tactical dilemma of how to reconcile his desire for Jennifer with his vision of himself as a moral man. The fall of Ridgeon in Act V is ultimately cathartic, it's true, but this kind of catharsis is peculiar to Shaw, where we feel less pity and terror than regret and removal. By the final punchline of *The Doctor's Dilemma,* in which Ridgeon learns that Jennifer has married again, not only has the character of Ridgeon been totally discredited, but the audience has lost all sympathy for him and may well even see him as a villain.

Ridgeon has suffered a fall at the end of *The Doctor's Dilemma*, but he is only slightly more isolated from the community of the audience than he was at the start, or than most people in the audience are from their fellow human beings in daily life. The play is thus designed purposefully to frustrate not only the sense of closure provided by artworks of a single, conventional genre, but also the sense of closure that even partial reintegration—of Ridgeon into the community of the audience, and of that audience into the society of man—would suggest. In fact, Shaw wanted to show that the ideals of this community are morally bankrupt, and all the devices he uses in the play, the metatheatrical ones as well as the ones associated with deliberate confusion of genre, are intended to aid in exposing such a bankruptcy. Because Shaw turns the audience's own inability to make moral judgments against it, that audience is left feeling unable to provide the means for Ridgeon's, or its own, moral redemption. Shaw's philosophy dictated that the theater should inspire positive change in the community of the audience, but the sense in the tragedy of *The Doctor's Dilemma* is that the community necessary for this change, and with it social reintegration, has not yet evolved. Such reintegration belongs instead to an audience of the future—one that would be able to understand the importance of the most tragic of all themes, in Shaw's words, "a man of genius who is not also a man of honor" (Henderson, 1932: 616).

Ibsen and Tragicomedy

Connected with the subject of social change and drama's role in it, Shaw had this to say about Ibsen's role in the development of modern tragedy:

> Ibsen was the dramatic poet who firmly established tragicomedy as a much deeper and grimmer entertainment than tragedy. His heroes dying without hope or honor, his dead, forgotten, superseded men walking and talking with the ghosts of the past, are all heroes of comedy: their existence and their downfall are not the soul-purifying convulsions of pity and horror, but reproaches, challenges, criticisms addressed to society and the spectator as a voting constituent of society. ("Tolstoy: Tragedian or Comedian?" [1921], in Shaw's *Pen Portraits and Reviews*: 263)

Faced with the challenge of writing his own modern tragedy, Shaw was careful to imitate the tragicomic Ibsen in *The Doctor's Dilemma*, in the sense that he followed his four-act comedy with a one-act tragedy, in "a play all about Death which [is] most amusing," as he himself put it in his reply to William Archer in *The Tribune* (Henderson, 1911: 390). Furthermore, in Shaw's view, the new, modern dramatic genre at which Tolstoy himself, together with Chekhov, was aiming was tragicomedy—which is to say, in Anna Obraztsova's words, "a play that was essentially a comedy but into which the tragedy of life boldly intruded" (45).

Shaw evidently believed, then, that true comedy is invariably tragicomedy in an era (stretching into our own) preocuupied with human suffering and world cataclysm, for it is too difficult to depict such a world with unrelieved seriousness, and it is somewhat irresponsible to impose a wholly comic vision on it. Such absolute and disparate froms no longer seemed relevant in the twentieth century, as they do not seem so today. And we get at the deepest reason for Shaw's liking of tragicomic situations when he says of Ibsen's that "they are miserable and yet not hopeless; for they are mostly criticisms of false intellectual positions, which being intellectual, are remediable by better thinking" ("Tolstoy: Tragedian or Comedian?" 276). The tragicomic dilemma of the doctor confronted by a case like Dubedat's thus has a remedy, as Shaw sees it: a social structure that would free both its artists and its scientists from competitive struggle and so alleviate the personal tragedy by solving the social problem.

Like the tragicomic Ibsen, Shaw followed exposition and situation in this play with discussion. In *The Doctor's Dilemma, discussion* forms the resolution (though it is unusually curtailed by Shavian standards, which in the end contributes to the play's tragic quality); the ideals on which the characters base their lives are shown to be false (as they often are in Ibsen's plays), because the culture in which they live is based on false ideals; the tragic figure lives on; and the drama's ultimate aim is didactic. Once an Ibsenian hero of comedy, Ridgeon has become—in Shaw's own words—through his very existence and downfall, not a soul-purifying convulsion of pity and horror, but instead a reproach, a challenge, a criticism addressed to society and the spectator at large. The genius of *The Doctor's Dilemma* is that after the dust clears upon the collapse of the play's metatheatrical structure, and Ridgeon is left alone with Jennifer among Dubedat's paintings, the play really does function as a tragedy—of the most open, abbreviated, unassimilated kind.

Works Cited

Bertolini, John A. *The Playwriting Self of Bernard Shaw*. Carbondale: Southern Illinois University Press, 1991.

Henderson, Archibald. *George Bernard Shaw: His Life and Works*. Cincinnati: Stewart & Kidd, 1911.

----------. *Bernard Shaw, Playboy and Prophet*. New York: Appleton, 1932.

Obraztsova, Anna. "Bernard Shaw's Dialogue with Chekhov." In *Chekhov on the British*
Stage. Ed. Patrick Miles. Cambridge, U.K.: Cambridge University Press, 1993. 43-53.

Shaw, George Bernard. *The Quintessence of Ibsenism*. 1891. London: Constable, 1913.

----------. *Collected Letters, 1893-1910*. Volume 2. Ed. Dan H. Laurence. New York: Dodd, Mead, & Company, 1972.

----------. *The Doctor's Dilemma, Getting Married*, and *The Shewing-Up of Blanco Posnet*. New York: Brentano's, 1911.

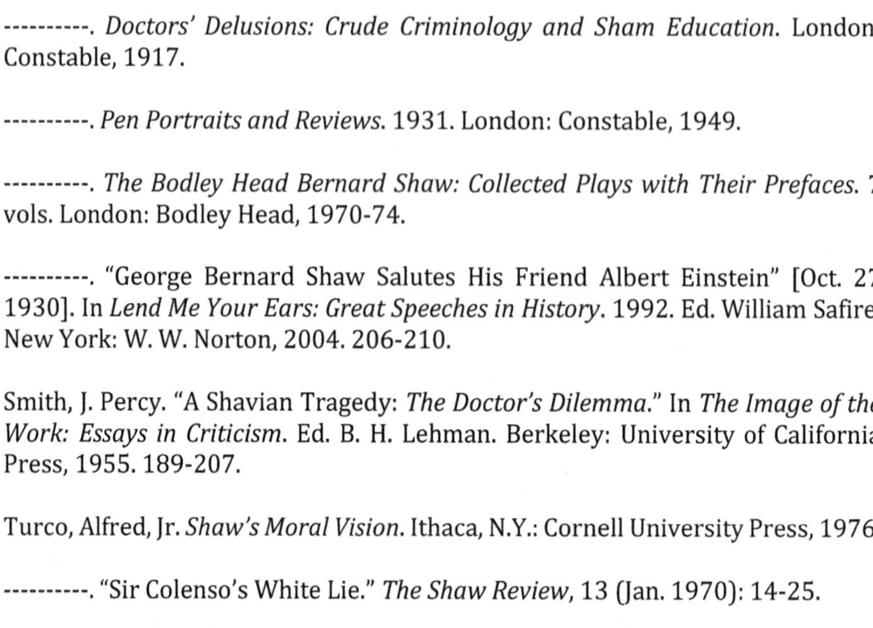

----------. *Doctors' Delusions: Crude Criminology and Sham Education.* London: Constable, 1917.

----------. *Pen Portraits and Reviews.* 1931. London: Constable, 1949.

----------. *The Bodley Head Bernard Shaw: Collected Plays with Their Prefaces.* 7 vols. London: Bodley Head, 1970-74.

----------. "George Bernard Shaw Salutes His Friend Albert Einstein" [Oct. 27 1930]. In *Lend Me Your Ears: Great Speeches in History.* 1992. Ed. William Safire. New York: W. W. Norton, 2004. 206-210.

Smith, J. Percy. "A Shavian Tragedy: *The Doctor's Dilemma.*" In *The Image of the Work: Essays in Criticism.* Ed. B. H. Lehman. Berkeley: University of California Press, 1955. 189-207.

Turco, Alfred, Jr. *Shaw's Moral Vision.* Ithaca, N.Y.: Cornell University Press, 1976.

----------. "Sir Colenso's White Lie." *The Shaw Review,* 13 (Jan. 1970): 14-25.

Weintraub, Stanley. *Shaw's People: Victoria to Churchill.* University Park: Pennsylvania State University Press, 1996.

----------. *Bernard Shaw: A Guide to Research.* University Park: Pennsylvania State University Press, 1992.

Wilson, Colin. *Bernard Shaw: A Reassessment.* New York: Atheneum, New York, 1969.

Wisenthal, J. L. *The Marriage of Contraries: Bernard Shaw's Middle Plays.* Cambridge, Mass.: Harvard University Press, 1974.

"Shaw, Brecht, and Saint Joan"

Introduction

Joan of Arc was an illiterate peasant girl, a mystic to whom Saints Margaret, Michael, and Catherine spoke directly, and a cross-dressing warrior whose mission, at the age of seventeen, was the liberation of France from English occupation in 1428 and the crowning of the dauphin Charles VII as monarch of a united France. After a number of astounding military successes in which she recaptured large parts of France from the English, she was taken prisoner, tried as a heretic by an international tribunal (run by the Rouen ecclesiastical courts but in collusion with the English), and burned at the stake in 1431, officially for heresy and witchcraft, but (as everyone knew) in reality for the political crime of revolt against the English occupation.

The Church, having accidentally created a martyr, cleverly decided to make her *its* martyr, so Joan of Arc was officially rehabilitated by the Church and King Charles after another international trial in 1456, which annulled the first trial on a number of different grounds: the procedure had been irregular, declared the new Court; the judges had been incompetent and partial; there had been no counsel for the defense; it had been improper to place Joan in an English prison (given that she had not been charged with violating secular law); there had been *post hoc* tinkering with the Articles of Accusation so that "heresy" would conform precisely to statements she had already made about her beliefs; her "confession" had been coerced and hence her "relapse"—in which she had withdrawn everything she had confessed—had been illusory; the sentence had been bizarre; and (as the archbishop of Rheims declared) her trial had been "contaminated with fraud, calumny, wickedness, contradictions, and manifest errors of fact and law. (The Church and King Charles also, somewhat mysteriously, declared "the execution, and all [its] consequences" null and void [Pernoud, 245, 247].)

So Joan was technically rehabilitated in 1456, but her real rehabilitation took place over the *longue durée*, not through formal legal proceedings but through cultural, literary, and (perhaps most often) dramatic representation: for instance, in the anonymous *Mystère du Siège d'Orléans* (1428-29), Shakespeare's *Henry VI* (1591), Voltaire's *La Pucelle* (*The Maid of Orleans*, 1752), and Schiller's *Die Jungfrau von Orleans* (1801). As mythic figure, she could become a leader of the religious wars of the seventeenth century, an eighteenth-century revolutionary, a nineteenth-century romantic figurehead (in Schiller, for instance, in which she tragically expires, having discovered the pangs of love; see Raknem in Works Cited). But the *political* Joan always dominated. For the late nineteenth century, she had been the champion of nations bound together by the words "blood and iron" (speech by Otto von Bismarck, 1862) as well as by the bonds of race (the German race as much as the French), and hence an icon not of resistance but of imperialist expansionism (see Marot, 85, 138). In the wake of the Franco-Prussian War, she had served as a paradigm of the slogan "France for the French," seen as the antithesis of

Alfred Dreyfus: the crowds protesting against Dreyfus had cried "Down with the Jews! . . . Long live Joan of Arc! Long live France for the French!" (Bancquart, 298; trans. mine).

But World War I changed Joan. She was a symbolic heroine of the Great War, representative of the struggle against tyranny, exemplar of courage under the dark fires of the trenches. Her suffering seemed to be reclaimed in the Allied victories of 1918 at Compiègne (the ground where she had been captured in 1430). And it was decided that her entry into official sainthood should mark an end of the War to End All Wars and the beginning of the new era. The Church had originally scheduled Joan for canonization in 1931, to celebrate the five-hundred-year anniversary of her execution. But in 1920—eleven years early—she officially became Saint Joan. It was a year after the League of Nations had been founded at the Paris Peace Conference, the year that decidedly ended the Russian Civil War in favor of the Bolsheviks, implicitly announcing a victory for International Socialism. In 1920 she was supposed to do something new for an ostensibly reunited and tolerant world.

A martyr at the hands of the intolerant Inquisition, a victim of a brutalizing and expansionist Northern European nation (Germany or czarist Russia in the role of the fifteenth-century English), she could become the antithesis of the nationalist spirit, the symbol of those who stood up to emperors and tyrants, of those who could transcend parochial national interests in the service of the larger truths of the spirit, truths that could unite nations and help to establish a new international order. Joan became a Soviet icon, imago of a new international socialism (see Levandovsky, 287). Her rehabilitation trial of 1456 became a model for what trials at the new Permanent Court of International Justice (established in 1920) could be, places for rectifying old wrongs. Oddly, for many, the warrior-girl became the "lark": a symbol of peace and conciliation, transcendence of differences, liberal harmony. She became the symbol of the new international world order: nations within their own boundaries, peaceably leagued together to combat aggression (even while, of course, the Allies were trading pieces of southern Europe).

Even before her official canonization Joan had occasionally played this role. One Joseph Fabre, revising the *Mystère du Siège d'Orléans* at the brink of World War I, has Joan cry out (contrary to all historians' accounts of the real Joan's views):

> Whether English or French, are they not humans?
> Oh! that the day would come, when instead of this slaughter,
> The brotherhood of nations!
> When all peoples, waging war no more,
> Would return peaceably to their hearths. (Bancquart, 311-312; trans. mine)

Such images of Joan became commonplace after the war, reflected in titles like William Paul Yancey's *The Soldier Virgin of France: A Message of World Peace*

(1926). As the Dutch legal historian Joseph van Kan put it apologetically in 1925, "She was a soldier [only] from stern necessity, a soldier completely ready to make peace. The soldier was—I say it emphatically—an angel of peace" (van Kan, 49). She still served for some as a proto-fascist nationalist, for instance for *Action française*, the far-right French royalists who adopted her as an incarnation of the purity of French blood. But oddly, even they could not fully resist the peace-loving, domestic Joan: "Joan of Arc is rebirth; she is the fertile peace after a cruel war; she is the motherland once again taking charge of its destiny" (see "Fête de Jeanne D'Arc" in Works Cited; trans. mine).

Joan-as-Pollyana, Joan proclaiming the world now safe for democracy: It was this portrait of Joan (in addition to the prelates' irksome glee at her canonization) that provoked George Bernard Shaw and Bertolt Brecht to offer their own versions. (Brecht in fact wrote three different Joan-of-Arc plays.) Shaw's and Brecht's Joan dramas are all quite different from one another, but each offers a critique of the sanguine belief that world peace really meant world peace—that it meant justice or equity or freedom from terror. In choosing the Joan-of-Arc story, with an international trial at its center, Shaw and Brecht were deliberately choosing a story that offered a false villain: Pierre Cauchon, bishop of Beauvais, the principal judge at the trial, with his sidekick, the Grand Inquisitor. In so doing, they could show that, however illegal the proceedings, it was not, in fact, the illegality that was responsible for the miscarriage of justice, but rather the legal system itself. They could show not the exceptional perversion of justice in the law, but the law itself as a perversion of justice.

To attack only the "illegalities" of the trial, as so many others had done, would have been to suggest that the legal system itself was not at fault, but merely plagued by corrupt and malevolent judges. To attack directly the laws of the Inquisition would have been to attack a historical relic, to suggest, as so many others had, that a world made safe for democracy would now be safe for its saints and saviors. (Shaw rejects such smug progressivism outright, arguing that in his time she would have been executed with hardly a trial or law at all [Preface to *Saint Joan*, 57]; Brecht would have agreed—in fact, his two modern Joans *are* essentially executed summarily.) Both Shaw and Brecht were attempting, through their refigurations of the Joan-of-Arc myth, more fundamental critiques of the legal system itself, both national and international.

Shaw's *Saint Joan*

Shaw's *Saint Joan* (first performed in 1923, three years after the canonization) is based largely on historical sources. In fact, a good deal of Shaw's trial scene follows the transcript of the actual trial, with Joan's clever evasion of the traps set for her by her interrogators. When, for instance, Cauchon asks her whether she believes herself to be in a state of grace, she answers, "If I am not, may God bring me to it: if I am, may God keep me in it!" (131, scene 6). When Thomas de Courcelles, one of the judges from Paris, asks her whether Saint Michael appears to her naked, she responds, "Do you think God cannot afford clothes for him?" (130, scene 6). But if he follows historical sources, in his long preface Shaw makes it clear that he is also drawing parallels between the events surrounding

Joan's trial and contemporary events (Preface to *Saint Joan*, 34-35). He compares Joan, for instance, to the

> Thousands of women, each of them a thousand times less dangerous and terrifying to our Governments than Joan was to the Government of her day, [who] have within the last ten years been slaughtered, starved to death, burnt out of house and home, and what not that Persecution and Terror could do to them, in the course of Crusades far more tyrannically pretentious than the medieval Crusades which proposed nothing more hyperbolical than the rescue of the Holy Sepulchre from the Saracens. (Preface to *Saint Joan*, 36)

Contemporary legal events, argues Shaw, compare badly with Joan's trial—in which she was not tortured, in which her judges insisted that they were bound by the law, in which there was no summary justice, no rush to the slaughter. Nothing in Joan's trial, Shaw writes, convicts Joan's judges of "as much anti-prisoner, pro-police, class and sectarian bias as we now take for granted in our own courts" (Preface to *Saint Joan*, 44):

> Can any of the modern substitutes for the Inquisition, the Special Tribunals and Commissions, the punitive expeditions, the suspensions of the Habeas Corpus Act, the proclamations of martial law and of minor states of siege, and the rest of them, claim that their victims have as fair a trial, as well considered a body of law to govern their cases, or as conscientious a judge to insist on strict legality of procedure as Joan had from the Inquisition and from the spirit of the Middle Ages even when her country was under the heaviest strain of civil and foreign war? From us she would have had no trial and no law except a Defence of the Realm Act suspending all law. (Preface to *Saint Joan*, 36-37)

As evidence, Shaw offers two cases: that of Roger Casement, the Irish revolutionary who exposed the exploitation of rubber gatherers in the Congo and South America and was eventually hanged for treason by the British; and that of Edith Cavell, the English nurse shot by a German tribunal in 1915 for releasing soldiers from the hospital without asking which side they were on. "The modern military Inquisition was not so squeamish [as Joan's]": Shaw writes. "It shot [Edith] out of hand" (Beck, 27).

Whether medieval or modern, whether in conformity with the law or not, trials, Shaw argues, serve merely as window dressing for political expediency, and this inevitably determines their outcomes. "The Church cannot take life," says Judge Cauchon piously (92, scene 4), and then hands Joan over to the secular arm of the law, which has the pyre burning in full view. The honest Brother Martin, who has been working to have justice done ever since Joan's execution, comments to King Charles after her rehabilitation trial in 1456:"The ways of God are very strange. . . . At the trial which sent a saint to the stake as a heretic and a sorceress, the truth was told; the law was upheld; mercy was shewn beyond all custom; no wrong was done but the final and dreadful wrong of the lying sentence and the pitiless fire" (145, epilogue).

Worse, perversion of the law and perjured testimony are as likely to bring about just outcomes as conformity with the law and true testimony are likely to bring about unjust outcomes. There is no correlation between law and justice. "At this inquiry from which I have just come," continues Brother Martin describing the 1456 rehabilitation trial,

> there was shameless perjury, courtly corruption, calumny of the dead who did their duty according to their lights, cowardly evasion of the issue, testimony made of idle tales that could not impose on a ploughboy. Yet out of this insult to justice, this defamation of the Church, this orgy of lying and foolishness, the truth is set in the noonday sun on the hilltop; the white robe of innocence is cleansed from the smirch of the burning faggots; the holy life is sanctified; the true heart that lived through the flame is consecrated; a great lie is silenced for ever; and a great wrong is set right before all men. (145, epilogue)

Charles's response suggests the extent to which the law has been his instrument all along: "My friend: provided they can no longer say that I was crowned by a witch and a heretic, I shall not fuss about how the trick has been done" (145, epilogue).

What is true of the national sphere is true of the international sphere, only the farce is usually less well played. In fact, Shaw stresses the internationalism of the Church and feudal authorities and their collaboration with the English precisely in order to highlight the collaboration of international law with state brutality. "Joan's trial was not," he writes in the preface to *Saint Joan*, "a national political trial. Ecclesiastical courts and the courts of the Inquisition were Courts Christian: that is, international courts" (27). Nationalism may be nasty at times. It may be "narrow and bitter in country folk" (99, scene 4). But international law underwrites precisely the conception of nations that permits them to serve as an excuse for that legalized form of murder called war. "[God] gave us our countries and our languages, and meant us to keep them," says Joan brightly. "If it were not so it would be murder to kill an Englishman in battle" (60, scene 1). Furthermore, international power acts as a check not on the dangers of nationalism but on the *liberating* potential of nationalism.

In *Saint Joan,* Shaw shows the great popular emancipators of the fifteenth century—nationalism and the nascent Protestantism inextricably intertwined with it—trying desperately to free themselves from the hegemony of the international Church, in league with an equally international feudalism. Cauchon, the representative of the Church International, sees the implications of (as he puts the matter) this "most dangerous idea": "Call this side of Joan's heresy Nationalism if you will. . . . I can only tell you that it is essentially anti-Catholic for the Catholic Church knows only one realm, and that is the realm of Christ's kingdom. Divide that kingdom into nations, and you dethrone Christ" (98, scene 4). The Nobleman, representative of Feudalism International, explains it to the English Chaplain from his perspective: "Men cannot serve two masters. If this cant of serving their country once takes hold of them, goodbye to the authority of their feudal lords, and goodbye to the authority of the Church. That is, goodbye to you and me" (87, scene 4).

Yet the tyrannical international order of the Church and the feudal aristocracy has not, after all, melted into air, but simply been replaced with another one, the tyrannical international order of colonialism. Britain's repression of Irish resistance, Shaw points out in the preface, is as violently intolerant as the Inquisition's repression of those who resisted its supremacy. "In 1920," writes Shaw, "the British Government slaughtered and burnt in Ireland to persecute the advocates of a constitutional change which it had presently to effect itself" (Preface to *Saint Joan*, 36). When the English Chaplain explains why Joan must be put to death, Shaw turns him into a modern British colonial administrator. "This woman," says the Chaplain, "denies to England her legitimate conquests, given her by God because of her peculiar fitness to rule over less civilized races for their own good" (99-100, scene 4). What Shaw suggests about the international order in *Saint Joan* he says more explicitly elsewhere.

In his farce *Geneva* (published in 1939, revised 1945), for instance, the League of Nations is a doddering body run by a maniacal British minister, an Anglican bishop from another era, a corrupt Soviet delegate, and an American who thinks the world arena is the "Wild West": Yet it is not merely League incompetence but general principles of the international law of war and general notions of the "New World" order that are hopelessly inadequate. Shaw notes, for instance, the international legal justification of British and American "liberation" of French cities, Dutch cities, Belgian cities, Italian cities. "That is," he writes,

> they were destroying them exactly as they were destroying German cities, and having to house and feed their surviving inhabitants after wrecking their water mains, electric power stations, and railway communications. From the national point of view this was conquest, glory, patriotism, bravery, all claiming to be necessary for security. From the European wider angle it was folly and devilment, savagery and suicide. (*Geneva*, in *Plays Political*, 316).

After the "Utopians carried the day triumphantly at the end of the War, the New World proved the same as the old one" (*Geneva*, in *Plays Political*, 323). We may hope for evolution: "It is conceivable even that the next great invention may create an overwhelming interest in pacific civilization and wipe out war. You never can tell" (*Geneva*, in *Plays Political*, 339). But "meanwhile here we are, with our incompetence armed with atomic bombs" (*Geneva*, in *Plays Political*, 338).

The critique of the international legal order (seen as a mere buffoonish façade for the play of power), in conjunction with Shaw's Fabian socialist politics, implicitly suggests an alternative: a legal system that might enforce social equity, if not egalitarianism (a concept hard for a social Darwinist to credit). But, in his more cynical moments, the rejection of international-law-as-it-is means a flirtation with totalitarianism that has disturbing ramifications. While on the one hand Shaw could protest racist colonialist police power and object to the Allied blockade of Germany on humanitarian grounds, on the other he could half-seriously champion "liquidations," hold up the Inquisition as a model (Preface to *The Simpleton of the Unexpected Isles*), and insist that if anything was to be done one had to get rid of the Parliamentary system. Moreover, in a pamphlet written soon after Germany's invasion of Belgium in World War I, *Common Sense About the War*, and in *Peace Conference Hints*, Shaw speaks favorably of Germany's violation of Belgium's neutrality.

More disturbing still, Shaw's view that all regimes are to some degree totalitarian, and that only totalitarianism can effectively resolve social and economic crises, allowed him not only to praise Stalin unequivocally, but, all the way to 1941, to embrace most of Hitler's domestic and international policies as well. (Though Shaw naturally praised Hitler's abolition of unemployment, he mercilessly attacked the latter's anti-Semitic program and his ideas about eugenics.) Shaw's view of totalitarianism allowed him to proclaim in a letter to fellow Fabian Socialist Beatrice Webb, "We are National Socialists!" (Cuomo, 439-440, 444, 450, 453). It allowed him to sanction Hitler's most flagrant flouting of international law—for instance, the German withdrawal from the League of Nations in 1933, which he terms "a masterstroke that completely changed [Hitler's] standing in Europe" ("G.B.S. and Europe," 19). Shaw commented on the *Anschluss* that Germany and Austria were bound to become one nation anyway, and that this was the logical consequence of the "criminal conditions" of the Versailles Treaty (Cuomo, 439; see also Shaw's *Geneva,* in *Plays Political*, 331).

There is a good deal of irony here—of desire to shock—but there is also an underlying political conviction. Perhaps Shaw, now in his eighties, could see no alternative to the "rule of law" that was still allowing tribunals to send modern Joan of Arcs to the stake. As he writes in the preface to *Saint Joan*, "We must face the fact that society is founded on intolerance" (35). He may have been right that (as he writes) "we may prate of toleration as we will; but society must always draw a line somewhere between allowable conduct and insanity or crime" (Preface to *Saint Joan*, 35), yet the assertion allowed him to minimize the difference in degree between regulation and totalitarian coercion. For Shaw, the only argument against extreme intolerance is that it breeds revolution:

> We must persecute, even to the death; and all we can do to mitigate the danger of persecution is . . . to bear in mind that unless there is a large liberty to shock conventional people, and a well informed sense of the value of originality, individuality, and eccentricity, the result will be apparent stagnation covering a repression of evolutionary forces which will eventually explode with extravagant and probably destructive violence. (Preface to *Saint Joan*, 36)

(Here Shaw sounds astonishingly like Oliver Wendell Holmes, in Holmes's essay *Natural Law* [1933] and in his letters [1912-34] to Learned Hand.)

Mitigation of the dangers of persecution so as to avoid igniting revolution, however, hardly seems a redemptive alternative to the judges (as Shaw describes them) "in the blindness and bondage of the law" (157, epilogue), or to the police state, or to the corrupt collaboration of the authorities (national and international) in the suppression of the great spirits. As Cauchon says, after he has returned from the dead after the rehabilitation trial in which he has been vilified and, he claims, unfairly found guilty of perversion of justice, "I arraign the justice of Man. It is not the justice of God" (149, epilogue). Joan is less surprised: "Still dreaming of justice, Peter? See what justice came to with me!" (149, epilogue).

When Joan reappears again in Shaw's epilogue, mightily pleased at the news of her canonization in 1920 and asking to be unburned so she can carry on with her work, those who have rehabilitated her are horrified at the thought. The English Chaplain who had most vigorously attacked Joan (threatening that "eight hundred men at the gate . . . will see that this abominable witch is burnt" whatever the law might say [134, scene 6]) had ended up in an anguish of remorse. But he is nevertheless dismayed at the thought of her resurrection, lamely crying out no, no, "peace in our time!" (158, epilogue) at the end of the play, in an odd premonition of Neville Chamberlain's famous claim on his return from Munich in the fall of 1938 that, in negotiating with Hitler, he had in fact brought "peace in our time."

In the preface to *Saint Joan*, Shaw quotes approvingly the letter of a priest who writes that he sees in Shaw's play "the dramatic presentation of the conflict of the Regal, sacerdotal, and Prophetical powers, in which Joan was crushed. To me it is not the victory of any one of them over the others that will bring peace . . . but their fruitful interaction in a costly but noble state of tension" (32). Shaw explains that "we must accept the tension, and maintain it nobly without letting ourselves be tempted to relieve it by burning the thread" (Preface to *Saint Joan*, 32). Seen one way, this is an insistence on toleration for the sake of a dialogue between the status quo and the future—the "Prophetical powers." But the echo between this passage and the Chaplain's plea that Joan stay properly dead suggests that the promise of "peace in our time" is the promise that the law will continue to uphold the collusion among the leaders of states, the Church, and the agents of terror at the cost of the suppression of the great spirits of liberation.

Brecht's *Saint Joan of the Stockyards*

Brecht shared Shaw's skepticism about the law as a tool of justice, but he was driven, unlike Shaw, by a Marxist program that offered, through a negative dialectic, at least an implicit image of what the national and global state might do while it was getting ready to wither away. In his first Joan-of-Arc play, *Saint Joan of the Stockyards* (1929), he places "Johanna Dark" (Joan Dark) in the Chicago meatpacking plants. There, she works for a Salvation Army-type outfit, the Black Straw Hats, doling out the pablum of religion and weak soup to the half-starved workers.

Life in the plants is gruesome: every once in a while a worker is sucked into the machinery and ends up in the tins of bacon and lard. The workers' destinies are ruled by the coterie of owners (in fierce competition with one another); by the wild fluctuations of the stock market, which often result in massive layoffs and wage decreases; and by invisible forces in New York that are mysteriously controlling international trade treaties. When the workers try to strike, the sentimental Pierpont Mauler, who weeps over the plight of the mooing cows on their way to slaughter and swears to give up his murderous occupation, calls in the army, which brings in its tanks and machine guns, firing into the crowd, just as Brecht had seen the German police do at a communist rally in Berlin in the year he wrote *Saint Joan of the Stockyards* (Hill, 75).

The law of international trade and the army are allied with the international "Laws of Economics"" (*GW* 2, 704, 735, 752: scenes 5, 9b, 9g; *CP* 3, 36, 67, 81), Brecht's recurrent phrase throughout the play. This is war, less a civil war than a world war, in which the Chicago stockyards are only one theater of battle. The lesson that Johanna Dark must learn is the inverse of the lesson that conventional twentieth-century portraits tried to place in her mouth: just as "patriotism is not enough" (as Edith Cavell said about her nursing of enemy soldiers [*CP* 3, 26]), pacifism is not enough in a world armed to the teeth to keep the poor poor. The soup Johanna has been serving is, like religion, an opiate of the people. As the leader of the Black Straw Hats gleefully tells his sponsor, who turns out to be the capitalist Mauler:

> If only we can scare up a band and some decent soup
> With some body to it, all God's worries are over
> And Bolshevism will give up the ghost. (*GW* 2, 761: scene 10; *CP* 3, 88-89)

Through the play, then, Brecht faces one of the central problems of the law, national or international, a problem both for those creating it and for those deciding whether or not to violate it: When does the individual or the individual's freedom have to be sacrificed for the greater good? Are there any absolute limits on that sacrifice? Johanna torments herself over the problem of violence, essentially the sacrifice of the individual under the banner of the greater good: "Force is not the answer to/Disorder and confusion" (*GW* 2, 753: scene 9g; *CP* 3, 82), she cries to herself. One who uses force, she muses, stands

> Moved by malice against his neighbour, and closed
> To all the understandings
> Customary among men.
> Cut off from all community, he would find
> No bearings in
> A world grown unfamiliar. The movement of the stars
> Over his head would no longer be governed by
> The old rule. Words
> Would change their meaning for him, innocence
> Forsake him, the pursued pursuer
> His vision would lose all candour. (*GW* 2, 754-755: scene 9g; *CP* 3, 83)

Brecht was repeatedly confronted with the problem of violence, as a committed pacifist who wrote a poem called "Legend of the Dead Soldier" (*GW* 8: 285; trans. mine) that got him a rank of No. 5 on the secret Nazi blacklist before even the 1923 Munich Putsch (Dickson, 162)—but as a committed Marxist who recognized violence as necessary to the revolution to come. Embracing it where necessary, he nonetheless recognized the losses that even necessary violence entails, losses not merely physical but moral and spiritual: the embrace of malice necessary to self-justification in war; the (at least temporary) refusal of negotiation and peaceful settlement; the alienation from the familiar comforts of settled order, from society, and hence the self-alienation (merely an intensification of the necessary alienation of the modern world); the loss of innocence; the entry into the bestial world of pursuer and pursued. But as *Saint Joan of the Stockyards* shows, the workers (who have become the stock of both stockyards and stock market) are already in the world of pursuer and pursued, long dehumanized, little different from the steer going to the slaughter. As in the world of Brecht's *Threepenny Opera* (1928), the play asks and answers the fundamental ontological and ethical question about the nature of the human: "On what does Man live? He feeds on others" (*GW* 2, 458: scene 6; trans. mine).

Johanna comes to realize that wordless oppression does not equal peace. As she says:

> Another night like this, another day of this
> Oppressive silence and no one
> Would hold himself back . . .
> True, violence builds up in the darkness
> Weakness and weakness build strength and
> Unfinished business accumulates. (*GW* 2, 753: scene 9g; *CP* 3, 82)

As she comes to realize, her "dreams were countless," and as a result she was one who "brought injury to the injured and was useful to the injurers" (*GW* 2, 779: scene 12; *CP* 3, 105). The crowd of Workers cries, "Force alone can help you and/ . . . you yourselves must wield it" (*GW* 2, 753: scene 9g; *CP* 3, 82). Having learned her Leninist lesson, she reluctantly leaves the "army of peace" and joins the war. But it is too late. The factories have started up again with two-thirds of the workers at two-thirds pay (*CP* 3, 101). The pacifist Johanna is, grotesquely, sainted by the plant owners, who intend to hold forth their "Saint Joan of the Stockyards," doler of soup, as proof "that with us humanity comes first" (*GW* 2, 778: scene 12; *CP* 3, 104). Liberal humanism is victorious and, as she says, "The world is back on its old course, unchanged" (*GW* 2, 779: scene 12; *CP* 3, 104). A third of the workers will die in the streets or the shelters.

As Mauler's hold on the police makes clear, the law is a tool not of the people but of those who rule through the state. As the *Great Soviet Encyclopedia* defines it, law is "the will of the state cast in legal form" (see Works Cited). In the early 1930s, this must have seemed painfully obvious to anyone watching the Third Reich entrench its power precisely through what it claimed was a legal revolution: first using emergency powers under Article 48, then consolidating them in the Enabling Act of March 1933, subsequently transforming the requirements for judges and the hierarchies of the legal system, and establishing the Nuremburg Laws in 1935. During this period, Brecht's attacks on the legal system and its collusion with capital intensified. In *Rise and Fall of the City of Mahagonny* (1930), for instance, the main character's creditors sentence him to death, while a placard above the stage reminds the audience that the law courts of Mahagonny are not worse than those elsewhere. In *The Resistible Rise of Arturo Ui* (1941), Ui recognizes that the law's purpose under a dictatorship is to legitimize the regime's crimes (Dickson, 148-150). In *The Private Life of the Master Race* (1938), a portrait of Nazi Germany, the legal profession has a motto, "Law is what the German people need" (*GW* 3, 1103; trans. mine).

Brecht's *The Trial of Joan of Arc at Rouen, 1431* and *The Visions of Simone Machard*

Only a few years after he had written *Saint Joan of the Stockyards*, Brecht clearly felt that he needed to revise the Joan-of-Arc story to resonate with the legal realities of the Third Reich. In *The Trial of Joan of Arc at Rouen, 1431*, which he adapted in 1934 from a radio play by Anna Seghers, he interspersed material from the actual trial with commentary by French onlookers in order to address simultaneously (if only implicitly) both the questionable socialism of "National Socialism" and the questionable legality of the Third Reich. When a young boy says in perplexity that the French have no grounds for bringing charges against Jeanne and no reason to put her on trial, the worldlier Dr. Dufour says, "All those doctors ought to be able to find one" (*GW* 6, 2505: scene 2; *CP* 9, 152). At the trial itself, Cauchon protests that he must proceed strictly according to law, which means suppressing questions that might demonstrate Jeanne's innocence and insisting on the paramount importance of speed (*CP* 9, 161). When Jeanne cries out, "This trial of yours is crooked" (*GW* 6, 2521; *CP* 9, 166), she is silenced.

In *The Visions of Simone Machard*, Brecht's third Joan-of-Arc play (written in collaboration with Lion Feuchtwanger in 1942-43, in response to the occupation of France), he transports Joan back into the twentieth century as a young French girl who, dreaming she is Joan of Arc, begins working for the Resistance by stealing food for the refugees and, when the Germans arrive, burning a storehouse of gasoline to prevent their access to it. At the end of the play, Simone (Joan) undergoes a "trial" in which Monsieur Soupard, the owner of the hostelry in which she worked, and Colonel Fetain (in a thinly disguised reference to Marshal [Philippe] Pétain), the neighborhood fascist who has welcomed the Germans with open arms—after cursory questioning that takes the form of ornate legalism—send Simone permanently to an insane asylum. Here, the illegal invasion is central to the constitution of the new legal system. But the invasion depends on those who see that they can protect their already substantial interests by collaboration, by capitalizing on the new market: the German occupiers.

"They're selling France the same as they sell their wine and *hors d'oeuvres*!"(*GW* 5, 1887: scene 3; *CP* 7, 41), says the elderly Père Gustave with disgust. The consumers of French food are cannibals, consumers of the refugees who line the streets. The war machine, similarly cannibalistic, lives on those who, in the end, get crushed by it. When Georges, a wounded French soldier, points out that "their forts are on wheels, they roll over us" and that "nothing is going to stop their tanks as long as they have gas," Père Gustave comments: "Tanks can get through any swamp, but in a human swamp they bog down. The civilian population has turned out to be a terrible nuisance in wartime" (*GW* 5, 1845: scene 1; *CP* 7, 5). If Brecht hated war as a pacifist by inclination, he hated it all the more as the unholy alliance he conceived it to be—of states with capitalism. Precisely what was wrong with international law was that it finally implicitly sanctioned wars between states (by acknowledging them and reinforcing the will of the victors through treaties), and so implicitly sanctioned the capitalist war machine whose purpose was to trade human lives for the propping up of the economy (just as the stockyard owners do).

If the central purpose of the law was to protect property interests, in international law it did this by protecting states and hence dividing the international worker's movement, establishing the rules for a perpetual game of imperialist conquest that successfully diverted the masses from mobilization. As Brecht points out in works like *Mother Courage and Her Children* (1941) and *The Caucasian Chalk Circle* (1945), even if a country loses the war, its war marketeers nearly always come out better than before. At the same time that international law implicitly sanctioned war, it refused to recognize the one unequivocal international right: as Friedrich Engels puts it, the "right to revolution" (Dickson, 152). Hence, the uprising of the masses never rose to the level of war (justified violence) but remained at the level of crime, not within the purview of international law and hence subject to the unmitigated violence of the state.

In both *The Trial of Joan of Arc at Rouen, 1431* and *The Visions of Simone Machard*, the stripping of the country for the pursuit of war is as criminal as the German violation of legal norms—that is, there is a parallel between fascist violation of the law of nations and the more ordinary capitalist violation of the law of justice. When, in *The Trial of Joan of Arc at Rouen, 1431*, a Well-Dressed Gentleman observes that Joan claims to be doing what she is doing for "her country," Dr. Dufour says (in characteristic Brechtian anti-nationalism): "Country! What difference does it make to the country who's on the white horse that's trampling it into dust? The Duke of Bedford or the Duke of Orleans? What difference does it make to the country who gobbles up its wheat and its wine, its venison and fruit, its taxes and tithes? The Lord of Beauvais or the Duke of Gloucester?" (*GW* 6, 2505: scene 2; *CP* 7, 153). As Shaw explains more cheerfully, "adventurers" interested in using the legal system "must come to terms with the captains of finance and industry, the bankers, and the Conservatives who really control the nations" (*Geneva*, in *Plays Political*, 330).

The collaborators in *The Visions of Simone Machard* use the rhetoric of peace, law, and order as a shield against the threat of popular resistance. As a wounded French soldier points out, "The first thing they announced over the radio was: 'No one who observes law and order has anything to fear'" (*GW* 5, 1882: scene 3a; *CP* 7, 37). In the last scene of the play, the owners of a hostelry who have welcomed the Germans lecture Simone: "We're quite capable of telling you when war is necessary, and we can also tell you when peace is better. *We* are France. Understand? Don't forget, we're at peace now!" (*GW* 5, 1909-1911: scene 4; *CP* 7, 59-61). Here, Brecht is enacting a mockery that echoes the Vichy government's version of Joan of Arc. (In Germany itself during this period, Joan was portrayed as the peasant hero of the national *Volk*, a natural *Führer* to be followed into battle to save the nation [never mind that it happened to be France; Cuomo, 445.])

In France under the Occupation, Joan was used to remind schoolchildren of the perfidy of the English and became, for the Vichy government, a renewed symbol of a unified and peace-loving nation, this time (as it so happened) unified in conciliation with its new German ally. As Marshal Pétain proclaimed in declaring a national Joan-of-Arc day, "Martyr of National Unity, Joan of Arc is the symbol of France." The Vichy Joan was a peculiar conjunction of humility and obedience (the government stressed her domestic work on her father's farm in Lorraine at the same time that it stressed her fascist iron will), but she served as an excellent tool. One play, for instance, performed throughout Vichy, France, in youth camps, had a decayed Englishman repeating over and over, "The French are rotten, rotten, rotten," and recommending that the entire camp recite in unison, "Like Joan, we believe in the resurrection of France" (Jacobs, 108; trans. mine).

If Brecht is offering a mocking echo of the Vichy Joan in *The Visions of Simone Machard,* he is also, in facing the Occupation and Resistance, returning to the more general question of resistance in a coercive legal system, whether that of the German occupiers or that of the capitalist occupiers. The international workers' Joan is, with the rise of Hitler, necessarily transformed for Brecht into a resistance fighter, one who again comes to realize the necessity of violence in the face of the exploitations of war and, in so doing, may bring about the revolution. If the world remains for the moment unchanged, if the legal system remains a pawn of international capital and the spokespersons of "peace and order" (*GW* 2, 772: scene 10; *CP* 3, 98) remain those who use it in the service of oppression, Brecht hints at a higher legal order, one that might declare the holding pens for slaves that are stockyards a "lawless world" (*GW* 2, 752: scene 9g; *CP* 3, 81), as he himself calls it, and that might actualize the "laws of justice" (*CP* 3, 84) in just laws.

In Brecht's *The Trial of Joan of Arc at Rouen, 1431,* Joan recants not in terror at the thought of being burned alive but in the mistaken conviction that the people of France have lost faith in her—that they have yielded up in spirit and become blindly obedient to the unified forces of Church and nobility, the representatives of the coercive state. But, as one observer recounts after her death, upon hearing of people's distress at her recantation, her courage came back and "she realized that a law court is as good a battleground as the earthworks before Orleans" (*GW* 6: 2546, scene 16; *CP* 9, 186).

Conclusion

If neither Shaw nor Brecht shared Joan's faith, both men were saying to the *international* Joan, the pacifist and harmonious and conciliatory Joan, that all is not right with the new international world order. In the decades that followed, international treaties and the development of customary international law tried to deal with some of the problems that Shaw's and Brecht's critiques raised:

identifying the nature of aggressive warfare; establishing norms for fundamental economic rights in addition to political and civil rights; actualizing a right to self-determination; establishing higher standards for the protection of civilian populations in wartime; establishing increased protections for labor. While the great human rights treaties of the postwar period were created largely in response to the horrors of World War II, in a world coming face to face as well with the brutalities of colonialism as well, they were also created by those who realized, with Shaw and Brecht, that absolute pacifism and principles of nonintervention were not always enough—and that if states were not always the best guardians of their citizens' interests, an international law whose only subjects were states (or, an international law that was, like Joan's tribunal, the mere tool of states) could never be such a guardian, either.

For Shaw this meant a comic resignation to the extremes of coercion and intolerance, to the temptations of fascism, which, when translated into real-world terms, had consequences for which the word "tragedy" is insufficient. For Brecht this meant an impossibly utopian vision to be brought about by violence that might never achieve its aim, an ideology that had consequences equally unspeakable. But each nonetheless offered a critique of the international world order that saw past its subterfuges to the possibilities beyond—possibilities that remain just that, even today, despite the respective political exhortations and artistic excellences of *Saint Joan, Saint Joan of the Stockyards, The Trial of Joan of Arc at Rouen, 1431,* and *The Visions of Simone Machard.*

Works Cited

Bancquart, Marie Claire. *Les écrivains et l'histoire: d'après Maurice Barrès, Léon Bloy, Anatole France, Charles Péguy.* Paris: Nizet, 1966.

Beck, James M. *The* Case *of Edith Cavell: A Study of the Rights of Non-Combatants.* New York: G. P. Putnam's Sons, 1916.

Brecht, Bertolt. *Gesammelte Werke* [*Collected Works*]. 20 vols. Ed. Elisabeth Hauptmann. Frankfurt am Main: Suhrkamp Verlag, 1967.

----------. *Saint Joan of the Stockyards.* Trans. Ralph Manheim. In vol. 3 (1970) of *Collected Plays* (201-314). 9 vols. Ed. Ralph Manheim & John Willett. London: Methuen, 1970-2004.

----------. *The Trial of Joan of Arc of Rouen, 1431.* Trans. Ralph Manheim & Wolfgang Sauerlander. In vol. 9 (1970) of *Collected Plays* (147-188). 9 vols. Ed. Ralph Manheim & John Willett. London: Methuen, 1970-2004.

----------. *The Visions of Simone Machard*. Trans. Ralph Manheim. In vol. 7 (1970) of *Collected Plays* (1-64). 9 vols. Ed. Ralph Manheim & John Willett. London: Methuen, 1970-2004.

Cuomo, Glenn R. "'Saint Joan before the Cannibals': George Bernard Shaw in the Third Reich." *German Studies Review*, 16.3 (Oct. 1993): 435-461.

Dickson, Keith A. *Towards a Utopia: A Study of Brecht*. Oxford, U.K.: Clarendon Press, 1978.

"Fête de Jeanne D'Arc." *Action française*, May 9, 1920: n.p.

Great Soviet Encyclopedia. Ed. A. M. Prokhorov. 3rd ed. 31 vols. New York: Macmillan, 1973-83.

Hill, Claude. *Bertolt Brecht*. New York: Twayne, 1975.

Jacobs, Gabriel. "The Role of Joan of Arc on the Stage of Occupied Paris." In *Vichy France and the Resistance: Culture and Ideology*. Ed. Roderick Kedward & Roger Austin. London: Croom Helm, 1985. 106-122.

Levandovsky, Anatole. "Jeanne d'Arc dans l'historiographie sovietique." In *Jeanne d'Arc: Une époque, un rayonnement*. Ed. C. T. Allmand *et al.* Paris: Éditions du Centre national de la recherche scientifique, 1982. 287-292.

Marot, Pierre. "De la réhabilitation à la glorification de Jeanne d'Arc: Essai sur l'historiographie et le culte de l'héroine en France pendant cinq siècles." In *Mémorial du vème centenaire de la réhabilitation de Jeanne d'Arc, 1456-1956*. Ed. René Coty. Paris: J. Forêt, 1958. 85-164.

Pernoud, Regine. *The Retrial of Joan of Arc: The Evidence* at *the Trial for Her Rehabilitation, 1450-1456*. Trans. J. M. Cohen. New York: Harcourt Brace, 1955.

Raknem, Ingvald. *Joan of Arc in History, Legend, and Literature*. Oslo: Universitetsforlaget, 1971.

Shaw, George Bernard. "G.B.S. and Europe." *Observer*, 432 (Nov. 5, 1933): 19, col. 3.

----------. *The Simpleton of the Unexpected Isles, The Six of Calais, & The Millionairess*. London: Constable, 1936.

----------. *Saint Joan: A Chronicle Play in Six Scenes and an Epilogue*. London: Penguin, 1957.

----------. *Plays Political:* The Apple Cart, On the Rocks, Geneva. Harmondsworth, U.K.: Penguin, 1986.

van Kan, Joseph. "Bernard Shaw's *Saint Joan:* An Historical Point of View" (1925). In *Saint Joan: Fifty Years After, 1923/24-1973/74*. Ed. Stanley Weintraub. Baton Rouge: Louisiana State University Press, 1973. 44-53.

Yancey, William Paul. *The Soldier Virgin of France: A Message of World Peace.* Gainesville: By the author, 1926.

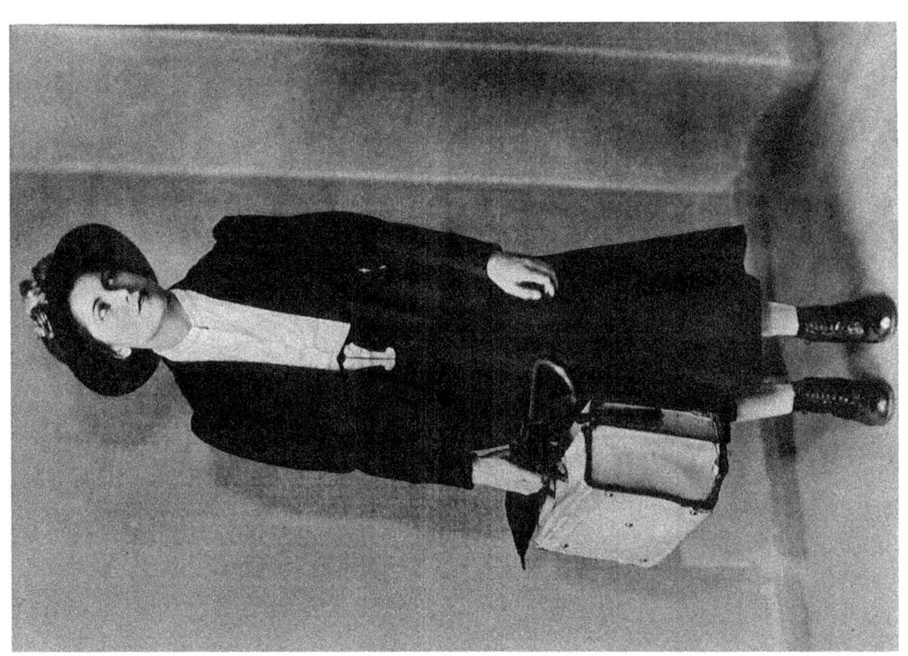

19. Carola Neher, *Saint Joan of the Stockyards*, 1930

20. Vera Komissarzhevskaya, *A Doll's House*, 1904

21. *A Doll's House*, dir. Patrick Garland, 1973

22. Mrs. Patrick Campbell, *Pygmalion*, 1914

23. *Pygmalion*, dir. Anthony Asquith, 1938

24. *How He Lied to Her Husband*, dir. Cecil Lewis, 1931

25. *The Good Person of Setzuan*, New York, 2013

POSTSCRIPT

"Ibsen's *Hedda Gabler* on Stage/*A Doll House* on Film"

In London during the summer of 1972, I saw a theatrical treasure: the Royal Court production of *Hedda Gabler* (1890) as adapted by John Osborne, with Jill Bennett (Mrs. Osborne at the time); the production was directed by Anthony Page. A young man at the time, I took prolific notes, which I'll now transcribe and polish.

Alan Tagg designed a setting, lighted by Andy Phillips, that transformed the small Royal Court stage into a large, Nordic nineteenth-century mausoleum. Osborne rendered Ibsen as he should have done: which is to say, he did not wrench the play to fit a theory or serve as hobby-horse; he simply seared the dialogue into language that showed why he admired the play and was attracted to it. This is urgent, supple, *useful* theater writing. For instance, after Hedda has offended her husband's aunt about the latter's hat, the younger woman says, "These things just seem to wait for me to do them." (Osborne's adaptation of *Hedda Gabler* was published by Faber & Faber only in 1989.)

The line is not only a sample of Osborne's diction, it is a clue to Hedda and to Jill Bennett's performance. (She was best-known in the United States in the 1960s and early '70s through her film performances: as the aunt with the heart attack in Bette Davis's *The Nanny* [1965, Seth Holt], as Trevor Howard's lady friend in *The Charge of the Light Brigade* [1968, Tony Richardson], as Calpurnia in *Julius Caesar* [1970, Stuart Burge].) This Hedda comes in finished, though only subconsciously aware of it, gliding airily to an end that is in her own nature and of her own doing. Some of the London critics in 1972 complained that Bennett's performance was not tragic, but *Hedda Gabler* is not a tragedy—it is the *dénouement* of a tragedy. Gooses were cooked long before the curtain rises. Hedda never tries to change her life, to pry herself free, to leave her husband, or take up again with Eilert Løvborg. She simply toboggans down the slope on which she has already started, and vindictively—she would say idealistically—takes Løvborg with her.

The *prior* tragedy is essentially one of gender. Hedda has the impulses and imagination of a man—romantic but male—in a society that provides no place for a woman but the conventional one. Her father, the General, is often mentioned; her mother, never. Her father's pistols (phallic symbols, need one point out?) are pivotal in the story. Her frigidity, her boredom, her loathing of her pregnancy, her terrible vengeances, are all unwitting functions of a biological doom that has condemned her to a role for which she is not psychologically or temperamentally fitted. This production even suggests, quite aptly, a lesbian touch toward (Mrs.) Thea Elvsted. All these matters Jill Bennett encompasses admirably.

For American theatergoers, who in 1971 had had Claire Bloom's inept Hedda visited upon them (in a Broadway production at the Playhouse Theatre, directed by Patrick Garland), here are a few comparisons to help make matters vivid. Bloom was a petulant, grown-up schoolgirl, striving for glacier force; Bennett was gracious, humorous, easy with superficial facets that contrast ironically with her depths. Bloom strove pathetically to be commanding; Bennett never bothered—her rich voice, her lynx-like presence allowed her, figuratively, to do as she pleased yet never lose us. Bloom wanted not to lose our sympathy; Bennett didn't care if we hated Hedda—she seemed to understand that Ibsen was after something larger than having us feel affection for a star. He wanted us to loathe a certain world: the one that made Hedda.

Ronald Hines was a perfect George Tesman: we could understand how Hedda might have slipped into marriage with him. Brian Cox, the Løvborg, played with a hulking, Marlon-Brando solidity, rather than the usual poeticizing, ethereal quality in the role. Denholm Elliott, long a favorite of mine, performed Judge Brack like a sadistic surgeon.

Anthony Page's direction bothered me at the outset, with its linear, angular movements and compositions, often quite neatly parallel with the footlights. Then these patterns began to suggest the corsets and stays of this society. At only one point would I have quarreled: Page has Hedda downstage of Brack when he tells her of Løvborg's suicide. The focus should be on her, not on Brack. As is, she has a difficult time controlling the moment. Bennett had a few other tonal difficulties toward the end. But if she didn't quite fulfill the character's desperate feeling of self-immolation, she was so captivating until then that I was willing to rationalize on her behalf: perhaps Hedda was so trapped in a mingy world that large-size Medea movements had become impossible for her by the finish.

With the 1973 film of Ibsen's *A Doll House* (1879), we are back with questions raised by every adaptation of a major play. Indeed, is there such a thing as a good *film* of a major play? Allowing for arguable exceptions like the films of Shakespeare's *Henry V* (1944, Laurence Olivier) and Shaw's *Pygmalion* (1938, Anthony Asquith), I think the answer is still no—in 2022, no less. The better the play, the less alterable the form. What we get here are some swatches of Ibsen, scissored apart, with some gussets of transition and transposition inserted, and the whole renovation stitched together again. And, as is the way with movie adaptations, although stuff is inserted, the whole altered thing is smaller than the original. This film runs only about 100 minutes—yet seems longer.

The picture was made for two reasons: first, the topicality of the theme; second, the success that Claire Bloom, the star, had had as Hedda *and* Nora in New York in 1971 (in repertory at the Playhouse) and then, with Nora again, in London in 1973, as directed by Garland at the Criterion Theatre. (Another film of *A Doll House* was made in 1973 [Joseph Losey], with Jane Fonda as Nora; two years later, in 1975, we got the first feature-length sound film made from *Hedda Gabler*: it starred Glenda Jackson and was directed by Trevor Nunn.) As to the first reason, it's dubious. I think the play is as much a struggle against nineteenth-century dramaturgy as against nineteenth-century marriage, but it does have some size; and that size is reduced by harping on topicality.

Over the years, some critics have pointed out, rightly, that *A Doll House* could have been about either Torvald or Nora Helmer; it is really about marriage, not the oppression of women. Indeed, five years after the play was written, the first great writer to discuss it, August Strindberg, argued vigorously that Ibsen had proved the direct opposite of what he intended to prove. (See the preface to

Strindberg's collection of stories titled *Getting Married* [1884/1886], translated by Mary Sandbach and published by Viking in 1972.) Even granting Strindberg's biases, his argument delivers a jolt. In any event the play still creaks and cranks along, driven through its mechanics only by the great mind that knew all along how it would end.

Claire Bloom (born 1931) proved here that she was a much better actress on screen than on stage: to put it properly, she is good on film and weak on stage. I had seen her in *A Doll House* as well as several other plays, I had even gone to a solo poetry recital of hers, and never once did she reveal a trace of *command*, let alone of conviction. Her voice and person simply are not able to cope with space. On film, with a compressed environment, with an opportunity to work almost completely for "interiorness," she is truthful and at ease. On film she looks a bit old for Nora, which she didn't on stage; but here, insofar as the shredded script permits, she can more clearly paint in the character's substructure: her concept of Nora as consciously playing little squirrel tricks, debasing herself deliberately to perform the itsy-bitsy wifey-pifey for Torvald, so that when she changes, we can see her throw off a role rather than suddenly alter character.

Anthony Hopkins bulges forcefully as Torvald and cracks credibly. Denholm Elliott, who was a fine Judge Brack in *Hedda Gabler* last summer in the Royal Court production discussed above, is an equally fine Nils Krogstad here. Anna Massey is a reedily affecting (Mrs.) Kristine Linde, while Ralph Richardson delights as Dr. Rank.

Christopher Hampton derived the screenplay from his own reasonably limber, 1972 stage version. (This theatrical adaptation was published by Samuel French in 1972; Hampton's screenplay was never published but is available, in second-draft form, from Internet booksellers.) Patrick Garland, like Claire Bloom, himself gains from the move to film. His directing on stage (in the 1971 *Doll House* on Broadway with Bloom, as well as in the 1971 *Hedda Gabler* with the same actress, in the same place) was like Schubert operetta *réchauffée.* He is much better off with less space to live in, moment by moment, and with enforced control of the audience's eyes. Sadly, this was Garland's first and only feature film; he made no others.

So, in 1972-1973, I got one theatrical treasure and a film that made Garland and Bloom look good: I was pleased to see them then . . . and still have them with me now. Thanks, Ibsen.

"Shaw's *Pygmalion*, Play and Film: A Self-Interview"

Interviewer: *Pygmalion* (1938, Anthony Asquith) is a film of significance, based on a major play from a major twentieth-century artist. As we sit in the twenty-first century, I think it is well worth beginning by recalling just what a towering figure George Bernard Shaw was, and is, for English-language theater. You once told me you'd fallen in love with his work as a young man.

J. R. Russo: At age fifteen. Younger than young. (*Both laugh.*)

Interviewer: So what is it about Shaw as an artist that's kept your interest for all these years? Because you have taught him at the undergraduate as well as at the highest graduate level, written about him, lectured on his work, and so on.

Russo: What's kept my interest is that every time I read him, I discover him. Which is true, of course, of any great artist. You think you know something about him and then you find out that you've only begun to investigate him. It's hard for me to talk calmly about Shaw.

Interviewer: Don't.

Russo: Because I think he is a titan. I think that there can be very little question that he's the second greatest playwright in the English language. He is also the greatest comic dramatist after Molière. Those judgments can be argued with a bit, but not decisively against. Those, for me, are data from the world of playwriting. In addition, talking about his reputation during the twentieth century, he was, you could almost say, through the first half of that century, omnipresent. Whenever anything happened—a flood in Johnstown, Ohio, a revolution somewhere in South America—the first thing, it seemed to me, that any newspaper did was to find out what Shaw had to say about it. There's a newspaper in Belgium, I was told, that for many years every day in a corner of its front page, where the *New York Times* ran the weather, this paper had a quotation from Bernard Shaw—every day! The man was inexhaustible in two senses: as a source and as a figure of energy.

Shaw's work in the theater just went on and on, but it began quite late. He didn't write his first play until well into his thirties, in 1892. He was thirty-six. He'd done mostly novels and criticism before then. Before he wrote a play, he was a famous music critic—a *great* music critic. When I talk about Shaw in seminars, it takes me three or four weeks just to get to his plays. Because first you have to deal with the fact that he was a fine music critic, who has the respect of every reasonably serious music critic I have ever read on the subject of Shaw. And second, he is the greatest theater critic—critic!—who ever wrote in the English language. I don't need anyone else's opinion on that; I know that! And, again, that's before you get to his plays. As a matter of fact, you can demonstrate—I've tried to—that the three books he wrote before he began writing plays are the source of a lot of the material in his plays. Books on Wagner and other subjects as well. You can see that this man devoured ideas.

Shaw got a reputation—misleading—as a "brain-box" playwright, when, as a matter of fact, he is one of the most sensitive (you see it in the film of *Pygmalion*), most humane writers ever. He couldn't be a great playwright if he were just a merchant of ideas. If there's anything that drives me nuts—and I suppose I am nuts on this subject—it is to hear the stale, false comment that all Shaw's characters are voices expressing different ideas of his. Nothing could be more false. If you want proof of that, ask any actor who's ever been in a Shaw play. Actors, finally, are those who keep plays alive. Not critics. Actors want to do plays or not, and they want to do Shaw.

Interviewer: There's a wonderful anecdote about that: Shaw sent a copy of one of his plays to the great actress Ellen Terry. And Terry was very busy in her dressing room, so she had her attendant simply read it to her. And somewhere through the first act, the attendant just stopped and said, "Madam, this is you, this is you. This has been written *for you*." And thus the recognition that Shaw's plays are not just about ideas, they consist of characters who have been gracefully molded with this or that actor in mind.

Russo: That leads to one more of the 10,000 things we could be saying about Shaw. He was his era's greatest casting agent. He knew the work of every available actor in Britain. And if you read his letters—which are fascinating in themselves—he was also a great letter-writer. You could read his advice, comments, and suggestions to the people who were going to do his plays. For example, apropos of a sad passing in the year 2000, he said in one of his letters around 1940, I think it was, "I suggest that you"—to whomever he was writing—"take a look at a young actor named Alec Guinness." That occurs as a passing note in one of his letters—it's fantastic! You can't talk about Shaw without beginning to sound hyperbolic. Because he was a living hyperbole and remains a hyperbole today.

Interviewer: So here we have someone of such a high level of professional accomplishment in so many different fields, but who also is one of the great creations—and manipulators—of celebrity culture in the twentieth century.

Russo: He often said that his greatest creation was G.B.S. And it wasn't an entirely beneficial one, as he knew. Because the fact that he made this public persona—he himself said—a little too facetious, a little too omniscient, interfered a bit with the appreciation of Shaw as a serious artist. People began to think of him as a jokester—as unthinking and superficial. He knew he himself was responsible for that. But he was one of the first of the twentieth century's infamous public personae. You know Daniel Boorstin's definition of celebrity (in the 1962 book *The Image: A Guide to Pseudo-Events in America*): someone who's famous for being famous. (*Both laugh.*) Shaw, in a certain sense, instigated that definition. He was famous for something, but he added too much to his fame.

Interviewer: Right. In a second, we are going to turn to *Pygmalion* the play and the film, but it is interesting to note that, if it were now 1935, if you were to be anywhere in the world, and I were to name two people in the entertainment world known everywhere, they would be Charlie Chaplin and George Bernard Shaw.

Russo: I think that's a very fair statement. They're quite comparable in terms of fame. There was a time until maybe the last decade of the twentieth century when you could say—in fact, I did say, and I bet someone a dollar on it once!—that at any given moment of any day in any year, somewhere on this globe, a Bernard Shaw play was being performed. It might be an amateur performance in

Korea, but somewhere someone was doing Shaw. He was almost as omnipresent as Shakespeare.

Interviewer: That's interesting because we think, you know, of "globalization" as the buzzword of today, but it's important to recover the degree to which an artist like Shaw had a fully global penetration in his time. Shaw would have been at the top of any list of "quantity of translations, and performances, from English into another language."

Russo: Additionally, the first books about Shaw's work were written in foreign languages. I think I'm correct in saying that the first book about him was written in Spanish; I once noted that in one of the many bibliographies of the writings about Shaw.

Interviewer: This makes for a good transition into our discussion of *Pygmalion*. I want our readers to know that we just saw the third film version of this 1913 play.

Russo: That's quite true. The first was a German one (1935, Erich Engel), the second Dutch (1937, Ludwig Berger).

Interviewer: Correct. Have you seen those other two?

Russo: No. The only person I know, or know of, who has seen them is a man named Bernard Dukore, who has done a good deal of work in the field of Shaw scholarship and has also edited a collection of Shaw's screenplays. And he wrote a long, detailed introduction to that collection. Moreover, he went to see what he was talking about. Just to add one more item. Henry Higgins in the German film of *Pygmalion* is played by Gustaf Gründgens, who, you may remember, is the leader of the crooks and thieves in Fritz Lang's *M* (1931).

Interviewer: Small world, as they say. (*Both laugh.*) Let's move to the play *Pygmalion* and talk a bit about where it stands in Shaw's overall trajectory. How do you evaluate it among all his plays, and where does it stand in our collective imagination today?

Russo: Its first production was in London in 1912. Shaw wrote it with a woman named Mrs. Patrick Campbell in mind as Eliza, and she did play it in this production, which he directed. Higgins was written for a then-famous actor named Herbert Beerbohm Tree—whose grandson, David Tree, plays Freddy Hill in the film! And, incidentally, Esmé Percy, who in the movie plays the Hungarian expert at the ball, played Higgins himself three times in revivals of the play in London.

Pygmalion comes in Shaw's career at a peculiar juncture, if you look at the whole line of that long career. He began in the 1890s as a playwright who took relatively accepted forms and used them in brand-new, explosive ways. I won't go into details because there isn't time. After the turn of the century, he began to experiment with innovative dramatic forms, as in *Man and Superman* (1903), *Getting Married* (1908), and *Misalliance* (1910). But by the time he got to *Pygmalion*, he had some kind of hankering to go back to the 1890s state of mind that he had already experienced, and to take a familiar form, refurbish it, and make it new—renovate it. He had already done this, after the turn of the century, in something called *Fanny's First Play* (1911). He did it again, I think in part, because of his infatuation with Mrs. Campbell.

Shaw had precedents for this play. W. S. Gilbert of Gilbert and Sullivan had written a play in blank verse called *Pygmalion and Galatea* (1871), I think. But Shaw had his own impetus for doing a *Pygmalion*, which was first of all to use the theater to dramatize and titivate a social subject. One of the many things I haven't done, which I'd like to do, is to write an essay on the subject of class in Shaw's plays. It runs all through much of his work, including this play, this film. And here is a play, *Pygmalion*, in which he says, "The only thing that keeps this girl in the gutter is the fact that she doesn't speak like someone of a better class. And I will show you how brains and education can burrow through and explode that false barrier." There's not a difference in humanity, not a difference in character, between Eliza and other people; there's a difference caused simply by the manifestation of class. One that still applies in Britain, to some degree.

Interviewer: And even in New York, in certain neighborhoods.

Russo: I know that's true. I could give you examples. In any event, class was one aspect of the play. The other was that Shaw always liked to lean toward classical antecedents, and what could be more classical than the legend of Pygmalion and Galatea? He once said that he stood on the shoulders of Shakespeare and Molière. And now he was also standing on the shoulders of Hellenic civilization. So these factors, plus his desire to do something for Mrs. Campbell, plus his ambition as a director—what they used to call "producer" in England—produced *Pygmalion*. He wrote a very interesting pamphlet once, by the way, called "The Art of Rehearsal" (1928), about directing.

There's an anecdote connected with the subject of directing or rehearsal and *Pygmalion*. It's well known that Shaw was a vegetarian: one might say a passionate vegetarian if that weren't an oxymoron. (*Laughs.*) He was directing a rehearsal of *Pygmalion*, the story goes, and really working on Mrs. Campbell—working on her and working on her to frazzle her nerves. He was in the auditorium of the theater; she was on the stage. Finally, she came down to the footlights and said, "George Bernard Shaw, some day you are going to eat a lamb chop, and then God help every actress in London." (*Both laugh.*)

Interviewer: If he could have that effect with vegetables, one can imagine . . .

Russo: The play was a success. But this production closed after a while, and one of the things that helped to close it was the approach of the First World War. When *Pygmalion* was first revived, about 1920, Mrs. Campbell continued as Eliza and Higgins was played by C. Aubrey Smith, who became something of an English figure in American films.

Interviewer: Quite so. Let's make a transition now to the film itself. The film of *Pygmalion* pleased Shaw and it was a worldwide success, deservedly so. Not only did it win Academy Awards, have a large box office, and garner critical praise, but it's also revived with some frequency.

Russo: More than that. Courtesy of the version you gave me, I saw it again the other day for the first time in, maybe, twenty years. I was bowled over by it as film: it is a very fine piece of filmmaking.

Interviewer: Absolutely.

Russo: Leslie Howard, I think, had much to do with the excellence of the acting. Anthony Asquith—the only film director who was the son of a Prime Minister (*laughs*)—had great skills, and he did wonders with the picture. But, after all, David Lean was the editor.

Interviewer: Arthur Honegger is the—

Russo: —composer, my next point. This is one of the prime film scores, an extraordinarily fine piece of movie-music writing. And it has been overlooked completely. When people talk about—as they should—Sergei Prokofiev and Nino Rota and Bernard Herrmann, wonderful film composers, what about what Arthur Honegger did for *Pygmalion*? He wrote a lot of other film scores, which I can't recall at the moment. But this is an excellent piece of writing.

About the screenplay: you know there was a good deal of wrangling back and forth about how it was to end. Shaw wanted to keep the ending unromantic: he was more interested—and you can see it in a number of his plays—in the teacher-student relationship. In *Caesar and Cleopatra* (1899), for example, he subverted history. In point of fact, Caesar and Cleopatra had a child, but they're father and daughter, so to speak, in Shaw's play about them. We won't go into some thirty-second psychoanalytical explanation about why it was true that Shaw was more interested in the teacher-student or parent-child relationship; it was true of him. And he fought a sentimental ending—a romantic ending—to *Pygmalion*. There were three endings filmed for this picture, as I'm sure you know.

Interviewer: Before we go into *that*, let's remind people of what the ending of the play as written is.

Russo: The ending of the play as written is that Eliza goes off to meet Freddy Hill, and Higgins—left alone onstage at the end—doubles up with laughter at "Freddy! Freddy!! Ha ha ha ha ha!!!!!" (Shaw had some precedent for this sort of last-act derailment of the well-made play: Henrik Ibsen's *A Doll House* [1879], about which he had written extensively as a critic.) But I must add that that's in the film, too. This is, I think, the best Shaw film. Not only because of the cast, but because, relatively speaking, most of the play has been retained. Only some of it has been taken out. The Doolittle scene in the first act, for instance, is so drastically condensed in the film that you never quite understand why he got all that money for being a great moralist.

But what the filmmakers kept almost pristine is that last scene between Eliza and Higgins in his mother's house, a very beautiful scene. "You devil, you know how to twist . . ."—in the middle of a quarrel, Higgins says something that turns her heart around. Anyone who thinks that Shaw didn't know how to write about human beings, just take a look at that scene in the film. It's wonderful. Shaw wanted Eliza and Higgins to part as satisfied, and yet not quite satisfied, with each other. And one of the three endings that he supplied for the film was that she does marry Freddy, who has a flower shop in South Kensington or somewhere, and who has muttonchop whiskers as he waits on a customer in the last shot. But the ending of the picture, as filmed, is, as far as I can remember, almost exactly like the ending of *My Fair Lady*, the 1964 movie musical (made from the 1956 Broadway version), which, of course, was based on Shaw's play: Eliza flees Higgins with Freddy but then returns to Higgins' home (though whether permanently or on her own terms is left deliberately ambiguous).

There's another interesting point to make here. Harry Stradling was the cinematographer for *Pygmalion*; he was also the cinematographer on *My Fair Lady* about twenty-five years later.

Interviewer: There's a whole progression from the play through this film and back to the stage once again as *My Fair Lady*.

Russo: Poor *film*, I think, *My Fair Lady*. I believe it's one of George Cukor's weakest pieces of direction.

Interviewer: It's one of those instances where a director seems overwhelmed by the phenomenon surrounding him.

Russo: Yes. There's no congeniality between him and the idea of making this picture. Whereas there's nearly absolute synchronicity between the co-directors or co-makers of the film of *Pygmalion* and the work itself.

Interviewer: Well, that brings us back to the central character of Eliza. Because while I am a deep admirer of many of Audrey Hepburn's performances, this seems to be one of her weakest ones. I mean, Cukor's using of all her features as if she were a model, whereas Wendy Hiller fully characterized the woman.

Russo: Wendy Hiller—whom I never saw on the stage, but I would have died just for a glance from her in the theater—had played Eliza in the stage production at the Malvern Festival in Britain, just before the film was made. And when Shaw saw it, he was simply captivated. He said, "If ever a film gets made of this" (in English, that is; there had been the other two), "you are Eliza." A lot of actresses wanted to play the film part. Marion Davies appealed to Shaw—a very big star at the time with some money behind her in the person of William Randolph Hearst—but she didn't get it. It's interesting apropos of this subject of casting to remark that, in order to ensure there was no romance, no romantic hint, between

Higgins and Eliza, Shaw's original choice for Higgins in the film was Charles Laughton—so that there would be a father/daughter relationship established right from the start.

Interviewer: Well, that casting would have changed the male-female chemistry altogether.

Russo: Without a doubt.

Interviewer: But the casting of Leslie Howard puts a very different spin on the matter: it adds a romantic element. Yet, as manipulated in the film, Howard's casting maintains a tension as well.

Russo: Shaw admired Leslie Howard as an actor, but he thought that Howard would add too much of a romantic flavor to the picture. Just a year or so before the film of *Pygmalion*, Howard had played Romeo in the film of *Romeo and Juliet* (1936, George Cukor) with Norma Shearer. And Shaw was afraid that that particular effluvium would carry over into the film. It does, to an extent.

Interviewer: Yes, no question. In closing, if there's one aspect of this film you would say you admire most, what is it?

Russo: My chief admiration for the film of *Pygmalion* is that, in somewhat distilled form, as incarnated by some very fine acting, it gives me the genius of Shaw.

"Shaw's First Movie: *How He Lied to Her Husband*"

The inevitable happened in 1931. For years George Bernard Shaw had turned a deaf ear to all proposals to put his plays on the screen. He at last relented, and one of his early works, the one-act *How He Lied to Her Husband* (1904), was made into a short sound film by an English company. There was doubtless great wisdom in Shaw's refusal to submit to the ministrations of the Hollywood experts. For one thing, he spared us the disappointment of seeing his showman's display of a nimble and effervescent mind brought down to the level of infantile understanding. He also spared us the painful experience of sitting through some of the worst movies that could possibly be made. For as silent pictures, shorn of their conversational brilliance, Shaw's plays, with the possible exception of *The Devil's Disciple* (1897; filmed 1959, Harold Hecht), would have been particularly lacking in the qualities that make the flesh and blood of a good motion picture. In the talkies, it is true, he is on safer ground, though one may still have grave doubts whether any of his bigger dramas (*Saint Joan* [1923], *Caesar and Cleopatra* [1901]) have been successfully adapted to the screen since 1931.

How He Lied to Her Husband, regarded as an augury of what is to come, is disappointing. The film was produced under Shaw's personal supervision; and it is rather a pity, for Shaw's ideas of direction, which cramp his plays even on the stage, are little short of disastrous when applied to the movies. He evidently does not sense the difference between the cinema and the stage. Though Cecil Lewis, who directed the picture, has given it a pleasant fluidity of alternating shots, Lewis has adhered to the dramatic original in practically everything else. So much so, indeed, that he has confined the entire action to a single room, showing even that setting exclusively from one end, as if, like a stage set, it had only three walls.

But what seems to matter even more, where quality is concerned, is the essential theatricality of the whole piece. The theatrical intimacy of contact with the audience that enables the actor to make his points on the stage is still unobtainable in the sound film, however. A deficiency affecting all the sound genres, it makes itself felt with special force in the conventional dramatic genre, and *How He Lied to Her Husband*, with its invented situation of a husband's welcoming and even demanding admiration for his wife from a lover who feigns indifference to her, has decidedly all the earmarks of a dramatic stunt. On the screen this simply does not work.

Yet even such a failure does not quite explain the paucity of effect produced by the film. The truth is that besides its situation—a not very happy conceit at best—the play has little to offer. What is most surprising of all, it has none of the Shavian brilliance of dialogue and none of the sudden twists of characterization that made Bernard Shaw's reputation as a dramatist. One is still kept in a state of amused bewilderment while watching the antics of his four-act comedy *You Never Can Tell* (1899), but *How He Lied to Her Husband* is not even mildly amusing. The one relieving feature of the picture is the acting of Vera Lennox (as Aurora Bompas). The finesse of her craftsmanship is admirable—if nothing else in the picture is.

"Brecht's Drama/Hare's *Fanshen*"

In an influential review, Michael Coveney once described David Hare's *Fanshen* as a "marvellous play that, in my opinion, is the nearest any English contemporary writer has come to emulating Brecht" (31). *Fanshen* does indeed resemble such *Lehrstücke* of Bertolt Brecht's as *He Who Says Yes* (1930), *He Who Says No* (1930), and *The Measures Taken* (1930). In Brecht's "plays for learning," as in *Fanshen*, there is, according to David Bathrick,

> an emphasis upon the open, tentative, and heuristic presentation of ideas; upon learning through involvement, through active, critical, testing participation. The quintessence of the "play for learning" . . . is the very opposite of "didactic," for it requires that the audience not accept action and characters as finished products, but rather as unhewn attitudes and behaviors which must be tested; as models for critical experimentation. (213)

Bathrick is right to point out that the *Lehrstück* exists "to a lesser or greater degree in all of Brecht's political plays, whether in the works he specifically referred to as *Lehrstücke* or in the 'epic' *Schaustücke* (*Mother*

Courage, *Galileo*, etc.) of the later years" (214). It is equally true that the concept of character Brecht employed in plays such as *Mother Courage and Her Children* (1941) and *Life of Galileo* (1939), which treat "main characters" or single protagonists and their victimization or alteration by society, is the same one he employed in the *Lehrstücke*, which emphasize the *group* and the individual's role in strengthening or improving it. This is the concept of character that David Hare employs in *Fanshen*, as well.

To recap the play's action for the sake of my discussion here: after World War II, Long Bow, located 400 miles southwest of Beijing, is turned by its one-thousand inhabitants from a village exploited by feudal landlords into one run on a rudimentary model of Chinese communism: land and goods are distributed to all as equally as possible, and decisions are made collectively. The change for the better in the social system leads to a change for the better in the nature of the citizens: a beggar becomes a leader of a women's organization; a quiet, shy man learns that he can be an eloquent and persuasive speaker; and the brutal, greedy, wanton Yu-lai is broken and eventually reformed. I would like to describe his character and anticipated change in detail, because he is probably the most conventional figure in the play on the surface—the villain—and therefore normally the one least susceptible to productive reform (as opposed to gallows repentance) in Western drama.

Yu-lai became vice-chairman of the Peasants' Association of Long Bow in the wake of the defeat of the Japanese and the establishment of Communist rule in North China. In *Fanshen: A Documentary of Revolution in a Chinese Village*, on which Hare's play is based, William Hinton describes him:

> [Wang Yu-lai] had once been a member of the local Kuomintang [American-backed, anti-Communist] army, had later taken up banditry as a way of life, and was said to have joined the "Red Rifle" secret society as a young man. He had always been poor. Throughout the ten years he had lived in Long Bow he had worked as a hired laborer. (133)

In Hinton's book we see Yu-lai immediately as a product of his social conditions, as a man who turned to theft and violence to relieve his poverty and feelings of powerlessness. Once he gets legitimate authority under the Communists in Long Bow, he proceeds to abuse it, assuming out of habit that "might makes right." Hare creates incidents involving Yu-lai in the play that either do not exist in the book or do but don't include this character, in order to dramatize his villainy. Conditions change for the better in the village—the people rule, everyone owns land—but Yu-lai will not change until both he and his fellow citizens understand the origin and substance of the new conditions.

As I've already made clear, certainly one of the points of a play like *Fanshen*, which exalts Communism, is that there is no main character. But Yu-lai may be considered its protagonist, not only in the sense that he is the only one to assume a large and dynamic role both early and late in the play, but also, and most important, in the sense that his change will be a model. It will prove that even the most incorrigible of men, and by extension of societies, can be reformed if approached with intelligence, perseverance, and foresight; and that these traits are necessary to the continued betterment of a people. Hare saw the possibilities for a model change in Yu-lai, and molded him accordingly from the raw data provided by Hinton.

The dramatist establishes the violent side of Yu-lai early in the play, in a scene not recorded in the book. Yu-lai wants simply to shoot Kuo Te-yu, collaborationist head of Long Bow for the last two years of the Japanese occupation. When T'ien-ming, the new village head, wisely says, "[Kuo Te-yu] must be tried, in public, by the peasants of Long Bow, by the people he's oppressed . . ." (17), Yu-lai accuses him of cowardice. But T'ien-ming wants to accustom the villagers to the kind of participatory government necessary if the Communists are to be successful in China. In another scene, recorded in the book but with the militiaman Man-hsi as the culprit, not Yu-lai, Hare further documents the latter's violent behavior. Another of the endless village meetings is announced, and the old peasant Tui-chin refuses to go, wanting to work his land instead. Yu-lai responds, "The meeting is for your own good. (*He hits him across the face.*) It's in your interest. (*He hits him again.*) You think I don't have my work cut out without chasing up idle cunts like you?" (41).

According to Hinton, Yu-lai is guilty of a kind of abuse of power called "commandism" by the Communists:

> Without realizing what was actually happening, many leading cadres in Long Bow began to issue orders instead of educating and persuading people, and because most people obeyed these orders . . . the leaders did not realize how much support they had lost. Those peasants who did not obey they condemned as backward—. . . "sour and slippery" troublemakers who needed to be taught a lesson. Some of these were arrested, beaten, and punished with extra work for soldiers' families, or extra terms of rear service such as stretcher-bearing or transporting supplies to the front. (224-225)

Hare creates two other incidents in which Yu-lai is ready to use violence to make villagers obey him. On the way to the meeting to which Tui-chin had refused to go, he notices a peasant hiding and yells, "You. Get out of that ditch and get to the meeting" (42). In Act II, after returning from prison, he replies to a cadre's complaint that he cannot get anyone to come to meetings, "(*Holding the gun with both hands at arms' length . . .*) Use force" (71).

Yu-lai was put into prison on suspicion of attempting to murder the "work team" member Chang Ch'uer, sent along with three others by the Communist government to supervise land reform in Long Bow. Hinton cites no evidence that Yu-lai tried to strangle Chang Ch'uer; there were no witnesses. (He is later released from prison on account of the insufficient case against him.) He and his son, Wen-te, were jailed on the following logic: "Were they not former bandits? Had they not made threats against the whole village? Surely none but these two could have attempted a deed so foul" (Hinton, 257).

Hare implicates Yu-lai in the attempt on Chang Ch'uer's life by adding a scene immediately preceding the near murder in which Yu-lai reacts uneasily to the arrival of the work team. He is the first to encounter the team members as they enter the village and seems threatened by them, for they will be evaluating the work that he and other Long Bow officials have done. Note the terseness of Yu-lai's responses in the following dialogue, his apparent unwillingness to comment on the team's mission:

> YU-LAI. I don't know you.
>
> HOU. I'm Hou Pao-pei, leader of the work team. . . .
>
> YU-LAI. I see. Wang Yu-lai, Vice-Chairman Peasants' Association.
>
> HOU. Ch'i-Yun. Chang Ch'uer. Magistrate Li. Members of the work team.
>
> YU-LAI. Welcome to Long Bow. (*Pause.*) We are all at a meeting, you've chosen a bad time.
>
> HOU. We will be starting work at once.
>
> YU-LAI. Yes?
>
> HOU. Talking to the people, finding out how they've prospered . . . Examining the progress of the movement. Elsewhere there have been shortcomings. Some landlords, rich peasants, riff-raff, have sneaked into the people's organizations,where they abuse their power, ride roughshod over the people, and destroy the faith of the masses in their new organizations.
>
> YU-LAI. You can sleep in the temple. I must go to the meeting. . . . (*He looks at them, goes out. The four of them left standing.*) (42-43)

Hare goes on to give evidence of grasping behavior on Yu-lai's part, as well as further proof of his brutality. During the distribution to poor peasants of wealth confiscated from landlords, rich peasants, and the Catholic Church, a woman asks, "The leaders, what do the leaders get? You [Cheng-k'uan], the Chairman of the [Peasants'] Association. Yu-lai over there, T'ien-ming. What do you get?" T'ien-ming responds, "[The leaders] get some but they get less" (32). Yu-lai listens to their exchange intently, then engages in the following discussion:

> YU-LAI. Why?
>
> CHENG-K'UAN. Mm?
>
> YU-LAI. Why less?
>
> T'IEN-MING. Less because you're the leaders and you must wait for the peasants to suggest you get some.

YU-LAI. Wait for them?

T'IEN-MING. Yes.

YU-LAI. Well it's not worth it. I'd be better off as a peasant. (33)

In the book, "the leaders get some but they get less" is the policy adopted by the village cadres and militiamen at the urging of the district Communist Party leader. But no discussion like the above one takes place: Hare invents it, not only to dramatize Hinton's description of the allocation policy for leaders, but also to continue the consistent characterization of Yu-lai as violent and greedy, as Long Bow's equivalent of a villain. He even makes Yu-lai suggest that the cadres start confiscating the goods of the so-called middle peasants, in order that the hundreds of remaining poverty-stricken peasants in the village can "fanshen," can gain the land, stock, agricultural implements, and shelter necessary for survival:

> YU-LAI. There are hundreds in the village who still don't have enough to make a living.
>
> CHENG-K'UAN. How's it to be done?
>
> T'IEN-MING. The land must be further redistributed.
>
> CHENG-K'UAN. What land?
>
> YU-LAI. We've scarcely begun. More soup.
>
> CHENG-K'UAN. There aren't many gentry left in Long Bow. Two landlords, four rich peasants, it's not going to go very far.
>
> YU-LAI. Middle peasants.
>
> CHENG-K'UAN. You can start on the middle peasants certainly.
>
> YU-LAI. Plenty of those . . . (*He strikes Hsien-e, who has returned with more soup.*) (38)

The policy of dispossessing middle peasants is eventually condemned by the Communist Party as "left extremism":

> You [the cadres and the work team] have sought support only from the poor peasants, thereby neglecting the middle peasants. . . . Everything the poor peasants wanted you have believed and tried to give them. You have elevated their point of view to the status of a line. That line is in clear opposition to the official policy of the Party. . . . Too many middle

> peasants have been pushed over to the enemy side. We need all the allies we can get. (Hare, 63-64)

In the dialogue given in the above paragraph, note how Hare skillfully underlines Yu-lai's grasping side by having him demand more food at the same time as he suggests that more land and goods be found by dispossessing middle peasants. Then the playwright connects Yu-lai's ravenousness with his brutality by having him senselessly strike Hsien-e, his son's wife, when she serves the soup. His violent treatment of Hsien-e and sexual abuse of her (described by Hinton in the book, not invented by Hare) lead, of course, to her climactic testimony against him and before the second "gate". This was a "council of delegates, elected by peasants at large, before which all the cadres had to answer for their motives and their actions" (Hinton, 238).

Yu-lai is crushed by Hsien-e's testimony and by the interrogation of the Long Bow citizens whom he had terrorized for so long. We last see him being questioned by Secretary Liu, a regional Communist Party leader who has come to the village to check on the progress of the work team. In the book, Liu questions Wen-te; Hare substitutes Yu-lai for his son in order to complete his Brechtian portrait of a villain. Yu-lai is about to face a People's Court and certain dismissal from the Party as well as imprisonment; he is disconsolate: the villain's tough façade has begun to crack. Then Liu enters the room where he is being detained:

> LIU. Tell me why you are crying.
>
> YU-LAI. I want to die.
>
> LIU. Why?
>
> YU-LAI. There's nothing . . . for me. If I'm sent to People's Court, I'll be shot. If I confess everything, I'll be lynched. Or they'll throw me out of the Party and that's as bad as being shot. People hate me, they want me dead.
>
> LIU. You can still decide your fate. It's up to you. I know people who have done much worse than you. They have faced the people honestly and the people have accepted them again as leaders.
>
> YU-LAI. I can't face living in this . . .
>
> LIU. You can. Everyone can face everything.
>
> YU-LAI. The people hate me.
>
> LIU. No. They hate what you've done. (77)

Significantly, Liu speaks to Yu-lai not as a villain whose fate is sealed, not as a unified and unchangeable personality—not, that is, as the last-minute penitent of Western drama who dies bravely to satisfy society's reflexive need to root out evil—but as a man who can determine his future for the better by changing his behavior. The people do not hate Yu-lai, says Liu; they hate what he has done wrong. And if he does right, they will like *it*. The focus here, as in Brecht, is on the external individual of observable actions rather than on the internal one of hidden motivations, of ineffable nature.

Yu-lai is not a villain *by nature*. He is the villainous product of once feudal social conditions in Long Bow, and he has remained so out of bad habit. Conditions have changed, and Yu-lai can change with them if he is given a chance and the proper guidance. The work team must realize, says Secretary Liu, that even as the social and economic structure of the village has been transformed, so too must its delinquent citizens be. (The team, like the villagers, had been in favor of eradicating Yu-lai's presence in Long Bow once and for all.) Not to transform them—and place them back in the community as models of rehabilitation to other miscreants—is itself to foster delinquency. The message is that human beings must not only make the changes in the social system, as the Communists did in Long Bow and throughout China; they must also help their fellows to change in harmony with an improved environment.

Yu-lai must be permitted to take his fate into his own hands, then, just as the village was enabled by the Communists to get out from under the feudal yoke and determine its destiny. Secretary Liu uses apt metaphors to win the work team members over to his position:

> You let [Yu-lai] lose hope. . . . Never, never let a man lose hope. It's a waste, to the Party. To the people. It's easy, it's so easy to stamp something out. It's what they do in every country in the world. They cure diseases by killing the patient. . . . You can't smooth trouble over, it will come back at you, always it will appear somewhere else unless you dig out the root. . . . There are no breakthroughs in our work. There is no "just do this one thing and we will be there." There is only the patient, daily work of re-making people. Over each hill, another hill. Over that hill, a mountain. (Hare, 77-79)

Liu recommends that Yu-lai be sent, not to prison, but instead to a "school for cadres . . . where [he will] be re-educated, taken out of [his] own life, given a chance to think, to learn, to be objective" (78). Liu sends Yu-lai out onto the streets of Long Bow to face the people honestly, and his final words to the work team leave us with the impression that the "villain" will indeed change, will become a happy man and a credit to his village: "The Party needs Yu-lai because he is clever and strong . . . We must save him. We can use him. He can be reformed" (79). But we never see Yu-lai the changed, finished product. The implication is that, once reformed, Yu-lai will continue to change in response to a dynamic society. *Fanshen* thus ends openly, "in process"—like Brecht's *Lehrstücke*.

Works Cited

Bathrick, David. "Brecht's Marxism and America." In *Essays on Brecht: Theater and Politics*. Ed. Siegfried Mews & Herbert Knust. Chapel Hill: University of North Carolina Press, 1974. 209-225.

Coveney, Michael. "*Fanshen*: Criticism." *Plays and Players*, 22.9 (June 1975): 31.

Hare, David. *Fanshen.* London: Faber and Faber, 1976.

Hinton, William. *Fanshen: A Documentary of Revolution in a Chinese Village.* New York: Monthly Review Press, 1966.

BIBLIOGRAPHY

IBSEN

Allphin-Hoggatt, Clela. *Women in the Plays of Henrik Ibsen.* New York: Revisionist Press, 1975.

Beyer, Edward. *Ibsen: The Man and His Work.* New York: Taplinger, 1980.

Bloom, Harold, ed. *Henrik Ibsen.* 1999. New York: Chelsea House, 2010.

----------, ed. *Henrik Ibsen: Comprehensive Research and Study Guide.* 1999. New York: Chelsea House, 2010.

Boyesen, Hjalmar Hjorth. *A Commentary on the Works of Henrik Ibsen.* New York: Russell & Russell, 1973.

Bradbrook, M. C. *Ibsen, the Norwegian.* London: Chatto & Windus, 1946.

Bryan, George B. *An Ibsen Companion: A Dictionary-Guide to the Life, Works, and Critical Reception of Henrik Ibsen.* Westport, Conn.: Greenwood Press, 1984.

Chamberlain, John S. *Ibsen: The Open Vision.* London: Athlone, 1982.

Clurman, Harold. *Ibsen.* New York: Simon & Schuster, 1977.

Downs, Brian W. *Ibsen: The Intellectual Background.* New York: Octagon Books, 1969.

----------. *A Study of Six Plays by Ibsen.* New York: Octagon Books, 1972.

Durbach, Errol. *Ibsen and the Theatre: The Dramatist in Production.* New York: New York University Press, 1980.

----------, ed. *Ibsen and the Theatre: Essays in Celebration of the 150th Anniversary of Henrik Ibsen's Birth.* London: Macmillan, 1982.

Egan, Michael. *Henrik Ibsen.* New York: Routledge, 2009.

Ferguson, Robert. *Ibsen: A New Biography.* 1996. London: Faber & Faber, 2010.

Fischer-Lichte, Erika, *et al.*, eds. *Global Ibsen: Performing Multiple Identities.* London: Routledge, 2010.

Fjelde, Rolf, ed. *Ibsen: A Collection of Critical Essays*. Englewood Cliffs, N.J.: Prentice-Hall, 1965.

Goldman, Michael. *Ibsen: The Dramaturgy of Fear*. New York: Columbia University Press, 1999.

Hornby, Richard. *Patterns in Ibsen's Middle Plays*. Lewisburg, Pa.: Bucknell University Press, 1981.

Lebowitz, Naomi. *Ibsen and the Great World*. Baton Rouge: Louisiana State University Press, 1990.

Ledger, Sally. *Henrik Ibsen*. 1998. Liverpool, U.K.: Liverpool University Press, 2008.

Lyons, Charles R. *Henrik Ibsen: The Divided Consciousness*. Carbondale: Southern Illinois University Press, 1972.

----------, ed. *Critical Essays on Henrik Ibsen*. Boston: G. K. Hall, 1987.

Marker, Frederick J., & Lise-Lone Marker. *Ibsen's Lively Art: A Performance Study of the Major Plays*. New York: Cambridge University Press, 1989.

McFarlane, James Walter, ed. *Henrik Ibsen: A Critical Anthology*. Harmondsworth, U.K.: Penguin, 1970.

Meyer, Michael L. *Henrik Ibsen: The Making of a Dramatist*. London: Hart-Davis, 1967.

Moi, Toril. *Henrik Ibsen and the Birth of Modernism: Art, Theater, Philosophy*. New York: Oxford University Press, 2006.

Rhodes, Norman. *Ibsen and the Greeks: The Classical Greek Dimension in Selected Works of Henrik Ibsen*. Lewisburg, Pa.: Bucknell University Press, 1995.

Robinson, Michael, ed. *Turning the Century: Centennial Essays on Ibsen*. Norwich, U.K.: Norvik, 2006.

Shafer, Yvonne. *Henrik Ibsen: Life, Work, and Criticism*. Fredericton, New Brunswick (Can.): York Press, 1985.

Shepherd-Barr, Kirsten. *Ibsen and Early Modernist Theatre*. Westport, Conn.: Greenwood Press, 1997.

Templeton, Joan. *Ibsen's Women*. New York: Cambridge University Press, 2000.

Thomas, David. *Henrik Ibsen*. New York: Macmillan, 1983.

SHAW

Baker, Stuart E. *Bernard Shaw's Remarkable Religion: A Faith That Fits the Facts*. Gainesville: University Press of Florida, 2002.

Bentley, Eric. *Bernard Shaw, A Reconsideration*. New York: New Directions, 1947.

Bloom, Harold, ed. *George Bernard Shaw*. 2000. New York: Bloom's Literary Criticism, 2011.

Boxill, Roger. *Shaw and the Doctors*. New York: Basic Books, 1969.

Crompton, Louis. *Shaw the Dramatist*. Lincoln: University of Nebraska Press, 1969.

Davis, Tracy C. *George Bernard Shaw and the Socialist Theatre*. Westport, Conn.: Praeger, 1994.

Dukore, Bernard. *Bernard Shaw, Playwright: Aspects of Shavian Drama*. Columbia: University of Missouri Press, 1973.

Ganz, Arthur F. *George Bernard Shaw*. New York: Grove Press, 1983.

Gibbs, Anthony M., ed. *Shaw: Interviews and Recollections*. Iowa City: University of Iowa Press, 1990.

Gibbs, Anthony M. *A Bernard Shaw Chronology*. Basingstoke, U.K.: Palgrave, 2001.

----------. *Bernard Shaw: A Life*. Gainesville: University Press of Florida, 2005.

Hill, Eldon C. *George Bernard Shaw*. Boston: Twayne, 1978.

Holroyd, Michael, ed. *The Genius of Shaw*. New York: Holt, Rinehart, & Winston, 1979.

Holroyd, Michael. *Bernard Shaw, Vol. 1: 1856-1898; The Search for Love*. London: Chatto & Windus, 1988.

----------. *Bernard Shaw, Vol. 2: 1898-1918; The Pursuit of Power*. London: Chatto & Windus, 1989.

----------. *Bernard Shaw, Vol. 3: 1918-1950; The Lure of Fantasy*. London: Chatto & Windus, 1991.

----------. *Bernard Shaw, Vol. 4: 1950-1991; The Last Laugh.* London: Chatto & Windus, 1992.

----------. *Bernard Shaw: The One-Volume Definitive Edition.* London: Chatto & Windus, 1997.

Innes, Christopher, ed. *The Cambridge Companion to George Bernard Shaw.* New York: Cambridge University Press, 1998.

Laurence, Dan H. *Bernard Shaw : A Bibliography.* 2 vols. Oxford, U.K.: Clarendon Press, 1983.

----------, ed. *Theatrics: Selected Correspondence of Bernard Shaw.* Toronto: University of Toronto Press, 1995.

Matthews, John F. *George Bernard Shaw.* New York: Columbia University Press, 1969.

Mills, John A. *Language and Laughter: Comic Diction in the Plays of Bernard Shaw.* Tucson: University of Arizona Press, 1969.

Morgan, Margery M. *The Shavian Playground: An Exploration of the Art of George Bernard Shaw.* London: Methuen, 1972.

----------. *File on Shaw.* London: Methuen, 1989.

Ohmann, Richard M. *Shaw: The Style and the Man.* Middletown, Conn.: Wesleyan University Press, 1962.

Peters, Sally. *Bernard Shaw: The Ascent of the Superman.* New Haven, Conn.: Yale University Press, 1996.

Pharand, Michel W. *Bernard Shaw and the French.* Gainesville: University Press of Florida, 2000.

Weintraub, Stanley. *Journey to Heartbreak: The Crucible Years of Bernard Shaw, 1914-1918.* New York: Weybright & Talley, 1971.

----------. *Bernard Shaw: A Guide to Research.* University Park: Pennsylvania State University Press, 1992.

----------, ed. *Bernard Shaw: The Diaries 1885-1897.* 2 vols. University Park: Pennsylvania State University Press, 1986.

Wisenthal, J. L., ed. & intro. *Shaw and Ibsen: Bernard Shaw's* Quintessence of Ibsenism *and Related Writings.* Toronto: University of Toronto Press, 1979.

Wisenthal, J. L. *Shaw's Sense of History*. Oxford, U.K.: Clarendon Press, 1988.

BRECHT

Bartram, Graham, & Anthony Waine, eds. *Brecht in Perspective*. London: Longman, 1982.

Bentley, Eric. *The Brecht Memoir*. New York: Performing Arts Journal Publications, 1985.

----------. *Bentley on Brecht*. 1998. Evanston, Ill.: Northwestern University Press, 2008.

Berlau, Ruth. *Living for Brecht: The Memoirs*. Ed. Hans Bunge. Trans. Geoffrey Skelton. New York: Fromm International, 1987.

Bloom, Harold, ed. *Bertolt Brecht*. Philadelphia: Chelsea House, 2002.

Cook, Bruce. *Brecht in Exile*. New York: Holt, Rinehart, & Winston, 1983.

Demetz, Peter, ed. *Brecht: A Collection of Critical Essays*. Englewood Cliffs, N.J.: Prentice-Hall, 1962.

Eddershaw, Margaret. *Performing Brecht*. London: Routledge, 1996.

Ewen, Frederic. *Bertolt Brecht: His Life, His Art, and His Times*. 1967. New York: Citadel Press, 1992.

Fuegi, John. *The Essential Brecht*. Los Angeles: Hennessey and Ingalls, 1972.

----------. *Bertolt Brecht: Chaos, According to Plan*. Cambridge, U.K.: Cambridge University Press, 1987.

Giles, Steve, & Rodney Livingstone, eds. *Bertolt Brecht: Centenary Essays*. Atlanta, Ga.: Rodopi, 1998.

Glahn, Philip. *Bertolt Brecht*. London: Reaktion, 2014.

Gray, Ronald D. *Brecht the Dramatist*. Cambridge, U.K.: Cambridge University Press, 1976.

Hayman, Ronald. *Brecht: A Biography*. New York: Oxford University Press, 1983.

Kleber, Pia, & Colin Visser, eds. *Re-interpreting Brecht: His Influence on Contemporary Drama and Film*. Cambridge, U.K.: Cambridge University Press, 1990.

Lyon, James K. *Bertolt Brecht in America.* Princeton, N.J.: Princeton University Press, 1980.

Mews, Siegfried, & Herbert Knust, eds. *Essays on Brecht: Theater and Politics.* Chapel Hill: University of North Carolina Press, 1974.

Mews, Siegfried, ed. *Critical Essays on Bertolt Brecht.* Boston: G. K. Hall, 1989.

----------, ed. *A Bertolt Brecht Reference Companion.* Westport, Conn.: Greenwood Press, 1997.

Morley, Michael. *Bertolt Brecht: A Study.* London: Heinemann, 1977.

Mumford, Meg. *Bertolt Brecht.* London: Routledge, 2009.

Parker, Stephen. *Bertolt Brecht: A Literary Life.* London: Bloomsbury, 2014.

Parmalee, Patty Lee. *Brecht's America.* Columbus: Ohio State University Press, 1981.

Subiotto, Arrigo V. *Bertolt Brecht's Adaptations for the Berliner Ensemble.* London: Modern Humanities Research Association, 1975.

Suvin, Darko. *To Brecht and Beyond: Soundings in Modern Dramaturgy.* Totowa, N.J.: Barnes & Noble, 1984.

Thomson, Peter, & Glendyr Sacks, eds. *The Cambridge Companion to Brecht.* 1994. Cambridge, U.K.: Cambridge University Press, 2006.

Völker, Klaus. *Brecht Chronicle.* Trans. Fred Wieck. New York: Seabury Press, 1975.

----------. *Brecht: A Biography.* Trans. John Nowell. London: Marion Boyars, 1979.

Weber, Betty Nance, & Hubert Heinen, eds. *Bertolt Brecht: Political Theory and Literary Practice.* Athens: University of Georgia Press, 1980.

White, Alfred D. *Bertolt Brecht's Great Plays.* London: Macmillan, 1978.

Willett, John. *Brecht in Context: Comparative Approaches.* 1984. London: Methuen, 1998.

Witt, Hubert, ed. *Brecht As They Knew Him.* Trans. John Peet. New York: International Publishers, 1974.

INDEX

www.ingramcontent.com/pod-product-compliance
Lightning Source LLC
Chambersburg PA
CBHW071414090426
42737CB00011B/1453

* 9 7 8 1 8 4 8 9 0 4 0 4 0 *